The UK Labour Market

The UK Labour Market

The *IMS* Guide to Information

**Kenneth Walsh, Ann Izatt
and Richard Pearson**

Kogan Page

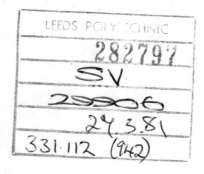
First published 1980 by
Kogan Page Limited
120 Pentonville Road
London N1 9JN

British Library Cataloguing in Publication Data
Walsh, Kenneth

    The UK labour market
    1. Labor supply — Great Britain — Information Services
    2. Labor supply — Great Britain — Bibliography
    I. Title
    331.1'2'07   HD5765.A6

ISBN 0 85038 372 2

Printed in Great Britain by
Billing and Sons Limited

Contents

Preface

This book has been prepared as an aid to those who need to make use of labour market information in the course of their work. It will be of value to a wide selection of practitioners in the field of personnel and manpower management and research in all sectors, including both private and public employers, government departments and bodies such as local authorities, the industrial training boards and trade unions, as well as individual researchers.

Each year the output of statistics, surveys, and reports relating to the labour market increases. Some of it is presented in the form of time series stretching back over a number of years, others in the form of one-off reports and some are a number of years out of date by the time they reach publication. The range of material covered is vast and while the majority is collected and disseminated by government agencies, this does not necessarily mean that each series or individual source is compatible, one with another. This Guide identifies the key sources of labour market information likely to be of use to employers and others, and to show the type and scope of the information contained in the various publications that are more generally available.

The Guide is intended as a reference document, structured so that the user can quickly and easily identify the range of labour market information available to meet the identified need, and then to pinpoint the most appropriate published source or point of contact.

The Guide is arranged in two distinct parts. Part I brings together key sources of labour market information under the following 19 distinct subject headings:

☐ population and its components
☐ economic activity
☐ employment
☐ unemployment
☐ vacancies and placings
☐ educational supply — school-leavers
☐ educational supply — further education
☐ educational supply — universities

7

- ☐ training
- ☐ travel-to-work areas
- ☐ labour mobility
- ☐ absence from work
- ☐ hours of work
- ☐ redundancy, temporary stoppages and short-time working
- ☐ labour turnover
- ☐ earnings
- ☐ labour costs and productivity
- ☐ trade union membership
- ☐ strikes

Each is laid out in such a way as to facilitate ease of identification of relevant sources, but at the same time giving both an appreciation of the relative merits and defects of the sources and sufficient detail of content for an assessment of usefulness to be positively made. The organisation of this part is explained in more detail in the introduction to Part I.

Part I concludes with an index of the published information sources referred to. This gives the publisher, frequency of update, latest price, and, where useful, brief commentary on the source.

Part II contains two sections concerned with the identification of further sources of advice and information, most of which are referred to in various sections of Part I. The first section describes the labour market institutions which are the most active organisations as far as advice and information are concerned and names, addresses and telephone numbers are also given. The second section lists the names, addresses and telephone numbers of a wide range of sources for further types of information.

Although labour market information is constantly being added to, it is intended that the Guide will remain useful for a fairly long time since the majority of the primary reference sources are well established and change little over time. New information sources, for example in the form of research reports, are most likely to originate from one of the organisations listed in Part II and where appropriate their future output should be monitored.

Acknowledgements

This study was produced as part of the Institute of Manpower Studies' Co-operative Research Programme. We would like to thank the following CRP members for their support in producing this volume:

Barclays Bank Ltd
British-American Tobacco Co. Ltd
British Gas Corporation
British Petroleum Co. Ltd
British Steel Corporation
Carrington Viyella Ltd
Civil Service Department
Equity & Law Life Assurance Society Ltd
Ford Motor Co. Ltd
IBM UK Ltd
Imperial Chemical Industries Ltd
Imperial Group Ltd
Legal & General Assurance Society Ltd
Marks & Spencer Ltd
Midland Bank Ltd
National Westminster Bank Ltd
Philips Industries Ltd
The Post Office
Prudential Assurance Co. Ltd
Shell UK Oil Ltd.

Particular thanks are due to the staff of these organisations, and to the staff of the Department of Employment, the Manpower Services Commission, the IPM, the Institute and other bodies who provided valuable advice and comments throughout the preparation of this Guide.

Finally, we would like to thank Valerie Raggio for her valuable help in the typing and preparation of the manuscript.

Kenneth Walsh
Ann Izatt
Richard Pearson

Institute of Manpower Studies
Mantell Building
University of Sussex
Falmer, Brighton

The Institute of Manpower Studies

The Institute of Manpower Studies, an independent, national centre, was founded in 1970 in response to the need for more effective deployment of human resources in employing organisations. The IMS is a national and international focus of knowledge and practical experience in manpower management, the labour market, issues of employment policy and manpower information. The Institute now has a staff of 35 who have built up extensive working relationships throughout the United Kingdom and in other countries.

IMS expertise and resources are available to all organisations working on manpower or labour market problems or requiring practical guidance on the solution of such problems. These organisations include public and private sector employers, trade unions, industry-wide and regional bodies and associations, and government departments and agencies. All have worked closely with the Institute, both benefiting from and contributing to its practical knowledge and experience.

Specific IMS activities include a wide range of manpower and labour market advisory work including analyses of particular local labour markets; detailed research studies into various aspects of the labour market requested by firms, government departments, industrial training boards and other agencies; the Co-operative Research Programme run with the participation of some 20 subscriber organisations who help develop the areas for study; the regular DE Manpower Commentary grant, aided by the Department of Employment and the Manpower Services Commission; Company Manpower Commentary, launched at the end of 1979 to report on key manpower issues affecting employing organisations; a highly successful and rapidly expanding programme of short courses and seminars on manpower planning and labour market topics; and an extensive publications list, including *Education and Employment 1980* and *Manpower Studies*, a twice-yearly, in-depth review of current developments. Full details on these and other publications are available direct from the Institute.

Introduction: The Employer's Need for Labour Market Information

Personnel specialists and manpower planners in all kinds of organisations — public and private, large and small, with highly technical or largely unskilled workforces — are becoming increasingly aware of the need for and use of labour market information. Some of the key questions they are facing are:

- ☐ Will I be able to recruit the people I need?
- ☐ Will I be able to retain my existing workforce?
- ☐ How do my employment conditions compare with my competitors?
- ☐ How effectively am I using my existing workforce?
- ☐ Are there changes going on in the external labour market that are likely to alter radically the *status quo*?
- ☐ Where can I get the necessary information to answer these questions? Is it published? Are there organisations to ask? Is the information up-to-date? Is it detailed enough?

How can individuals keep themselves informed about the external labour market? Each year the output of statistics and reports on the labour market is enormous. For example, there are more than 16 volumes published each year which simply deal with the output of the education system, the number of school-leavers, graduates, etc. Not all are of relevance, even if the time were available to digest them. There is no sense in collecting labour market information for its own sake; the key thing is to establish why it is needed, the contribution it can make to the planning or management process both now and in the future, and to be able to identify the key sources of information and help. To do this requires an understanding of the way the organisation interacts with the labour market. It means identifying the types of staff involved and the events and circumstances that affect this interaction, and the problem to be resolved. This Guide will make the task easier by setting out what is contained in all the main sources of labour information publicly available. However, the more localised the problem facing an employing organisation, the more the employer will need to go beyond published sources and seek answers to specific

11

questions by contacting local bodies such as the local office of the Manpower Services Commission, and the local authority. Details of such organisations are also contained in this Guide.

Just as manpower management within the organisation requires the internal labour market to be analysed, described and understood in terms of its different dimensions and component parts, so a similar understanding of the working of the external market has to be acquired before information can usefully be gathered and interpreted. The internal market can, for example, be analysed in terms of locations, occupational structure, pay grades, career streams, recruitment and wastage flows. Similarly the external market can be studied at national, regional or local level, in terms of employment structure, workforce characteristics, labour availability and the future supply. The labour force can be described in terms of age, sex, skills, qualifications, occupation and

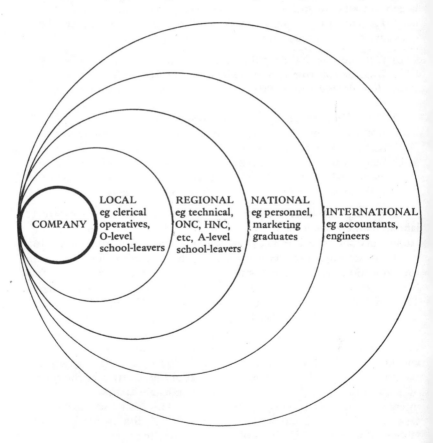

Companies are part of wider labour markets

location. Two of the most influential factors determining the relationship between the internal and external markets are the location(s) of the organisation and the characteristics of the workforce in terms of their skills, qualifications and occupations. The figure opposite shows how a company may relate to different labour markets, geographically defined, by virtue of its employment of different categories of staff. Many organisations draw the vast majority of their recruits from a limited area. When recruiting workers and determining pay and conditions of employment, an important dimension will therefore be the dynamics of the local labour market and this will often require the use of more informal data sources and local opinion.

Labour market information for recruitment and retention

A manager responsible for recruitment in an organisation of any size will, of course, be in continual touch with conditions in the labour markets from which the organisation regularly draws personnel. This contact, however, will sometimes need to be supplemented by more detailed information, if, for example:

- [ ] there are large numbers of personnel in a particular job or occupational category. (Sheer size may indicate a steady and high replacement requirement, and changes in the labour supply may therefore be critical.)
- [ ] there is a sudden increased requirement for a large number of recruits. (It may be impossible to meet this from traditional sources.)
- [ ] there is a persistent shortage or recruitment difficulty. (Is demand growing, supply falling, how do pay and conditions of employment compare?)
- [ ] wastage among employees is high. (Why, are competitors faring better or worse, will replacements be available?)
- [ ] expansion is planned, especially if this involves relocation or starting up in a new location. (Will suitable recruits be available, how do we choose the location?)
- [ ] the organisation depends heavily on a supply of externally trained people. (Is the market, both supply and demand, changing?)

All managers will, from time to time, face one or more of these issues. Having identified the categories of people involved (occupation, skill, experience, etc), there is a need to consider which labour market, or catchment area, you are normally operating in. This can be done by analysing:

- [ ] the sources of previous applicants and recruits, including their previous job or place of study, and their place of residence

13

- ☐ the ages, qualifications, skills, previous experience, places of residence and travel-to-work patterns of current employees
- ☐ the characteristics of people leaving the organisation, reasons for leaving and subsequent employment, which give an indication of the likely competition.

Such an analysis of the existing workforce will indicate the current (and past) geographical limits of the labour market for a particular category of worker, but may give no hint of how it is changing. For example, in the past it has been assumed that managerial and professional workers operate in a national labour market while manual workers and those in low paid jobs are known to be largely geographically immobile. However, there is increasing evidence that even those previously highly mobile are becoming less so, perhaps due to the difficulty of the housing market, pay policy constraints, attachment to children's schools, and the increase in the number of married women with jobs. Therefore there is a need to consider what factors may be influencing these mobility patterns and whether the changes are for better or for worse (see Part I, subject heading 11).

In assessing the likely future supply of suitable recruits there is a need to know:

- ☐ Do such people exist in the labour market? This may require reference to the sections of this Guide on *population, employment* and *unemployment*.
- ☐ Is there a new or additional supply likely to become available? Here reference should be made to the sections on *educational supply, training* and *redundancy*, while the *labour turnover* section will indicate the possible level of job seekers.
- ☐ What is the competition for these people? The *vacancies* data will be important as will those relating to *earnings*.
- ☐ What catchment should we consider? Here the relevant sections include *labour mobility* and *travel-to-work areas* together with the analysis of the internal data outlined above.

In planning a relocation or expansion in a new area, there will be a need for similar data relating to labour supply, but if there is a choice of location then other types of labour market information that may also be important in influencing that choice could include, for example, patterns of shiftworking, hours and holidays (see the section on *hours of work*), the industrial relations record of the area in terms of *strikes* and *trade union membership*, while consideration may also want to be given to local *absence from work* and *turnover* rates.

Information for comparing and monitoring

One of the most frequent and well-established uses of labour market information is in the monitoring and comparative assessment of company performance and conditions of employment. The basis of comparison varies, of course, in accordance with what is being compared, and very few aspects of labour markets can be compared in a simple and straightforward way. Among the topics organisations monitor and compare regularly against external standards or movements are: earnings (including pay and other benefits and conditions of service); *labour costs and productivity*; *strikes, stoppages* and *absence* levels; *hours of work*; and *turnover* rates.

Some organisations know clearly with which labour markets, whether defined in geographical, industrial or occupational terms, they want to compare themselves. They may exchange information with other organisations operating in the same markets, either informally or through groups such as trade associations. They may also subscribe to surveys carried out by bodies who undertake inter-firm comparisons. However, there are circumstances in which identifying information for comparative purposes may be more difficult. This is particularly true of information on local labour markets, but may also be the case where the organisation has no previous experience of the subject with which it is concerned, for example shiftworking.

Part I of this Guide identifies the major sources of readily available information that will be needed for comparing organisations' performance levels and conditions of employment. It also indicates the types of information that are not available and where possible suggests other sources of help and advice, such as government agencies, independent consultancies and research bodies. Additionally, in fields where comparison may be difficult due to problems of data definition, such as productivity and labour wastage, the major pitfalls are pointed out, and reference is made to further useful books or articles where these exist.

Sources of local labour market information

As suggested earlier, some of the needs for labour market information are most concerned with the local level but in many cases the published sources only provide regional or national data. Recourse therefore has to be made to local sources of data, some of which may not normally be published.

The local labour market for an employer can be defined as the area within which a substantial proportion of the firm's workforce lives. The size and boundaries of this area will be influenced by the type of worker concerned, occupation, sex, age, etc, the transport facilities which make for easy or difficult journeys, the availability of work and competition from other employers. These factors will vary in their effects from one part of the country to another and between urban and rural areas. Officially, local labour markets centre on the Employment Service's local offices and are based on 'travel-to-work patterns' (see

15

Part I, subject heading 10), but an individual firm may find that its catchment area for workers covers more than one official travel-to-work area.

Defining the geographical area over which data are to be collected can be done in a number of ways. If the organisation already operates in the area, the limits of the catchment area can be drawn by analysing where the current employees live. Alternatively, if the area is unfamiliar then the likely catchment area for the new location can be estimated from official travel-to-work statistics for the locality (see Section 10). The type of data which may be required at a local level could include:

- ☐ population characteristics and trends
- ☐ employment structure of the area
- ☐ size and characteristics of the local workforce, their ages, sex, skills and qualifications
- ☐ levels and type of unemployment and vacancies
- ☐ travel-to-work patterns
- ☐ transport and housing facilities
- ☐ rates of pay and conditions of employment
- ☐ labour turnover rates
- ☐ pattern of recent redundancies
- ☐ education and training facilities and the supply of people leaving them
- ☐ trade union membership
- ☐ other employers

Whether these categories of data will in fact be readily available for the defined area will depend on a number of factors. The amount of local labour market information available from the Employment Service is a matter for local discretion and so some offices may be in a better position than others to help with a firm's inquiries, but in any case the Employment Service should be the first place to seek advice. Some offices will be able to provide a description of their local area and may also offer informal information. The main types of information available through the local employment office will usually include most of the following:

- ☐ a general description of the locality in relation to employment
- ☐ population of the locality, showing totals of men and women, and those who are economically active
- ☐ Census of Population data for the travel-to-work area, showing where the resident population is employed and the places from which workers commute into the locality
- ☐ future labour supply of skillcentre trainees and school-leavers
- ☐ trends in the local labour market which indicate developing shortages or surpluses
- ☐ local unemployment data, analysed to show industry and

occupation

- ☐ age of the unemployed and length of their unemployment
- ☐ numbers of vacancies notified and of those filled or still unfilled in each occupation
- ☐ a general bulletin on employment in the district
- ☐ a news sheet on some particular aspects of the local labour market

For information about a larger area than that served by the local office, an approach can be made to the Regional Manpower Intelligence Unit of the MSC (see Part II for addresses).

Information on local schools and other teaching establishments should be available from the local education authority or Careers Service, showing numbers by age and sex, and recent output by level of qualifications. Where the leavers go, and, importantly, what proportion are available for work, can usually be ascertained from the local Careers Office or the Employment Service. A further important source of information is the local authority and in particular its structure plan which contains development plans covering population changes, transport, housing, employment and so on. Structure plans are available for each County and Metropolitan County Council (addresses are in Part II), but many authorities now have local plans prepared for smaller areas. Finally, local offices of trade associations, employers' federations, and trade unions often have valuable information about local earnings, fringe benefits and conditions of employment. Many also have useful information about the extent of any local skill shortages as do the local offices of the industrial training boards.

From the employer's point of view the main difficulty, unless its local labour market lies entirely within a well-defined travel-to-work area, will be in relating information, collected by a variety of agencies and on varying geographical areas, to its own catchment area.

The foregoing examples provide an indication of the range of applications of labour market information. In all, it becomes clear that a sound information base is essential for the right manpower decisions to be made and, having first identified the need, it then becomes necessary to access that information. This Guide provides a rapid assessment of what information is available and with what degree of ease and cost it can be gathered.

PART I:
Sources of Labour Market Information

How to Use this Section

This part of the Guide provides a comprehensive listing of sources of labour market information under nineteen subject headings which can be useful on their own or in conjunction with each other. The information under each subject heading is presented in a uniform way so that the sources can be identified easily and quickly.

The *Introduction* to each subject heading provides details of the type and nature of the sources available and the main collectors and presenters of the information. Terms used in the published data are defined, and the breakdown adopted for the quick reference table is explained in detail. The *Points to note* section lists the most important considerations to be aware of when using the regular, published statistics, and draws attention to such problems as aggregation, sample size and limitations of the range of data presented in the published sources.

Each section has a *Quick reference table* showing the primary and secondary sources of published information on the subject concerned and the analyses which each contains.

The *Primary sources* consist of the major sources of regular published information on each subject heading and they usually contain the most detailed analyses of the statistics. They should be regarded as the first sources to be consulted. The *Secondary sources* include those published sources which are less rigorous in their analysis of the information, but usually appear regularly and contain statistical series in many cases based on those first appearing in Primary sources. The choice between Primary and Secondary sources for the user of labour market information will obviously depend on the degree of detail required; in many cases the Secondary sources have the advantage of being presented in a much simpler way.

The *Tertiary sources* of information include those providing brief basic detail on a regular basis and one-off studies, articles and books which represent a significant contribution to the level of information on each subject. Not all of the sources listed in this section will contain a wealth of statistical data, and many will be more concerned with discussing the problems of information gathering in the particular subject area. A brief outline of the content of each source is given

21

which should be sufficient to enable the user to decide whether or not the source will be useful. Tertiary sources do not appear in the Quick reference tables.

Many publications provide information relating to a number of subject headings, and their publication details will be found at the end of Part I in the *Index of Key Publications.* Publication details for specialised sources are given at the point of reference. Details include latest price, although due to fluctuations this should be treated as a guide only.

The final section under each subject heading lists *Further sources* of information which consist in the main of points of contact for further inquiries. Government bodies such as the Department of Employment and the Manpower Services Commission appear frequently. Details including addresses and telephone numbers of these further sources will be found in Part II of the Guide.

It is intended that this part of the Guide should be used in a systematic way to pinpoint the relevant sources of information and, at the same time, to gain an appreciation of the problems inherent in the regular sources. Having decided on the subject heading of labour market information that is relevant, it is recommended that both the *Introduction* and *Points to note* sections are read before proceeding to the *Quick reference table* for sources of information. The *Tertiary* and *Further sources* are alternatives if the information is not available in either *Primary* or *Secondary sources.*

The details presented for each published information source reflect the contents of the latest volumes available at the time of publication of this Guide. Minor changes in content and layout may be found in subsequent editions of the various publications, and some indication is given (if possible) where change in established practice is likely.

1. General Statistics: Population and its Components

Introduction

The outstanding source of information on the UK population is the decennial Census of Population. This has been carried out every ten years since 1801 (with the exception of 1941) and is by far the most accurate assessment of the actual number of people in the country. The Great Britain and Northern Ireland censuses are normally carried out on the same date (on one specific day) although question coverage can differ between the two. In April 1966, the Office of Population Censuses and Surveys (OPCS) in Great Britain held a 10 per cent sample (interim) census, while Northern Ireland held a full census in October of the same year, although generally the results are compatible.

Most of the other sources of population data listed, including the OPCS mid-year estimates, are derived from the decennial census results.

The term 'population' needs to be clarified as it can have different definitions:

Census population includes all enumerated persons on the census date (in Great Britain or Northern Ireland) and includes all those involved in coastwise shipping, ships in port, and armed forces at home, whether British or foreign.

Total population differs from the census population in that it includes British armed forces and merchant seamen at home and abroad, but excludes Commonwealth and Allied armed forces in this country.

Civilian population is the same as the total population but excludes all armed forces and includes (as it has done since 1968) the merchant navy.

Home population consists of the civilian population plus all armed forces stationed in the UK and all merchant seamen in home waters. In many ways it is similar to the census population being of the *de facto* type (see Points to Note 4 below), and is usually estimated annually on a detailed regional basis.

Working population includes those working and seeking work in the total population of working age (ie between the ages of 16 and 65)

23

and is composed of employees in employment, unemployed, the self-employed, and HM Forces. Adult students are not included.

Population projections attempt to assess the future trend in population and most are carried out by sub-dividing the population into its components such as sex and age groups, with more sub-divisions for the more sophisticated projections. The following breakdown of the statistics has been applied:

- ☐ sex
- ☐ age distribution — usually shown by age groups and usually quinquennial
- ✓☐ working population
- ☐ births — shown in total and frequently by the rate per 1000 population, age of mother and legitimacy
- ☐ deaths — again by numbers and frequently by rate per 1000 population and by age group and cause.
- ☐ marital condition — single, married, widowed, divorced
- ☐ migration — to and from the UK, sometimes by broad area of residence or intended residence
- ☐ projections — mostly made for decennial periods and coinciding with designated census years.

These are the main divisions in the information sources but others may be found amongst the large amount of data available on population.

Points to note

1. In order to guard against misinterpretation, especially when using information from different sources, it is important to be aware of the population definitions listed above.

2. The use of the term 'projection' in demographic statistics is important. A projection only shows how the population will change on the basis of assumptions on the determinants (components) of population change such as birth or death rates. It is distinct from a 'forecast' which tends to imply a strong likelihood of becoming fact. A projection takes into account the factors which might lead to ultimate change.

3. Although the decennial Census of Population results must be seen as the best source of information, it must be remembered that many of the results are published some time after the census date, often four or more years later. In addition some census results are based on a ten per cent sample rather than the full returns.

4. The UK censuses are of the *de facto* type which enumerates persons in the places where they spent the census night irrespective of whether or not they lived there. The *de jure* census enumerates persons ordinarily resident at the time of the census whether or not they were resident on the census night and, for this reason, is considered to be less accurate than the *de facto* type. Nevertheless, the *de jure* approach is still widely used, for example in the USA.

1. Population and its components

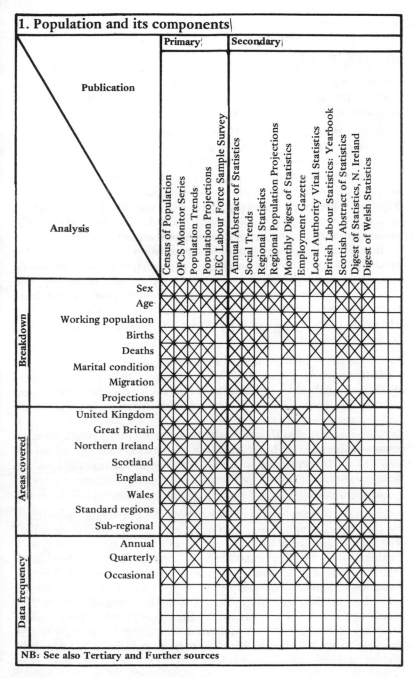

Publication

Primary | **Secondary**

Columns (publications):
- Census of Population
- OPCS Monitor Series
- Population Trends
- Population Projections
- EEC Labour Force Sample Survey
- Annual Abstract of Statistics
- Social Trends
- Regional Statistics
- Regional Population Projections
- Monthly Digest of Statistics
- Employment Gazette
- Local Authority Vital Statistics
- British Labour Statistics: Yearbook
- Scottish Abstract of Statistics
- Digest of Statistics, N. Ireland
- Digest of Welsh Statistics

Analysis

Breakdown
- Sex
- Age
- Working population
- Births
- Deaths
- Marital condition
- Migration
- Projections

Areas covered
- United Kingdom
- Great Britain
- Northern Ireland
- Scotland
- England
- Wales
- Standard regions
- Sub-regional

Data frequency
- Annual
- Quarterly
- Occasional

NB: See also Tertiary and Further sources

Primary sources

Census of Population

In discussing the output from the decennial censuses, reference will be made to the latest one available — that for 1971 — but this can be used as a guide to previous and future censuses.

1. *Census 1971: England and Wales: Preliminary Report*
   Census 1971: Scotland: Preliminary Report
   Census of Population 1971 (Northern Ireland): Preliminary Report
These contain the first provisional figures on the total population, by sex, together with figures from earlier censuses by way of comparison. Figures are presented nationally and for the standard regions (England and Wales report only). All reports show further analyses by sub-regions and for Scotland by local government regions.

In England and Wales provisional population figures are given for counties, county boroughs, local authority areas, new towns, the rural/urban mix and in addition some analysis of population density. For Scotland provisional figures are given for cities, counties and local authority areas. For Northern Ireland the analysis covers local authority areas, and towns and villages containing 50 or more houses (not having legally defined boundaries).

2. *Census 1971: Great Britain: Advance Analysis*
Contains data on population totals for Great Britain, England and Wales and Scotland by sex, marital status and year of birth (with five-year bands). Similar analysis is given for standard regions in Great Britain and for the conurbations. For smaller areas down to counties, county boroughs and local authorities with populations over 15,000, separate county leaflets should be consulted in the series *Census 1971: England and Wales: Advance Analysis County Leaflets* and *Census 1971: Scotland: Second Preliminary Report*.

3. *Census 1971: Great Britain: Summary Tables*
Information is given on the final totals of the enumerated population by constituent country, sex, age (in single years) and marital condition. The data covers Great Britain, England and Wales, and Scotland, with further analysis for the standard regions, conurbations and sub-divisions of the regions. For Scotland only, the *Census 1971: Scotland: Scottish Population Summary* contains details of final population totals by sex only, but for hospital board areas and local government areas. For Northern Ireland, the *Census of Population 1971 (Northern Ireland): Summary Tables* gives the enumerated population by sex, age (single years up to age 25, then bands of five years) and marital condition for district councils, counties and county boroughs.

4. *Census 1971: Great Britain: Age, Marital Condition and General Tables*
This duplicates some of the information contained in the *Summary Tables* including analysis by age, sex and marital condition for Great Britain, England and Wales and Scotland separately.

5. *Census 1971: England and Wales: County Reports*
   Census 1971: Scotland: County Reports
   Census of Population 1971 (Northern Ireland): County Reports
For the English and Welsh counties the statistics are given in three volumes and for Scotland each county is given a separate volume with an additional one for Scottish new towns. The data shows the enumerated population by sex and density (persons per hectare) for the counties, local authority areas, wards (in towns), parishes (in rural areas of England and Wales), electoral divisions (in Scotland), conurbation centres and new towns. For local authority areas only there is some age analysis of the numbers of people, with further analysis by sex and marital condition.

In the case of Northern Ireland, each county is given a separate volume and shows the population by sex with some analysis by age and marital condition for each county, local authority area, ward, rural district and district and electoral division.

6. *Census 1971: Great Britain: Qualified Manpower Tables*
This contains analyses of those people aged 18 or over holding at least qualifications of a standard above GCE Advanced level showing them by age and sex, and by industry and occupation. There are further analyses by economic activity, area of usual residence and employment status. Most of the information relates to Great Britain and its constituent countries although there are some regional analyses.

A broader analysis of qualifications held is given for Northern Ireland only in *Census of Population 1971 (Northern Ireland): Education Tables.*

Much of the above census information has not been redefined to take into account the boundary changes brought about by the 1972 Local Government Act, but a useful publication — *Reorganisation of Local Government Areas: Correlation of New and Old Areas* (HMSO, 1975, price 48p) — gives a comparison between the old and new areas.

OPCS Monitor Series

This is a series of OPCS information bulletins designed for the quick release of figures on specific topics. As such, they represent the first publication of many of the regular series of statistics to be embodied in a final publication at a later date. Currently the *Monitors* of interest are as follows:

☐ *Population estimates* (ref PP1)
☐ *Population projections* (ref PP2)
☐ *Deaths and mortality* (ref DH1)
☐ *Deaths by cause* (ref DH2)
☐ *Deaths from accidents* (ref DH4)
☐ *Births* (ref FM1)
☐ *Births and deaths* (ref VS)
☐ *Migration* (ref MN)

Each *Monitor* will vary in content slightly so it is difficult to describe the range of information given, but as a guide *Population projections* summarises the main features of the latest mid-year population projections for England and Wales and gives the projected figures for Great Britain and the UK as well.

All OPCS *Monitors* can be obtained free of charge from OPCS, Information Branch (for address see Part II).

Population Trends

This contains articles on key features of the population and vital statistics of the UK. Recent articles have covered such topics as migration, birth intervals (that is, how much time elapses between first and second child, and so on), and population density. Regular tables show population for the UK and 19 other selected countries at mid-year for the latest five years plus two others (usually the latest available census years). The population change each year is analysed by its components (birth and death rates) and the total relative change. For the UK and separately for its constituent counties, mid-year estimates of population are given for the latest 18 years plus two other years, with the latest year to publication only broken down by broad age groups.

The components of population change (births, deaths, net migration and other factors) are given annually for about 18 years (mid-year to mid-year), with separate tables for the UK, Great Britain, Scotland, England and Wales. A summary of vital statistics in the UK, Great Britain, Scotland, England and Wales is given, with each table showing the number of live births (legitimate and illegitimate), marriages, deaths and a comprehensive analysis of infant mortality, with numbers and rates (per 1000 population) all for the latest four years quarterly, and the latest six years plus another two annually.

Further analyses for England and Wales only show population by age group, sex, and marital status for 14 years annually (very recent), with the latter data also supplemented by a graph. In addition birth and death rates and numbers are given with an age group analysis in both cases, for five years quarterly and annually for eight years. There are also tables on international migration to and from the UK, including analysis of broad area of last or intended residence and some broad occupational analysis. Some of the data are given quarterly but most are presented on an annual basis.

Population Projections (Series PP2)

The annual OPCS projections of population are based on the mid-year estimate of two years prior to publication and utilise the projections of the components of population change to predict the final population figure. Full details of methods and formulae used are given. The main tables show the base population (ie that at the beginning of the period) by sex and age range for the UK and its constituent countries. Also given are the projections of total UK population based on these components, by sex and age group, for the future four decennial census years, numbers and percentages in each age group and indices of population change from the base year. Graphs supplement the indices.

The appendices section contains a more detailed analysis of the projections. Actual and projected total mid-year populations are given by sex and age group, usually for actual figures back five years plus two previous census figures and projections forward for 30 years annually. There are separate analyses for the UK and constituent countries. Changes in the projected total population are given annually for 30 years for the UK and its constituent countries. For the UK, Great Britain and England and Wales only, the analysis also shows the marital condition of the projected population. Finally, projected mortality rates by sex and single ages are given for 30 years annually, but only for England and Wales, Scotland and Northern Ireland.

EEC Labour Force Sample Survey

This contains details of the total population of each of the nine EEC member countries plus the EEC total, all by sex and broad age group for the survey year only. Similar analysis is given for the UK standard regions and the other member EEC countries by regions. There is also an analysis of the composition of the total population of each country, also broken down regionally, which shows the principal characteristics of activity with such groups as those with a main occupation (full- or part-time separately), housewives, and schoolchildren.

Secondary sources

Annual Abstract of Statistics

This contains a summary of the UK population by sex and constituent countries showing the home population for the censuses of 1801, 1851 and from 1901 onwards, and the mid-year estimates annually for about 30 years. Total population projections are also given decennially for about four future census years. An analysis of population changes in the UK and its constituent countries shows the population at the beginning of the period, births, deaths and net civilian migration during the period, and the resultant new figures at the end. Decades are given from 1901 to about 2011. There is also some analysis of the projected population change by sex and age group but for the UK only.

The geographical distribution of both the enumerated and the home estimated population is given by region with the former by UK standard regions, conurbations and cities for the last four census years plus one other and the latter by constituent UK countries, standard regions, metropolitan counties, London boroughs and county districts with a population in excess of 300,000, for seven consecutive years (the latest being about two years prior to publication). Separate tables show the age group distribution of the enumerated population and its constituent countries by sex, for recent census years. Similar details are given for the home population but are based on mid-year estimates for the latest 11 years in the case of the UK only, and for just the latest year for the constituent countries.

Births are given comprehensive treatment with an analysis of live births by sex, legitimacy, still births, and age range of mother, for the latest 17 consecutive years plus a further eight (at long gaps), all separately for the UK and its constituent countries. Live births by age of mother and for legitimate births by duration of present marriage are given in separate tables for England and Wales and Scotland, for the latest 11 consecutive years. Deaths are analysed by age, sex and cause for the UK and its constituent countries for a number of recent years. The UK death rates (per 1000 population) are also presented for a long run.

Marital condition, showing numbers for single, married, widowed or divorced, is given for the enumerated population and for the total population, with broad age ranges. These are given for the UK and constituent countries. There are also tables on migration into and out of the UK showing the country of last or next residence and the broad occupation (ie professional, manual and clerical, not gainfully employed), all for the latest 12 years.

Finally, there is an analysis of the total working population showing the composition annually for the latest ten years, with separate tables for the UK and Great Britain.

Social Trends

UK population is given by sex and broad age group with, in addition, the sex ratio (that is, males per 1000 females) for all censuses since 1901 plus the latest year's estimate, with projections for a further four decennial periods. The past changes in UK population (all census years back to 1901) and projections (decennially for next four census years) are analysed by the components of change showing births, deaths and migration over a ten year period. For Great Britain only a bar chart shows the population structure by age, sex and marital status for one year. A graph also shows some variant projections forward for about 35 years.

Birth and fertility rates are given by the age group of the mother for the UK only for the latest five years plus the two previous census years. For Great Britain, death rates are shown by sex in six age ranges for the latest three or four years, and some historical analysis is also given.

There is some analysis of UK migration, by losses and gains for about seven years plus graphs. For Great Britain the estimated total of married persons for the latest four years plus a further 50 years (decennially) is given and the marital status of the household population over 15 years of age is given, by sex.

Finally, there is an international analysis of population in selected countries, showing such factors as density, change over time, birth rates, infant mortality and life expectation.

Regional Statistics

The 'Regional profiles' section shows for each UK standard region, the total population by sex and the percentage under 15 and over 65, the number of persons per square kilometer, the number of births per 1000 women aged 15-44, and the deaths per 1000 population, all for the latest year and with UK comparisons. For each county within each standard region similar information is given, but in addition there are details of perinatal mortality rates, some population projections (not far ahead) and an analysis of net migration to and from the region and counties within it.

Regular statistics show the home population by sex and standard region annually for the latest four years plus three further years (over a ten year period), and by broad age group for the latest year plus one other. Projections of the home population are given for the UK and its constituent countries by sex and broad age ranges for the next two census years.

The vital statistics of the standard regions are summarised for the latest two years plus a further three years (over a ten year period), showing live births (numbers and rate), stillbirths, legitimacy, and deaths, the latter also shown by cause.

Regional Population Projections

These contain projections on the population of the individual standard regions of England and Wales (post 1972 Local Government Act boundary changes), counties, London and the metropolitan districts, all by sex and by age group. Similar analyses for Scotland and its regions are contained in the *Quarterly Return of the Registrar General, Scotland* which includes projections for health boards and hospital regions.

Monthly Digest of Statistics

This contains home population mid-year estimates by sex annually for the latest 18 years, for the UK and its constituent countries separately. For the latest mid-year estimate (the full year prior to publication) total population is shown by sex for the UK only, with the home population analysed by age group for the UK and its constituent countries. Births and deaths are shown in total for the UK and its constituent countries, quarterly for 16 quarters (the latest quarter about three months prior to publication) and annually for six years.

Also, the UK working population is given (in unadjusted and seasonally adjusted form) quarterly for 14 quarters (the latest about six months prior to publication) and annually for a further seven years.

Employment Gazette

A regular table shows the working population for the UK and Great Britain separately by its component parts and in total. Figures are unadjusted and seasonally adjusted, and quarterly for 18 quarters (the latest being about six months prior to publication).

Local Authority Vital Statistics (Series VS)

This covers England and Wales only and shows the estimated home population in total for the latest year with live births by sex and legitimacy and rate per 1000 population. Deaths are given by sex and rate per 1000 population plus a separate analysis of deaths under one year old, all for England and Wales (separately), the standard regions, counties, Greater London and its constituent boroughs, and the local authority areas of the counties. Another lengthy analysis on the same basis is given for the regional and area health authorities of England and Wales.

For Scotland similar information can be found in the *Quarterly Return of the Registrar General Scotland* and for Northern Ireland in *The Registrar General's Quarterly Return for Northern Ireland.*

British Labour Statistics Yearbook

Total working population and the components of the total are shown by sex, based on estimates from the Censuses of Employment, quarterly for the latest eight years. There are separate tables for the UK and Great Britain. Also the seasonally adjusted working population in total only, but by sex, is given.

Scottish Abstract of Statistics

Extensive population statistics show the enumerated population of Scotland by local government regions and districts, by sex, with details from the last census only. For all previous censuses, the population of Scotland is given by sex and age group (with numbers and percentage in each), together with the changes between censuses shown by the components of that change (births, deaths and migration), the latter for about 25 years annually. The home population of Scotland by local government areas and islands areas is given by age group for the latest available year (numbers and percentages in each group), and in total for these areas for about eight years annually. There are also projections of home population by age and sex for local government regions.

Births and deaths (the latter by cause) in Scotland are given for the latest available year.

Digest of Statistics — Northern Ireland

This shows the Northern Ireland home population by district council areas for four years (up to the full year preceding publication)in total only, and for the latest mid-year estimate plus the previous three censuses by sex and broad age group, for Northern Ireland in total only. Projections of the future population of Northern Ireland only are given by age group, for the next full year plus a further eight periods (usually quinquennial). The distribution of the total Northern Ireland working population is given, by sex, annually for seven recent years.

Births and deaths are given comprehensive treatment showing the overall numbers and rates per 1000 population by sex, all for two years quarterly and four years annually, plus usually some odd years.

Digest of Welsh Statistics

The mid-year estimates provide the basis for an analysis of population by Welsh administrative area for the latest eight years plus two other years. For the counties only, population is shown by age and sex for the latest year with some analysis of the components of population change. Population projections are given for Wales and its counties by age group and sex, for the latest year plus three census years. There is also some analysis of Welsh population by occupation and status, with further analysis by socio-economic group and social class, all by sex and based on the latest census results.

There is extensive analysis of births and deaths in Wales, the former shown by legitimacy and age of mother, the latter by cause and age, all for a long run. Finally the 'County statistics' section shows for each Welsh county, the total population, the percentage under 15 years old and over 65, and the number of persons per hectare (for population density), with the projected percentage change over a long period.

Tertiary sources

British Labour Statistics: Historical Abstract 1886-1968

This contains historical statistics on the working population of Great Britain by sex, annually for the period 1938-68, and for the UK quarterly for the period 1950-68. Also, separate tables for males and females show the UK and Great Britain components of the working population for a long period annually.

Yearbook of Labour Statistics (ILO)

This shows the total population by sex and broad age group for about 180 member nations of the ILO.

Demographic Trends 1950-1990

(OECD Paris, 1979)

A report of a study of demographic and labour force trends carried out by the OECD and based upon information supplied by the member nations. There is a description of the main components of demographic change together with tables showing actual and projected birth and death rates for all member countries over the period of the publication. Tables also show the anticipated growth in both total population and working population for member nations over a number of years, with some analysis by age.

Further sources

Office of Population Censuses and Surveys
County and Metropolitan County Councils (especially the structure plans)
General Register Office (Scotland)
General Register Office (Northern Ireland)

2. General Statistics: Economic Activity

Introduction

Broadly defined, economic activity refers to the working activities of the population and includes the sub-categories of economically *active* and *inactive*. The usual distinction is that those considered to be economically active will include:

- ☐ those in employment (employed and self-employed)
- ☐ those out of employment (unemployed and temporarily sick) but seeking work.

Those considered to be economically inactive include:

- ☐ the retired
- ☐ the permanently sick
- ☐ students
- ☐ others, such as housewives
- ☐ school children (under 16 years old).

This section will focus in particular on the sources of information on activity rates.

An *activity rate* (or ratio) can be described as the proportion of the total population in any age and sex group who are in the working population (employed, unemployed or temporarily sick). It is sometimes referred to as a *participation rate*, and quoted as a percentage.

The most accurate source on activity rates is the decennial census, but this does have the disadvantage of being dated by the time detailed results are published. In the interim periods the best sources are the surveys carried out annually in the General Household Survey and biennially in the EEC Labour Force Sample Survey.

The statistics have been broken down as follows:

- ☐ sex
- ☐ age — usually broad age groups
- ☐ activity rates — provided in some publications but can be worked out from the raw data if necessary
- ☐ status — by this is meant whether in or out of employment and further sub-divisions of these two

☐ occupation — usually very broad groups
☐ industry — broad groups
☐ marital condition — an important distinction for economic activity, with many sources at the very least giving details of married women separately.

These are the main forms of presentation but others may be found in the regular statistics.

Points to note

1. Much of the information derived from the Census of Population (see Primary sources 1 below) is based on a 10 per cent sample of the census returns, although this must still be regarded as indicative of the total population.
2. Projections of activity rates should be treated with caution as the determinants of economic activity are notoriously difficult to predict with accuracy.
3. Other information on the working population and the numbers in employment will be found in the relevant sections of this Guide. These components can be useful in providing the raw data for the calculation of activity rates.

Primary sources

Census of Population

The relevant publications based on the 1971 Census of Population are given below and can be taken as a guide to the range and content of past and future censuses.

1. *Census 1971: Great Britain: Economic Activity (Parts I–V)*
   Census of Population 1971 (Northern Ireland): Economic Activity Tables
The Great Britain analysis is presented in five separate parts. Part I only is based on the actual results of the census and shows economic activity for males, females and married females, and by age group quinquennially, all for Great Britain in total and for counties, conurbations, regions and sub-regions.

Parts II to V are based on a 10 per cent sample. Part II gives analyses of economic activity by status, sex (married females separately), age group, area of usual residence and workplace, occupation and industry. Most of the analysis covers Great Britain in total but there is also some county analysis. Part III shows economic activity by industry and status which are further shown by occupation, sex and age group for Great Britain, standard regions, counties and conurbations. Part IV

2. Economic activity

Analysis / Publication	Primary			Secondary			
	Census of Population	General Household Survey	EEC Labour Force Sample Survey	Annual Abstract of Statistics	Social Trends	Digest of Welsh Statistics	British Labour Statistics: Historical Abstract
Breakdown							
Sex	X	X		X	X	X	X
Age	X	X					
Activity rates		X		X			
Status	X			X	X		
Occupation	X		X				
Industry	X						
Marital conditon	X	X			X		
Areas covered							
United Kingdom		X		X			
Great Britain	X	X		X		X	
Northern Ireland	X						
England	X						
Scotland	X						
Wales	X				X		
Standard regions	X		X				
Sub-regional	X				X		
Data frequency							
Annual		X	X				
Occasional	X	X	X	X	X		

NB: See also Tertiary and Further sources

concentrates on analyses by social and socio-economic class by sex, age group and marital condition for Great Britain, England, Wales and Scotland. There are further analyses of married women by social and socio-economic class of their husband for Great Britain, England, Wales and Scotland, conurbations and regions. Also, a useful analysis is given of those retired but economically active, by sex, industry and age group, with the main analysis for Great Britain only, although also some for counties, conurbations and regions. Part V shows (for males only) economic activity by area of usual residence and socio-economic class for Great Britain, England, Wales and Scotland, conurbations, regions, counties and local authority areas.

The Northern Ireland analyses show economic activity by occupation and industry, by sex, age, marital condition, employment status (ie self-employed, etc) and socio-economic group. Most of the data cover Northern Ireland only but included are some analyses of local authority areas.

2. *Census 1971: England and Wales: Economic Activity: sub-regional volumes*
Census 1971: Scotland: Economic Activity: sub-regional volumes
These volumes contain details derived from a 10 per cent sample and contain analyses by counties, county boroughs, urban areas with populations of 50,000 or more, and the conurbation centres. Main details given are occupation and status by sex and area of usual residence, with some industrial and workplace analysis. Similar details, but for specific areas analysed by smaller divisions (eg local authorities, cities, etc) are contained in a further series of publications:

☐ *Census 1971: England and Wales: Economic Activity: County Leaflets*
☐ *Census 1971: Scotland: Economic Activity: County Leaflets*
☐ *Census 1971: England and Wales: Economic Activity: New Towns*
☐ *Census 1971: Scotland: Economic Activity: New Towns*
☐ *Census of Population 1971 (Northern Ireland): County Reports*

3. *Census 1971: England and Wales: New County Reports as Constituted April 1973*
Census 1971: Scotland: New Region Reports
These contain a similar range of information to the old county reports listed above, but have been redrafted to take into account boundary changes following the Local Government Act 1972.

General Household Survey

The percentage of people economically active (with those employed and those unemployed separately) and the percentage inactive are given by sex and age, with females shown by those married and those not married, for the survey year and for Great Britain only. The percentage of women working is further analysed by age, number of dependent children and whether working full- or part-time.

Those reported as economically inactive are also shown by their major activity during the week of the survey, for example, whether they went to school, were retired or kept house, etc. They are further analysed by age and sex and by whether they have ever worked.

There might be some variations in the range of information contained in the GHS each year, but some aspects of economic activity are usually covered, and most of these are not normally found elsewhere.

EEC Labour Force Sample Survey

This survey assesses the UK population by principal activity and includes a comprehensive table which shows for each constituent country and for males and females separately, those with a main occupation, and those unemployed, and thus the total of economically active persons. It shows the economically inactive by those with an occasional occupation, those seeking employment, school children and students, and housewives. Numbers and percentages are given in each category. A similar analysis is given by UK standard region and for the regions of the other EEC member nations.

Also shown are the activity rates (ratios) of the UK population and the other EEC nations by sex and age group beginning with 14 years of age.

Secondary sources

Annual Abstract of Statistics

This shows for Great Britain only, by sex, the total economically inactive population aged 15 and over by reason for inactivity, and those economically active by status (in employment, self-employed, managers, foremen and supervisors, other employees), including those out of employment (separately those sick and those not sick). All the above are given by eight age groups, for the latest year.

Social Trends

For Great Britain only, a summary of economic activity is given (with numbers and percentages) for those economically active or inactive for the three latest census years. Economic activity rates for the population of Great Britain are given by age group and sex based on the GHS results for four years annually (the latest year being about two years prior to publication). Bar charts comparing the Census of Population and GHS activity rates are given for a number of years. Also there is an international analysis of those economically active based on ILO data and covering the UK plus about 14 other widely selected countries. It shows the percentage economically active in three age groups for one year only (although not necessarily the same year for each country).

Digest of Welsh Statistics

Based on the latest census results, this shows the enumerated population aged 15 and over by sex and whether economically active or inactive (with reasons). The analysis is for one year only and covers Wales and its counties.

British Labour Statistics: Historical Abstract 1886-1968

For the census years of 1951, 1961 and 1966, the components of the economically active population of Great Britain are shown by activity rate and numbers by broad age group, with separate analyses for males, females, married females, and single, widowed and divorced females.

Tertiary sources

Yearbook of Labour Statistics (ILO)

This contains tables showing the numbers economically active and the activity rate by sex and age group for a large number of ILO member countries (including the UK) for one year only, although the actual year may vary from country to country.

Regional Civilian Labour Force Projections
(*Employment Gazette*, September 1978, pp1040–43)

This article concentrates on the anticipated growth in the civilian labour force in Great Britain and includes analysis of activity rates by sex and standard region for the years 1961, 1966, 1971 and 1975, and those projected for 1981, 1986, 1991, with commentary on the key trends.

Changing Composition of the Labour Force 1976-1991
(*Employment Gazette*, June 1979, pp546–51)

A summary of a research study carried out by the DE, it includes a graph showing married women's activity rates in Great Britain in broad age groups over the period 1911–91 with commentary.

Demographic Trends 1950–1990
(OECD, Paris, 1979)

This publication shows for the UK and other OECD member countries, trends in activity rates by age and sex, with graphs and tables in addition to the commentary. Most of the data are projected ahead to 1990 (quinquennially).

An Increase in Earlier Retirement for Men
(*Employment Gazette*, April 1980, pp366–69)

This article examines the changing retirement patterns of men and women since 1975, including an assessment of possible reasons for these changes. Economic activity analysis is given for those age ranges below the official retirement ages.

Further sources

Office of Population Censuses and Surveys
County and Metropolitan County Councils (particularly the structure plans)
General Register Office (Scotland)
General Register Office (Northern Ireland)

3. Employment

Introduction

The *working population* is taken to comprise the employed labour force plus those unemployed. This section covers data relating to the *employed labour force* which by definition consists of:

- ☐ employees in employment
- ☐ employers and the self-employed
- ☐ those in the armed forces.

The most accurate information on employment numbers is that derived from the censuses of Population, Employment and, to a lesser extent, Production and Distribution. The decennial Census of Population is the most thorough survey but has the disadvantage of being rather dated by the time the results are published, the time lag between census and publication of any results relating to employment being in the region of four years. The Census of Employment is carried out annually (since 1970) and is the most regular and thorough of the reports on employment. Each June a postal enquiry is sent to employers requiring them to give a range of employment details about their paid workforce. All sectors of the economy are involved except for agriculture which has its own employment survey carried out by the relevant ministry, but which makes the information available to the Department of Employment. A full census is only carried out every three years (1979 being such a year), the years in between omitting those employers who at the last full census had less than three employees.

The censuses of Production and Distribution include some information on employment in the industries covered by them. The Census of Production is carried out annually but covers only those manufacturing industries employing 20 or more employees in the UK; it is, nevertheless, useful for industrial analyses of employment. The Census of Distribution is less useful, the last one, covering all retail establishments, being in 1971. Some of the relevant results are published in the *Employment Gazette* (see Primary Sources below). Other main sources of information on employment include the regular surveys carried out by the DE on a monthly and quarterly basis, and the biennial EEC Labour Force Sample Survey. They are a valuable supplement to the more thorough census information.

The DE's main coverage of employment data comes from the annual Census of Employment, providing the basis for monthly and quarterly estimates which cover all industries and services. The ratio of change since the last available census is then used to update the employment series. Some data are supplied directly on a regular basis by the central government departments and the nationalised industries, for example, and added to the survey results. The monthly and quarterly series are issued in a provisional form until their revision when new census data become available.*

The information has been broken down as follows:

☐ sex
☐ age — given coverage in a limited number of the regular publications by either exact years or age bands
☐ manual/non-manual — the relative proportions of the two of total employment, but can sometimes be a subjective distinction.
☐ industry — with much of the analysis distinguishing between the large groups of production, manufacturing and service industries, but with some analysis by SIC and MLH
☐ occupation — usually by broad group but occasionally by a more detailed analysis
☐ Establishment size — showing in most cases the number of establishments (firms or plants, for example) within a size range of employees — a conventional measure of firm size — or by the numbers of employees within certain employee size bands
☐ Full/part-time — distinguishing between the two types of employment (more details of part-time employment will be found under subject heading 13).

Points to note

1. The term *employees in employment* as used in the offical statistics includes those persons temporarily laid off but still on employers' payrolls and persons unable to work because of short-term sickness. Full- and part-time workers are both included, and the latter are counted as full units.

---

*The derivation and use of employment statistics is given a thorough examination in Buxton, N K and Mackay, D I *British Employment Statistics — A Guide to Sources and Methods* (Basil Blackwell, Oxford, 1977), which looks at the validity of the data over a long period as well as commenting upon the current statistics

2. The self-employed definitions, as used in the official statistics, includes managing directors (but not other directors) of companies and those who declare themselves to be self-employed (as in the decennial Census of Population).

3. The current range of official data on employment is not of a uniform standard for each industrial sector. Taking the *primary* sector first, because of the omission of employers from the regular DE estimates, this source tends to underestimate the total employment. The most significant omission occurs in agriculture, where a large proportion of the total workforce are the employers themselves. From this it would seem that the best source of information on agriculture and, therefore, on the total primary sector must be the Census of Population.

In the *manufacturing* sector there seems to be little difference between the decennial Census of Population and the annual DE Census of Employment results and from this it could be assumed that the Census of Population is the most thorough of the two. In the intervening years the DE census would be a reliable measure.

In the *service* industries sector again the Census of Population is probably the best source of information. The problem again is that posed by the omission of employers in the DE annual census, but this is aggravated by problems of accurate measurement of specifically two service groups, miscellaneous services (SIC XXVI) and public administration and defence (SIC XXVII). So the Census of Population should be used where possible.*

4. The Census of Employment uses the distinction of below 30 hours per week to indicate part-time work.

5. The following categories are excluded from the Census of Employment questionnaire:

☐ working proprietors
☐ partners
☐ the self-employed
☐ directors not under a contract of service
☐ wives working for husbands
☐ husbands working for wives (other relatives who are paid are included)
☐ persons working in their own homes (for example, taking in sewing machine or assembly work)
☐ former employees still on the payroll as pensioners only
☐ private domestic staff working in private households.

---

*A detailed discussion of the different sources for each industrial sector appears in *British Employment Statistics*, Buxton, N K and Mackay, D I, op cit

3. Employment

Breakdown / Areas / Frequency	Primary					Secondary											
Analysis	Employment Gazette	EEC Labour Force Sample Survey	Census of Population	British Labour Statistics: Yearbook	DMS Gazette	Monthly Digest of Statistics	Economic Trends	Annual Abstract of Statistics	Social Trends	Regional Statistics	Digest of Welsh Statistics	Scottish Abstract of Statistics	Scottish Economic Bulletin	Digest of Statistics – N. Ireland	Welsh Economic Trends	Census of Production	British Labour Statistics: Historical Abstract
Breakdown																	
Sex	X	X	X	X	X	X		X		X	X	X	X	X	X		X
Age		X												X			
Manual/non-manual			X														
Industry	X	X				X		X		X	X	X		X	X		X
Occupation		X	X														
Seasonally adjusted	X			X													
Employment unit size												X	X				
Full/part-time	X	X		X													
Areas covered																	
United Kingdom	X	X	X	X		X		X									X
Great Britain	X	X		X													X
Northern Ireland	X		X	X										X			X
England	X		X	X						X							
Scotland	X		X	X						X		X	X				
Wales	X		X	X						X	X				X		
Standard region	X			X						X							
Sub-regional			X							X							
Data frequency																	
Annual		X		X		X		X		X	X	X	X	X	X		X
Half-yearly						X											
Quarterly	X				X	X							X				
Monthly	X				X	X								X			
Occasional	X	X	X														

NB: See also Tertiary and Further sources

Primary sources

Employment Gazette

This provides the best range of regular employment data on a monthly and quarterly basis. Monthly statistics show employees in employment in Great Britain by SIC order and by sex and MLH for the Index of Production and manufacturing industries. Three consecutive months are given (the latest month usually being about two months prior to publication). For the UK and Great Britain separately, a table shows employees in employment, by sex, the self-employed, HM forces labour, and the total employed labour force, all quarterly for 18 quarters. There is also a separate table giving the seasonally adjusted figures.

Employees in employment for standard regions in Great Britain are given, by sex, for all industries and services, and separately for agriculture, fisheries and food, the Index of Production industries, all manufacturing industries and all service industries, for seven quarters. Also shown are the regional totals for all employees in employment as a percentage of the total for Great Britain. Regional indices of employment, showing the relationship to Great Britain, are given separately for the Index of Production industries, manufacturing industries, and service industries.

The total number of employees in employment in Great Britain in all industries and services is shown monthly for 19 quarters; employees in the Index of Production industries are shown monthly for under five years. Manufacturing industries are shown by full SIC order together with mining and quarrying, construction, and gas, electricity and water, for each month for over four years, but service industries by SIC are only given quarterly. A seasonally adjusted index for all Index of Production and all manufacturing industries (separately) is given, showing the relative monthly change over these years.

Quarterly series provide the most comprehensive industrial analysis of employees in employment. Estimates are given, by sex, for Great Britain with full SIC and a comprehensive MLH analysis, plus totals for all industries and services, Index of Production industries, and manufacturing industries and services. Estimates are made for the quarters ending in March, June, September and December, and appear in the Gazettes of January, April, July and October, showing three quarters with the latest being about four months prior to publication.

Also shown (for five quarters in each case) are employees in employment by standard regions of Great Britain, for all industries and services, by sex, and totals only in 14 other selected SIC groups.

There is quarterly analysis of manpower in the local authorities which covers England, Wales and Scotland separately, and shows a breakdown of numbers by 15 service groups (for example, education, construction, etc), with full- and part-time workers separated. The analyses cover the quarters ending March, June, September and December and the latest six are shown in the *Gazettes* of February, May, August and December.

Other occasional studies published in the *Gazette* will be found in the Tertiary sources section.

EEC Labour Force Sample Survey

The results relevant are those relating to 'persons with an occupation' which can be equated with the DE definitions of employees in employment plus the self-employed. Persons with an occupation during the reference week are shown by sex, with the following divisions: those with a main occupation (that is, a job which occupies most of their working time) shown separately as those working full- or part-time; those with an occasional occupation (jobs of a short, sometimes fluctuating nature) shown separately for full- and part-time: and the total persons with an occupation (being the summation of the previous two) again by full- and part-time separately. In total for the UK only. There is a separate table showing the percentages in each case.

Persons with a main occupation by occupational status — employers and self-employed, employees, family workers and total — and by sector of activity — agriculture, industry and services — are shown by sex for the UK only. Also by sex, they are shown by economic activity giving 11 sub-categories for the total UK only. Separate tables give the corresponding percentages. An extension of this analysis shows employees only by economic activity, together with a separate table of percentages.

A standard regions analysis for the UK shows the main occupational divisions by sex, together with the unemployment totals to give the total civilian workforce.

Similar tables are given for the other EEC member nations based on their own domestic survey results.

Census of Population

Relevant employment data are to be found in those census reports dealing with economic activity. A range of summary reports cover economic activity at a sub-regional level showing an analysis of those self-employed — with and without employees separately — and employees by various broad occupational groups such as managers, foremen and supervisors (this by manual/non-manual distinctions) and professional employees. All of the categories are analysed by age for males, females, and married females in each case.

Economic Activity County Leaflets cover each separate county in England and Wales and give details of the self-employed and employees (as outlined above) but by smaller areas. There are details of counties, county boroughs, urban areas with a population of 50,000 and over, conurbation centres and local authority areas, with occupational and industrial analyses of employment, all by males, females and married females separately.

British Labour Statistics Yearbook

A table showing total UK working population gives, by sex, employees in employment, HM forces labour and employers and the self-employed, all quarterly for nine years. There is a similar analysis for Great Britain only with the addition of employees in employment by sex, seasonally adjusted. Employees in employment are shown, by sex for UK standard regions, annually for six years, and by full SIC order and MLH (totals only) for the latest available year for males only.

Separately for the UK and Great Britain, employees in employment are shown by full SIC/MLH, by sex, with full- and part-time distinctions for the latest year only. A monthly analysis for the latest year with quarterly details for a further four years, shows UK employees in employment, by sex, and by SIC order. Similar tables for Great Britain give figures monthly for the latest three years and annually for the latest ten years.

Great Britain employees in employment in the Index of Production industries are given by sex, quarterly for the latest year. There is also analysis of employees in two broad occupational groups for Great Britain manufacturing industry, by sex, for April and October of the latest year.

Numbers of part-time females in manufacturing industries (SIC divisions) in Great Britain are shown, quarterly for the latest year. These numbers, expressed as a percentage of all female employees, are also given for each industry and, finally, indices of numbers in civil employment, by sex, are given quarterly for ten years, Great Britain only, with separate tables for those in manufacturing and those in production industries.

Department of Manpower Services Gazette

For Northern Ireland the first issue (Spring 1978) contained quarterly estimates of employees in employment by full SIC/MLH breakdown, by sex, with further distinctions between full- and part-time employees given for the period 1971 to 1976. The second issue (1979) contained employees in employment by SIC order and by sex for the four quarters of June, September and December 1977, and March 1978.

Secondary sources

Monthly Digest of Statistics

This contains details of the working population and its constituents based on the Census of Employment and shows the total employed labour force, employees in employment (in seasonally adjusted form also), the self-employed and those in HM forces. There are separate analyses for the UK and Great Britain for about the latest three and a half years quarterly and for a further seven years annually. Employees in employment are shown for the UK and Great Britain separately, by sex, for all industries and in total for 14 selected SIC orders, annually for nine years. For production industries only, employees in employment are given, by sex, for the total of all industries and in total only for the 21 SIC groups composing the Index of Production industries. All monthly for the latest 18 months and annually for a further four years.

There are also analyses of particular groups appearing regularly. Civil Service staff are shown in total by ministerial responsibility for the UK over a period of six years. The numbers employed in agriculture in the UK are given six-monthly for seven years with distinctions between regular workers and seasonal or casual workers, full and part-time (all by sex), and those who are salaried managers. Constructional workers in Great Britain are shown for a period of four years quarterly and annually for three of those years.

Finally, local authority manpower in England and Wales (with a separate table for Scotland) is given in total for the latest six quarters.

Economic Trends

In a table showing UK employment and unemployment, the employed labour force and employees in employment are shown in total monthly for the latest 18 months, quarterly for the latest five years and annually for 12 years. For GB manufacturing industry only, indices of employees in employment are given for the same period.

A longer run of this range of information will be found in *Economic Trends Annual Supplement*.

Annual Abstract of Statistics

For the UK and Great Britain separately, the employed labour force, HM forces and women's services, employers and self-employed persons and employees in employment (this only by full SIC order) are shown, by sex, annually for ten years. Employees in employment by full MLH are given in total annually for four years, with separate analyses for UK and Great Britain.

Males employed in engineering and related industries are analysed by broad occupational categories and by MLH for Great Britain only for the latest available year. Administrative, technical and clerical workers in manufacturing industries in Great Britain are shown by MLH, annually for nine years. Civil Service staff in Great Britain are shown by a comprehensive breakdown by ministerial responsibility, annually for 11 years. Finally, the number of agricultural workers in Great Britain is shown annually for 11 years, with distinctions (by sex) between regular and seasonal or casual workers, full- and part-time, and salaried managers.

Social Trends

For Great Britain, new entrants to employment are shown annually for six years, with boys and girls under 18 years old separately analysed according to those entering an apprenticeship to a skilled craft and the total number of entrants to employment, with the former expressed as a percentage of the latter. An analysis of economic activity shows, by sex, those in employment (self-employed and employers; employees and part-timers) and those out of employment, annually for three years quinquennially. Bar charts supplement the analysis. Also UK employment by sector is given for four years by sex, showing the numbers and percentages in the public sector (that is, central government, HM forces, civilian, local authorities and public corporations) and in the private sector (showing employees, employers and self-employed).

Regional Statistics

The 'Regional profiles' section provides an analysis for each UK standard region with employment in agriculture, engineering, other manufacturing, construction, mining, quarrying, gas, electricity and water, and service industries. It shows the percentage of employees in each by county, all for one year only and that being about three years prior to the publication date. Employees in employment, the self-employed and those in HM forces are shown separately for UK standard regions, by sex, for seven years annually. A similar regional analysis shows the industrial distribution of employees in employment by SIC groups, by sex, annually for two years (about three years apart). Finally, self-employed persons (with or without employees) are shown by seven major industrial groups for two years annually.

Digest of Welsh Statistics

Employees in employment, employers and self-employed, and the total in civil employment are shown separately for Wales and for Welsh sub-regions, by sex and by SIC order, annually for ten years. Employees in employment in Wales and the UK are given by sex and by SIC order (with percentages in each) for the latest year only; estimates of employees in employment by comprehensive MLH are given (for Wales only) by sex, annually for three years.

There are also analyses covering the numbers employed as non-industrial civil servants, by sex and by age group, those employed by local authorities and in the police force (with full- and part-time distinctions) and a comparative analysis carried out by the Joint Manpower Watch Survey, all annually for a number of years. There is also an analysis of manufacturing units by employment size, with seven size groups (measured by the number of employees) showing the numbers and percentages in each group for Wales, the assisted regions, the unassisted regions and the UK, for one year only. A smaller analysis covers Welsh sub-regions.

Scottish Abstract of Statistics

For Scotland, employers and the self-employed and employees in employment are shown, by sex, annually for 27 years. Employees in employment are shown by local government regions and island areas by broad industrial groups (primary, manufacturing, gas, etc) and services. Total and males separately are given, all annually for six years. A full SIC analysis shows Scottish employees in employment annually for 12 years with totals and males separately.

Further industrial analyses are based on the Census of Employment and give a comprehensive MLH breakdown annually for three years. Males and total are shown by full- and part-time working.

Special analyses show the amount of employment wholly related to North Sea oil for all Scotland and some sub-regions, quarterly for four years. Local authority manpower in Scotland is shown by full- and part-time and by department, quarterly for two years, and finally, manufacturing units by employment size are given for one year only showing the number of units in each group and total numbers employed.

Scottish Economic Bulletin

The 'Quarterly economic series' includes tables on employees in employment by sex, quarterly for 11 years. For the same period total employment in agriculture, all industries, manufacturing and services is given (separately for each). Employment by SIC order shows the total of employers and the self-employed and, by sex, employees in employment. Also the annual percentage change in total Scottish employees in employment is given, annually for 10 years.

Digest of Statistics — Northern Ireland

For Northern Ireland, employers and self-employed persons and employees in employment are shown by sex, with the latter also shown by totals in Index of Production and manufacturing industries separately. There is also a breakdown of civil employment (that is, the sum of employers, self-employed and employees in employment) by SIC order, all annually for seven years. Agricultural manpower (as in the June census) is shown annually for 17 years, with distinctions between owners of farms, family workers, hired workers, seasonal or casual workers, and males and females. Finally, an analysis by establishment size shows the number of units and the number of employees in nine size bands, with separate figures on primary (SIC I and II), secondary (SIC III–XX) and tertiary orders (SIC XXI–XXVII), all for one year only.

Welsh Economic Trends

The self-employed are analysed by numbers and percentage of total workforce for all Welsh regional sub-divisions and for Great Britain in total for the latest Census of Population year. The distribution of the self-employed by broad sector (extractive, manufacturing, construction and services) is given by the same breakdown and for the same period. Maps supplement the tables.

Based on the EEC Survey, persons in employment in Wales and Great Britain are shown by 18 broad occupational groups, with the percentage of the total in each group and the average age. The percentage of married females in employment is also given.

Employees in employment are presented by sex, as indices of regional growth annually for 13 years, for Wales, Scotland, the UK and some standard UK regions, including some analysis of assisted and unassisted regions. Total civil employment, employers and self-employed, employees in employment and those in the Index of Production industries are shown by sex, and by Welsh statistical sub-division, for one year only. Changes in the number of employees in employment by broad industry group and by sub-region are shown over a five year period, by sex, and with some percentages. There is also an analysis of the size of firm and numbers employed based on the latest available Census of Employment data, by selected SIC orders.

The appendices contain details of employment by employment office and/or travel-to-work area, by sex, and are based on the latest available Census of Employment details. This is supplemented by county and employment office area employment with a limited industrial analysis and the relative change in employment levels over a five year period.

Census of Production

For each industry report in the *Business Monitor PA Series* there is an analysis of employment by UK standard region, with numbers and percentages shown in total only. UK employment is shown by sex (percentages of each) and by full- and part-time distinctions, and there is some analysis of establishments employing 20 or more people in the UK for about 12 months.

British Labour Statistics: Historical Abstract 1886–1968

The decennial census results provide the basis for analysis of the occupied population from 1841, with some industrial analyses up to the 1966 interim census. An occupational analysis of the numbers in civil employment is given for 1961 and 1966 only, with the latter year broken down by employers and self-employed and employees separately for Great Britain only.

The numbers of insured employees at each mid-year over the period 1923–47 are given in total by UK standard region and for the same period, totals showing employed and unemployed numbers by broad industry group are given, by sex.

The total of employees (employed and unemployed) is shown for UK standard regions, annually over the period 1951–68. For the same period corresponding UK figures are given for males, females and the total separately, with further tables for Great Britain only.

Employees in employment are given comprehensive treatment; by UK standard region 1951–68, by SIC order (of 1948) for the UK in total and for Great Britain separately, and by MLH (of 1948) for the UK, both over the period 1948–68, by sex. Those in Great Britain Index of Production industries are given in total, monthly for the period 1952–68 and quarterly for 1948–51. Numbers of employees in each development area of Great Britain are given in total over the period 1956–68.

Quarterly indices of the numbers in civil employment in manufacturing and production industries in Great Britain are given, by sex, annually over the period 1948–68. Those employed part-time are shown as a percentage of all employees, by sex and by SIC order (of 1958) for the period 1961–68. The percentage of females employed part-time in manufacturing industries in Great Britain is given for the period 1950–68. There is also some analysis of the age of employees (employed and unemployed) by sex, with nine age groups showing the percentage in each for Great Britain only. The period covered is 1950–68.

Wage earners/manual workers as a percentage of the total employees in Great Britain are given by sex and by SIC order (of 1958), for the period 1961–68. Selected occupational analyses show administrative, technical and clerical staff in manufacturing industry as a percentage of total employees in employment, by sex, for the period 1948–68, for Great Britain only. This is supplemented with an analysis covering the period 1964–68 by broad occupational groups, by sex, including those in training shown separately.

Other analyses cover those employed in large shops by broad occupation category, type of shop and full- or part-time, for 1966–68, for Great Britain only. Public sector employment is given separate treatment for Great Britain and the UK; UK armed forces manpower is also analysed by sex, in selected periods going back as far as 1886. Great Britain local authority and police force employment are given more recent treatment from 1952. Finally, the numbers of young persons entering employment over the period 1950–68 are shown by sex, age and class of entry (for example, apprenticeship, clerical employment, employment with planned training or employment leading to a recognised professional qualification), for Great Britain only.

Tertiary sources

OECD Labour Force Statistics

This contains details of employment in the 25 OECD member countries, drawing mainly on domestic sources for the data but occasionally using some of its own statistics. Indices of total employment, the civilian labour force and the sectors of agriculture, industry and other activities are given for 14 years annually, with most of the series also presented in numbers. Bar charts or graphs show the percentage of women and of wage earners and salaried employees of the civilian employment, with a graph plotting the 'evolution of the civilian employment' showing indexed curves over 12 years.

For each country there are separate, more detailed analyses showing those in civilian employment and those in the armed forces by sex, with numbers and percentages annually for 12 years. Some analysis of change is also given. Civilian employment is broken down by professional status and by three broad areas of activity (all activities; agriculture, hunting, forestry and fishing; and non-agriculture). A further industrial breakdown is given by ten ISIC groups, with numbers and percentages. There are separate tables for males and females. Wage earners and salaried employees are given by sex, for 10 ISIC groups, with a further analysis for manufacturing industry only by nine ISIC sub-groups, plus some small occupational assessment. All tables are for 12 years.

OECD Economic Surveys.

The annual UK survey contains analysis of employment by sex, by those in production and manufacturing, and the percentage of males and females of total employees. All are shown by the percentage change over a year and for two years half-yearly, five years annually and an average taken over ten years. This is supplemented with a graph plotting the key employment trends. Comparisons with other OECD members are given in a basic statistics table which shows employment by total civilian and, separately, by agriculture, forestry and fishing, industry, and a residual 'other'.

Yearbook of Labour Statistics (ILO)

For a wider international coverage of about 180 member nations, the structure of the economically active population shows separately employers and workers on their own account (that is, the self-employed), salaried employees and wage earners, family workers and others, all by broad branch of economic activity. All are for the latest years available, but not necessarily the same years for each country. Persons employed by major divisions of economic activity and an index of the general level of employment are given for a 10 year run (where possible). Also employment in the five separate sectors of non-agriculture, manufacturing, mining and quarrying, construction, and transport, storage and communication are given, mostly in index form.

Bulletin of Labour Statistics (ILO)

This contains data similar to, but less extensive than, the *Yearbook* and appears on a quarterly basis.

Social and Economic Trends in Northern Ireland

Bar charts show the annual trend over five years of the self-employed and employees in employment separately for the service industries, manufacturing, construction and agriculture, forestry, fishing, mining and quarrying.

New Earnings Survey

Although details of employment as such are not contained in the annual survey, it is possible to find from the sample the percentage of males and females classified as manual workers, by all SIC groups, for Great Britain only. See Part E, *Analysis by Region and Age Group.*

Part-time Working in Great Britain
Employment Gazette, July 1979, pp671–75, 677)

A valuable study on part-time working in Great Britain which contains analyses of numbers working part-time by SIC order, by sex and by marital status. There is a limited analysis of females' part-time employment by occupational groups.

Employment and Unemployment in the English Inner Cities
Employment Gazette, August 1979, pp746–49, 752)

Shows employees in employment by inner city and travel-to-work area for the five cities of Newcastle, Manchester, Liverpool, Birmingham and London, with some commentary.

Further sources

Office of Population Censuses and Surveys
Department of Employment
Manpower Services Commission — Employment Service Division
Department of Manpower Services, Northern Ireland
Industrial Training Boards
EEC Commission

4. Unemployment

Introduction

Unemployment statistics are collected and disseminated in Great Britain by the Department of Employment based on those persons notified to the local employment offices and careers offices as being 'unemployed'. In Northern Ireland similar statistics are compiled by the Department of Manpower Services from notifications to its local offices. The unemployed are defined as:

'. . . persons registered at local offices who on the reference date have no job and are capable of and available for work. Included are both those who are claiming benefit and those who are not. Severely disabled persons, unlikely to obtain work other than under special conditions, are excluded from the count. Also excluded are adult students, non-claimants registered only for part-time work and the temporarily stopped.'*

The statistics are based on a monthly count usually made on the second Thursday of each month (prior to October 1975, it was on a Monday). Thus, it is clear that the monthly figures represent the situation as it appeared on one day only.

Official statistics are produced on a monthly, quarterly and yearly basis (also with some combination of these such as half-yearly) with the occasional *ad hoc* survey published in the *Employment Gazette*.

The inclusion or exclusion of such groups as school-leavers or adult students has been a matter for some concern. The problem is that the appearance of such groups in the unemployment statistics at predetermined times (such as the summer holidays) distorts the overall picture and so makes it difficult to discern the trend accurately. The current DE statistics exclude all adult students from the analyses and school-leavers are included except where the figures are 'seasonally adjusted'. Because of the combined effects of all seasonal factors such as school-leavers, seasonal work, holiday periods and such, the DE presents many

*From the *CSO Guide to Official Statistics*, No. 2, HMSO, 1978

of the unemployment series seasonally adjusted. This is a weighting based on the experience of previous years such that the figures so adjusted will reflect the underlying trends more accurately.*

Because of the reliance on unemployed people to register at their local employment office as being unemployed, the official DE statistics may not be an accurate reflection of the *total* numbers unemployed (see Points to note 2). This underlines the importance of the alternative sources of unemployment data, notably the Census of Population, the General Household Survey and the EEC Labour Force Survey (see Primary sources) which do not rely on registration but in the main depend on the individual's own assessment of his unemployment status.

The available data have been broken down as follows:

☐ Sex: married women are sometimes shown separately because of their special position in the ranks of the unemployed (especially difficult to measure accurately because many tend not to register as being unemployed).

☐ Age: an important breakdown for unemployment statistics, this can show the extent of youth unemployment as well as the situation as age increases.

☐ Duration: this is shown by number of weeks for the unemployed person's current spell of unemployment.

☐ Industrial: this is based on broad SIC orders in most cases but full or partial MLH is given quarterly by the DE. The classification is based on the industry in which the unemployed person last worked and there is also a category to include those for whom the last place of work cannot be easily identified.

☐ Occupational: the extensive DE quarterly analysis is based on those occupations which the unemployed wish to enter, which is perhaps a more useful way of presentation when attempting to match those unemployed to the existing vacancies.

☐ Entitlement to benefit: this shows the proportion of the unemployed eligible for unemployment benefit payments. This presentation has recently been discontinued by the DE in its published statistics.

☐ Seasonal adjustment: this is an important aspect of the unemployment series.

Points to note

1. The monthly DE and DMS count of the unemployed is a static

---

*For a fuller discussion of this, see *Seasonal Adjustment of the Unemployment Series, Employment Gazette*, August 1979, pp780–86

analysis representing the situation as it appears on *one day* in each month.

2. The official DE/DMS statistics are based on those *registered* as being unemployed and this precludes certain people from the analysis. Most likely to be left out are the self-employed, part-time workers, married women, and other groups not eligible for benefit, but also excluded might be those who are between jobs who do not consider it worthwhile to register for a short period. Therefore, the official figures will tend to understate the degree of frictional unemployment in particular, at any one time.

The General Household Survey, however, assesses unemployment on the basis of a sample survey and past results have shown a divergence between its results and those of the DE. In 1976 this difference was such that it appeared that the DE annual average represented only 81 per cent of the total number unemployed, that is, 19 per cent of those classing themselves as unemployed did not bother to register at the local employment offices. This illustrates the order of the discrepancy.

3. Some changes have taken place in the compilation of regular unemployment statistics. These changes are significant if a long time series of data is being used, but more recent results are quite compatible.

4. With unemployment statistics, those being measured are in a situation which makes their classification by industry and occupation somewhat difficult. This is overcome to some extent by basing the industrial classification of an unemployed person on the last position occupied (ie before becoming unemployed), or in the case of the quarterly analysis by occupation, on the type of job being sought.

5. The regional classification differs in that the person is regarded as being unemployed in the region which encompasses the local employment office at which that person is registered, irrespective of the area where the last job was held.

Primary sources

Department of Employment Press Notice

This is issued monthly 12 days after the second Thursday in each month (the reference date for the unemployment count) and is the first publication of the figures. Notices contain the month's figures on the unemployed by total (with school-leavers shown separately), and the total seasonally adjusted (excluding school-leavers). Both numbers and percentages are given with the corresponding change from the previous month. There is a small analysis of the month's figures by age and duration (under and over 60 years, and four weeks or less and over four weeks). The number of adult students registered during the month is also given, separately.

4. Unemployment

Breakdown / Analysis	Primary						Secondary												
Publication →	DE/DMS Press Notice	Employment Gazette	DMS Gazette	Census of Population	General Household Survey	EEC Labour Force Sample Survey	British Labour Statistics: Yearbook	Monthly Digest of Statistics	Annual Abstract of Statistics	Economic Trends	Social Trends	Regional Statistics	Scottish Abstract of Statistics	Scottish Economic Bulletin	Digest of Welsh Statistics	Welsh Economic Trends	Digest of Statistics – N. Ireland	Social & Economic Trends in N. Ireland	British Labour Statistics: Historical Abstract
Breakdown																			
Sex	X	X	X	X			X	X	X			X	X				X		X
Age	X	X		X			X					X	X				X		X
Duration	X	X					X										X		X
Industrial		X					X										X		
Occupational		X					X										X		
Entitlement to benefit	X	X					X		X									X	
Seasonal adjustment	X	X					X												
Areas covered																			
United Kingdom	X	X	X			X	X	X	X		X	X							X
Great Britain	X	X		X	X	X	X	X	X		X	X						X	X
Northern Ireland	X	X	X			X	X	X	X		X	X					X	X	X
England		X		X			X					X							
Scotland	X	X		X			X					X	X	X					
Wales	X	X		X			X					X			X	X			
Standard regions	X	X		X			X					X							
Sub-regional	X	X		X								X	X	X	X	X			
Data frequency																			
Annual				X			X		X	X	X	X	X		X		X	X	X
Half-yearly																	X	X	
Four-monthly																			
Quarterly	X						X	X					X	X					X
Monthly	X	X					X	X									X		X
Occasional				X	X	X													

NB: See also Tertiary and Further sources

For a longer period the notices contain the seasonally adjusted unemployment figures for 13 months (including the month under review) with total numbers, percentage rates, seasonally adjusted figures (excluding school-leavers) and, for these, change and average over the past three months. The flow of unemployed for Great Britain (seasonally adjusted), and the average per month (taken over three months) of those joining and leaving the register, is given for nine consecutive months from the previous month (does not include the review month).

For Northern Ireland the *Department of Manpower Services Press Notices* carry a comprehensive monthly account of unemployment in the province with more detail than the DE press notices, including an industrial classification (by SIC order) for the review month, with comparative figures giving the change over the month prior to the review month and a comparison with the same month a year earlier. Another table covers an analysis of numbers and percentages of persons registered as unemployed in travel-to-work areas and shows, for each area and for each employment service office within that area, numbers unemployed including and excluding school-leavers and comparisons with the same month in the previous year. Percentage rates are also shown and all the data are analysed by males, females and total. There is also a graph showing unemployment (excluding school-leavers) with actual and seasonally adjusted curves plotted quarterly for about eight years.

Employment Gazette

The most comprehensive regular unemployment statistics for Great Britain appear in the *Gazette* including finalised versions of those issued provisionally in the press notices. Regular statistics each month include an area analysis, showing unemployment in development, special development and intermediate areas, counties and certain local areas (usually in large towns) for the latest month. These are given for males, females, total, and percentage rate represented by the total. The unemployment summary analysis shows the total (including school-leavers) by number, precentage rate, and the total broken down by sex and school-leavers. Separately is shown the number of adult students registered for vacation work. All this is given monthly for five years. An analysis by UK standard regions shows for each one the total (including school-leavers) by the same breakdown as for the summary analysis, monthly for 13 months, with a more detailed analysis for the latest month which includes married women, school-leavers and adult students separately.

A simplified analysis by duration and age gives, for the UK and Great Britain, estimates for those months when age/duration analysis is not available, and shows those unemployed in the divisions of under and over 60 years, and up to and over four weeks, monthly for five years. There is a quarterly industrial analysis for Great Britain with ten broad industry groups showing total numbers (seasonally adjusted and unadjusted) and percentage rates for each quarter over four and a half years. An occupational analysis shows, for six broad groups, quarterly figures on the unemployed in Great Britain by sex, with percentages for a three and a half year period. Unemployed males and females in Great Britain are analysed within eight age groups, with figures quarterly* for the current year, four-monthly for the previous full year, and six-monthly for a further three and a half years back. A detailed Great Britain analysis shows numbers and percentages unemployed in seven duration divisions the largest of which is 'over 52 weeks'. Figures are quarterly for four years.

Up to 1980, when the table was discontinued, unemployed persons by entitlement to benefit were given showing those in Great Britain receiving unemployment benefit, those receiving supplementary allowance, and those registered for work at three times each year (February, May and November) for five years. The flow of unemployment is shown in a table alongside vacancies flow and gives the situation at employment offices in Great Britain (seasonally adjusted) with those joining and leaving the register and the excess of the inflow over outflow broken down by sex, monthly for five years.

Finally, in the regular monthly series, there is a table of unemployment numbers and rates for a number of countries compared (based on OECD members and with national definitions retained), with unadjusted figures for the latest six months, quarterly for the latest quarter and the previous full year (with possibly a further quarter), and annual averages for five years from the previous full year. Seasonally adjusted figures show the latest six months and quarterly averages for six quarters from the latest.

Regular quarterly statistics (appearing in the March, June, September and December issues) show more detailed analysis of certain areas. There is an industrial analysis of Great Britain and UK unemployed by sex as at the previous month's count by full SIC order and MLH.

An occupational analysis by KOS is given for the total unemployed, and by sex for Great Britain only. Also useful is an analysis of unemployed minority group workers given quarterly by standard region, showing numbers by sex and percentages (of each group) for the main areas of emigration to the UK. An analysis of minority group workers by age is published annually.

Other information on the unemployed appears occasionally in the *Employment Gazette* and some of these are listed in the Tertiary sources.

---

*This quarterly analysis was introduced in October 1978; before that they were for January and July each year

Department of Manpower Services Gazette

The first issue (Spring 1978) contains an analysis of unemployment in Northern Ireland, giving monthly details for the period June 1959 to December 1977. It contains numbers unemployed, by sex, including and excluding school-leavers (the former also with percentages) and also unemployed school-leavers shown separately (numbers only). Seasonally adjusted unemployed (excluding school-leavers) are given with totals and percentage rates only up to April 1964, after which they are also analysed by sex.

In the second issue (1979), details are given of the methods of classifying the unemployed by industry and of the method used for seasonal adjustment. A table gives details of unemployment by full SIC order, monthly for the period June 1959 to August 1978, numbers only, but males, females and the total all shown separately. There is further analysis of unemployment in Northern Ireland monthly over the period January 1976 to August 1978, both including and excluding school-leavers (but showing them separately) and with some seasonal adjustment to the series that excludes school-leavers, all by sex.

Census of Population

The relevant information on those unemployed appears in the *Economic Activity Tables* and they show those reported as being unemployed by occupation, industry, social and socio-economic class, all by sex, and mostly by age group. In addition to the UK constituent countries there are breakdowns by county, city and local authority areas. For details of specific publications see *Index of Key Publications*.

General Household Survey

The section on trends since 1971 includes comparisons of unemployment rates for males, married females and non-married females together with some commentary. The regular survey results provide a table showing the numbers and percentage rates of unemployed in the sample for males, married females, and non-married females, with numbers further split for each of four categories:

☐ looking for work
☐ waiting to take up a job
☐ unable to seek work because of temporary sickness
☐ registered but self-described as economically inactive.

Total numbers are split into those registered and those not registered as unemployed, also shown as a percentage for each group.

A table showing women who reported that satisfactory child-minding arrangements would mean they would work earlier than intended could also be useful in providing an indicator of the degree of the so-called 'hidden' unemployment amongst women.

EEC Labour Force Sample Survey

This survey contains details of unemployment in each of the nine EEC nations (including the UK), and the nine in total. Those who declared themselves as being unemployed are shown by sex and by whether looking for work or not. Further analyses show unemployment rates by sex and age group, and usually there is some analysis of reasons for being unemployed (such as dismissal, resignation, or retirement). Finally, unemployment for each standard region of each EEC country is given.

Secondary sources

British Labour Statistics Yearbook

General statistics are presented on the numbers and percentage rates of unemployed, both including and excluding school leavers (shown in unadjusted and seasonally adjusted form). Males and females are shown together and separately, with coverage for Great Britain and the UK monthly for five years (including the review year). A table shows numbers by age and sex (with 12 age groups) annually for seven years, with a further coverage of age and duration of unemployment with 12 age groups and 14 duration divisions.

A regional analysis is given for Great Britain standard regions by age and duration (with three age groups and seven duration divisions) with males and females shown separately for January and July of the review year. More broadly for the UK standard regions, numbers and percentage rates are given annually for 10 years by sex. For the review year a monthly analysis shows numbers and percentage rates with and without school-leavers and adult students, some seasonally adjusted. For the development areas, intermediate areas, and certain local areas (usually large towns) there is an analysis monthly for the review year (quarterly in the case of certain local areas), of numbers and percentage rates, with the assisted areas having a more comprehensive breakdown by sex.

An analysis by region and industry groups (by full SIC order) is also given for January and July of the review year (with males only shown separately). There is a broad industry analysis (eight groups) for Great Britain only of numbers, annually for 11 years and monthly for one and a half years (including the review year). This is supplemented by a full MLH industry analysis of numbers by sex, presented quarterly for the review year. A full occupational (CODOT) analysis of men and women (separately) is given for the beginning and end of the review year, and this is linked with vacancies figures for the interim period in order to show the flow over the year. There are also separate tables each for men and women showing numbers by 18 broad occupational groups and by standard region, quarterly for the review year.

There is an analysis of minority group workers by standard region and area of origin for two months in the review year (usually February and August).

An analysis by sex and age group and by type of benefit or allowance received, is given quarterly for ten years, and the expenditure on unemployment benefit is given for a long annual run.

Monthly Digest of Statistics

This contains an analysis of UK unemployment (numbers and percentage rates) with and without seasonal adjustment, and for Great Britain and Northern Ireland separately there is an unadjusted analysis by sex. Adult students are shown separately, and each series is presented annually for five years and monthly for the current year and at least two further years. An analysis by standard region gives overall numbers annually for four years and monthly for 18 months. Also an industrial analysis is given in seasonally adjusted, unadjusted, and percentage rate form for two and a half years quarterly. There is an analysis by duration with males and females (shown separately) with annual averages for three years and selected monthly figures for 15 months.

Annual Abstract of Statistics

This contains figures on the number unemployed in Great Britain by sex, monthly and with a monthly average for the year for about seven years. A similar table for Northern Ireland (but in total) has a longer run of about 12 years. Rates of unemployment are analysed by UK standard region for about eleven years annually. There is also an industrial analysis (with full SIC order and MLH breakdown) showing in total the numbers unemployed annually for four years (UK and Great Britain separately). There is also an analysis of unemployed by entitlement to benefit (located in the section on 'National Insurance and other Social Security') giving numbers (by sex) in seven categories of benefit, as at each May and November for eight years.

Economic Trends

UK unemployed numbers and percentage rates (seasonally adjusted) and numbers unadjusted are given, for 12 years annually, five years quarterly, and one and a half years monthly, with a seasonally adjusted analysis by UK standard regions of percentage rates, quarterly for six years. Both tables are supported with graphs. The *Economic Trends Annual Supplement* contains a similar series of figures to the monthly issue but for a longer run.

Social Trends

This shows monthly averages of numbers and percentage rates unemployed in Great Britain, by sex, for seven years (current year plus the four previous years and another two odd years). There are also graphs showing the duration of unemployment and the age structure over a long period.

Regional Statistics

The 'Regional profiles' section lists for each UK standard region and county separately, numbers and percentage rates unemployed for the reference year. There is also some commentary on conditions in the region. A table gives numbers and percentage rates unemployed for a few years supported by graphs. The duration of male unemployment is given for the regions of Great Britain (ie excluding Northern Ireland) for six duration categories. Relativities of duration (for males only) are also given, with an index of regional versus Great Britain unemployment (GB = 100) for a nine year run. There is an industrial analysis by broad industry groups for the reference year, and an occupational analysis by major categories taken at one point in the reference year. Also there is some analysis of unemployed racial minority group workers by area of origin, showing numbers and percentage rates by standard region for the reference year only, and an additional table shows an age group analysis along similar lines. Finally, there is a table showing comparative EEC (all countries by major regions) unemployment rates for one year.

Scottish Abstract of Statistics

This contains numbers and percentage rates unemployed (with some seasonal adjustment and with adult students shown) monthly and annually for about 27 years. There is an analysis of the Scottish unemployment rate relative to that of the UK as a whole shown as an index (UK = 100), monthly for about 24 years. Numbers and percentage rates unemployed, by local government regions and island areas, are given monthly for four years, and a regional analysis gives the numbers and percentage rates as at June each year for about 13 years, in total. An analysis by age and duration, by sex, is given, with eleven age groups and seven duration divisions, annually for eight years.

An occupational analysis (broad groups) by sex is given quarterly for three years, and an industrial analysis (SIC order) gives the numbers of males and females together annually for 12 years and quarterly for two years. There is also a table showing those unemployed by entitlement to benefit (six divisions) annually for seven years.

Scottish Economic Bulletin

This simply lists the numbers and percentage rates unemployed in Scotland for ten years.

Digest of Welsh Statistics

The registered unemployed, by sex, are given monthly for ten years. There is also an analysis by SIC order to show the industrial distribution of unemployment at six-monthly intervals over five years. Unemployment rates are analysed by local area sub-division, again at six-monthly intervals for five years, and this is supplemented by an analysis of numbers unemployed by statistical sub-division and industrial sector (ie where last employed). There is a table giving age and duration of unemployment (broadly, and by sex) at six-monthly intervals for about two years.

Welsh Economic Trends

Regular tables include numbers and percentages unemployed in Wales and Great Britain annually for 21 years with a corresponding graph. There is a regional analysis of percentage rates with a monthly average shown as a percentage of the Great Britain average for about 20 years, again with supporting graphs. Percentage rates by local area (statistical sub-division) are given half-yearly for ten years, with graphs. A map shows a comparison of percentage rates of unemployment in Welsh travel-to-work areas with a Great Britain average, and occasionally there are other relevant statistics, such as a measure of the effect of the government's job creation programme on Welsh unemployment.

Digest of Statistics — Northern Ireland

This contains a table giving numbers and percentage rates unemployed (total, males, females and married women, shown separately) monthly for two years and half-yearly (June and December) for about seven years. An industrial analysis by 17 broad SIC groups gives numbers unemployed monthly for two years and annually for about 12 years. The duration of unemployment (three broad bands) is shown by sex with monthly and some half-yearly analysis. Finally there is a table showing numbers unemployed by entitlement to benefit, half-yearly for about 11 years.

Social and Economic Trends in Northern Ireland

Graphs show the composition of the unemployed and the geographical distribution monthly for two years.

British Labour Statistics: Historical Abstract 1886–1968

For the period 1948–68, monthly tables give numbers and percentage rates unemployed (Great Britain and UK) for males and females (combined and separately), and an annual analysis by UK standard regions. Numbers and percentage rates unemployed in the development areas (men, women, boys and girls separated) are given annually for the period 1956–68.

Industrial analyses give the numbers unemployed by industry (SIC order) quarterly for the UK 1948–68 (separate table for males), and for the same period similar figures for Great Britain are given but on a broader base (eight industry groups). An occupational analysis (broad groups) gives the numbers unemployed annually for the period 1954–68, males and females shown separately. Numbers and percentages unemployed by duration in Great Britain are given quarterly 1948–68, covering (separately) males, females and young persons. Finally there are analyses covering those unemployed by benefit entitlement (quarterly 1960–68), and a series showing Great Britain's expenditure on unemployment benefit (current prices) over the period 1913–68.

Tertiary sources

Social Security Statistics

This contains details of unemployment by those claiming and entitled to benefit or supplementary help. There is a regional analysis (excluding Northern Ireland) of those claiming benefit over a six year period and of those receiving benefit over eight years. Unemployed persons analysed by entitlement to benefit (seven divisions) are given six-monthly (May and November) for eight years, and there is a similar analysis on a regional basis, but for the reference year only. Other tables contain details of the age structure of those entitled to benefit and of the degree of dependency (how many children, etc).

Economic Progress Report

This presents a regular series of seasonally adjusted numbers and percentage rates unemployed in its 'Economic indicators' section, for the latest two months and usually for the previous five quarters and perhaps one year before that. There is also some commentary on trends in unemployment in the 'Monthly economic assessment.'

Industrial Relations Digest

This presents a range of statistics on unemployment with a monthly table showing numbers and percentage rates (seasonally adjusted and unadjusted) for Great Britain and UK separately, with a measure of the relative change over time. A similar analysis is given for UK standard regions for the review month. A short analysis of numbers unemployed by duration and age is given for Great Britain and the UK separately, and there is also some commentary on the main unemployment trends and an occasional article.

How Should We Measure Unemployment?
(by Hughes, J J, in *British Journal of Industrial Relations*, Vol. 13, No. 3, November 1975, pp317–33)

This article explains some of the problems in measuring unemployment and offers some alternatives. See also the article by Hughes, 'The measurement of unemployment: an exercise in political economy?' (in *Industrial Relations Journal*, Vol. 7, No. 4, Winter 1976/77, pp 4–12).

How Little Unemployment?
(by Wood, J B, Institute of Economic Affairs, Hobart Paper 65, 1975)

This presents a useful analysis of the concept of unemployment and the usefulness of the statistics used to measure it, with some critical suggestions for future developments in thinking about the subject.

Statistics of Unemployment in the United Kingdom
(by Thatcher, A R, in Worswick, G D N (ed), *The Concepts and Measurement of Involuntary Unemployment*, Allen & Unwin, London, 1976)

A good descriptive account is provided of the official DE statistics on unemployment, outlining their drawbacks and analysing some trends.

Statistics on Long-Term Unemployment
(*Employment Gazette*, June 1978, pp678–81)

A comprehensive analysis is made of those unemployed for long periods — with some of the analyses from the period 1957–78 and with tables giving an age structure analysis, and also (for one year only) by region, broad industry group and broad occupational group.

The Young and Out of Work
(*Employment Gazette*, August 1978, pp908–16)

This article examines the available evidence to explain changes in the levels of unemployment amongst young people over time, with some useful results and conclusions.

Employment and Unemployment in the English Inner Cities
(*Employment Gazette*, August 1979, pp746–49, 752)

This article brings together the available data on five inner cities (Newcastle, Manchester, Liverpool, Birmingham and London), with unemployment examined for six years by city and TTWA, including an occupational analysis. There is some discussion of the problems involved in defining areas and inner city unemployment rates in isolation from other factors.

Measuring Employment and Unemployment
(OECD, Paris, 1979)

An examination is made of the OECD's member countries' treatment of employment and unemployment statistics, with some of the problems in comparing unemployment internationally coming to the fore. It also contains recommendations of an OECD working party on the measurement of employment and unemployment.

The Long-Term Unemployed: Some New Evidence
(*Employment Gazette*, January 1980, pp9–12)

A synopsis by Maureen Colledge and Richard Bartholomew of MSC of a full report carried out by MSC entitled 'A study of the long-term unemployed' (available from the Manpower Intelligence and Planning Division of MSC) which looked at the background and influencing factors of those unemployed for a long time. The article provides a useful overview.

The Anatomy of Youth Employment
(*Employment Gazette*, March 1980, pp234–36)

A survey article based on research into youth unemployment using national statistics as carried out by the DE, it provides a brief introduction to the larger report on the research by Peter Makeham of the DE in *Youth Unemployment* (DE Research Paper No. 11, HMSO, 1980).

A Review of Unemployment and Vacancy Statistics
(*Employment Gazette*, May 1980, pp497–508)

This gives a thorough assessment of the current DE unemployment statistics in terms of their purpose, concept and use. It describes the problems in using the statistics and draws on data from other sources for comparison.

Further sources

Department of Employment (Statistics Branch)
Department of Manpower Services (Northern Ireland)
Trades Union Congress
Manpower Services Commission (Employment Service Division)
EEC Commission
Organisation for Economic Co-operation and Development
International Labour Office

5. Vacancies and Placings

Introduction

The official statistics on vacancies in Great Britain are compiled by the Department of Employment from information received through the various employment and careers offices located throughout the country. At one point each month, the vacancies notified to these offices but remaining unfilled on that day are counted and this forms the basis of the monthly series. The quarterly series provides occupational and industrial analyses, supplanting the procedure prior to June 1976 when an industrial analysis was carried out monthly. In Northern Ireland the official data are compiled in a similar way, co-ordinated by the Department of Manpower Services.

The regional analysis of the official data is not extensive, with only Wales being treated on a sub-regional level in regular published form, despite the fact that the statistics are assembled on a local office basis. Therefore, it is important to stress the benefits of using the local offices of the ESD directly as they could be in a position to provide local analyses.

The official DE/DMS statistics are to some extent complemented by the results from the General Household Survey and the EEC Labour Force Sample Survey, which do not produce vacancy statistics as such, but do record responses to questions on methods used to seek work. This enables the official employment service to be put into context with the total employment services in the country.* Unfortunately the private employment agencies do not produce regular, co-ordinated statistics and other methods used to fill vacancies, such as advertisements in newspapers or word of mouth information exchanges, are even more difficult to quantify.

---

*A study by MSC put the official employment services' share of total vacancies existing at 35.9 per cent in May 1977. See Tertiary sources *Fast Service* for further details

The available data have been broken down as follows:

- ☐ Sex
- ☐ Vacancy flows: these show, by occupation, the number of vacancies notified during a quarter, the placings, the number of vacancies cancelled and the number remaining unfilled at the end of the quarter; also given is a monthly series of vacancy inflows and outflows published as an average of three months ended.
- ☐ Unfilled vacancies: notified vacancies are all those reaching the Employment Service offices, of which those remaining at the offices on the day of the count represent the unfilled portion. The unfilled vacancies represent some measure of the degree of employers' unsatisfied demand for labour, given the shortcomings of the official data (see Points to note below).
- ☐ Placings: this is a measure of the performance of the Employment Service in allocating jobs to people.
- ☐ Occupational: this is a quarterly analysis of the occupations in which the vacancies are offered.
- ☐ Industrial: this analysis is of the industries in which vacancies are offered.
- ☐ Seasonally adjusted: this takes account of seasonal fluctuations, as was done for part of the unemployment series (see section on employment).

Points to note

1. The most important point concerning the official vacancy figures is that they do not measure the *full* extent of vacancies existing at any one time. This is because they rely on those vacancies notified by employers to the Employment Service and careers offices only and take no account of other methods used for filling any existing vacancies. These other methods include mainly private employment agencies, media advertisements, and word of mouth information exchanges. (The last of these alternatives was the way in which 36 per cent of employees in their present job for less than a year, first heard about that job, in 1977.)*

2. The distinction between those vacancies notified to employment offices and those notified to careers offices is not clear. Not all the vacancies notified to employment offices are suitable only for adults; some could be filled by young persons. Equally, not all the vacancies notified to careers offices are only suitable for young persons. So the

---

* Information from the *General Household Survey* of 1977

73

5. Vacancies and placings.

Analysis \ Publication	Primary				Secondary									
	DE Press Notice	DMS Press Notice	Employment Gazette	BR Labour Statistics: Yearbook	Monthly Digest of Statistics	Regional Statistics	Economic Trends	Annual Abstract of Statistics	Welsh Economic Trends	Digest of Statistics — N. Ireland	Scottish Abstract of Statistics	Digest of Welsh Statistics	Scottish Economic Bulletin	British Labour Statistics: Historical Abstract
Breakdown														
Sex		X						X		X		X	X	
Vacancy flows	X	X												
Unfilled vacancies	X	X			X			X	X	X	X	X		
Placings		X	X											
Occupational								X						
Industrial														
Seasonally adjusted	X						X							
Areas covered														
United Kingdom	X		X		X			X						
Great Britain	X	X	X		X			X						X
Northern Ireland		X	X							X				
England														
Scotland		X	X								X		X	
Wales		X	X						X			X		
Standard regions	X	X				X								
Sub-regional														
Data frequency														
Annual			X		X			X	X					
Half-yearly			X											
Quarterly		X	X				X				X			
Monthly	X	X	X		X				X			X	X	
Occasional		X	X											

NB: See also Tertiary and Further sources

figures taken together are *not* a measure of total officially notified vacancies.

3. The official monthly series of unfilled vacancies based on the regular count represents the situation as it appeared on the day of the count only.

Primary sources

Department of Employment Press Notice

This is issued monthly and shows unemployment and vacancies data together. Total unfilled vacancies notified to employment offices and those notified to careers offices are shown for the month with the change since the previous month (Great Britain and UK shown separately). Those notified to employment offices only are shown seasonally adjusted. For Great Britain only the flow of vacancies through employment offices is shown monthly for a period of nine months from the current month back, and total vacancies are presented over a 13 month period, giving a monthly figure and change in the month, plus the average change over a three month period, for those notified to employment offices only; all are seasonally adjusted. For the same period those vacancies notified to careers offices are given in unadjusted form only.

There is also a UK standard regional analysis of notified vacancies for the month, showing separately those notified to employment and careers offices, with the former also shown seasonally adjusted. Numbers and monthly changes are given in each case.

Department of Manpower Services Press Notice

This contains the monthly details of unemployment and vacancies in Northern Ireland, with separate analyses showing notified and unfilled vacancies for adults and young persons alongside the month's placings figures. A table shows for adults only vacancies notified to employment offices and placings for six months, with the average monthly level and the average monthly change calculated over three-monthly periods. Finally, notified vacancies remaining unfilled are shown for adults and young persons separately, monthly for over 12 months, all alongside a comprehensive analysis of the unemployment situation.

Employment Gazette

This contains by far the most comprehensive regular series of vacancies and placings data. Each month notified vacancies remaining unfilled are shown for those at employment and careers offices separately, for all standard regions of Great Britain for the latest month available. There is also some commentary on the monthly change. For a long run of about 28 months, similar data are given for all UK standard regions. For employment offices only, unfilled vacancies are also shown seasonally adjusted, monthly for about five years, by UK standard regions. Vacancy flows at employment offices, seasonally adjusted, are given for Great Britain only showing the inflow, outflow and the net excess of the two, monthly (but based on averages over a three month period) for about five years. There is also a graph showing vacancies notified to employment offices plotted over 17 years, alongside one for unemployment.

Quarterly series show total notified vacancies remaining unfilled by SIC industry group (with a few odd sub-groups), with separate analyses for employment and careers offices. Vacancies and placings at employment offices in Great Britain are given by occupation. Detail here includes summary results for the latest month available of all unfilled vacancies by six broad occupational classifications; notified vacancies by full KOS breakdown for the latest available full quarter; placings for the quarter, shown by sex; vacancies cancelled during the quarter; and vacancies remaining unfilled at the end of the quarter. This series of results provides a flow analysis for vacancies over the latest available quarter. Also quarterly, there is an analysis by broad occupational group of unfilled vacancies during one month only, by UK standard regions.

Most of the quarterly statistics usually appear in the February, May, August and November issues and cover the previous full quarter, that is, December, March, June and September respectively. Occasional surveys and articles are published and some of these are listed below in the Tertiary sources section.

British Labour Statistics Yearbook

This puts together many of the monthly series on vacancies into a mostly annual series and gives separate analyses for men and women of notified vacancies, placings and cancelled vacancies. It gives some analysis of the flow, by comprehensive occupational breakdown for Great Britain only, and for one year (up to the first week in December of the latest available year). Vacancies notified and remaining unfilled are given for men, women, and in total seasonally adjusted, for Great Britain only. The figures are monthly for five years and annual averages for the same five years. Unfilled vacancies are also presented by SIC industry group (with some MLH breakdown), for Great Britain only, all quarterly for the latest available year.

UK standard regional analysis shows unfilled vacancies by SIC industry groups for males, and males and females in total, as measured in January and July of the latest available year. A quarterly analysis for one year only shows a similar breakdown but by 18 broad occupational groups, with separate tables for men and women. There are also analyses of numbers placed in employment by local employment offices and youth employment service careers offices by standard regions of Great Britain, annually for five years and for a longer run of ten years. Figures are given in total, and by sex for Great Britain only.

Secondary sources

Monthly Digest of Statistics

This shows in total the notified vacancies remaining unfilled by UK standard regions, with separate tables for those at employment and careers offices. The figures are monthly for a period of about 21 months.

Regional Statistics

For UK standard regions the total unfilled vacancies are shown, together with the percentage of the total UK figure represented by each region. The figures are monthly averages given annually for six years (usually the latest four plus another two odd years going back up to ten years).

Economic Trends

This shows total vacancies notified to employment offices seasonally adjusted, monthly for 21 months, quarterly for five years and annually for 12 years, for the UK only in each case. A graph shows total notified vacancies in the UK for about six years (although the observations are taken monthly, with three-monthly averages). For a longer run, *Economic Trends Annual Supplement* consolidates much of the monthly series covering the period of the last 25 years.

Annual Abstract of Statistics

This gives separate analyses of unfilled vacancies at employment and careers offices by sex, monthly for 6 years, for Great Britain only. Also, for Northern Ireland only, total unfilled vacancies are given monthly for 14 years.

Welsh Economic Trends

On a table with unemployment data are given total unfilled vacancies and vacancies expressed as a percentage of the total unemployed annually for ten years, with separate analyses for Wales and Great Britain. There are also graphs which show the total Welsh unfilled vacancies, and unfilled vacancies in Wales and Great Britain separately, as a percentage of the unemployed, for the same ten year run.

Further analysis of unfilled vacancies as a percentage of the unemployed shows, by six broad occupational groups, what are termed the 'occupational demand factors', that is, unfilled vacancies as a percentage of the unemployed within each occupational group. This is given for Wales, the assisted regions, the unassisted regions and the UK. The ratio of occupational demand factors in each area is compared with the UK average, all for the latest year only.

Digest of Statistics — Northern Ireland

This shows for Northern Ireland vacancies filled and unfilled, for males and females separately, with the total placed, for those under and those over 18 years of age, monthly for 30 months and annually for 12 years. Another table concentrates on placings monthly for nine months and shows those placed in total, by sex, and those under and over 18 years old. Unfilled vacancies are shown separately for adults and young persons.

Scottish Abstract of Statistics

The total unfilled vacancies are given by broad occupational groups, with managerial (two sub-divisions), professional (three sub-divisions) and processing (13 sub-divisions), Scotland only, quarterly for two and a half years.

Digest of Welsh Statistics

Unfilled vacancies are shown for Wales only by sex and total, monthly for six years. Separate analyses for employment and careers offices show unfilled vacancies by sex, monthly for five years, for Wales only.

Scottish Economic Bulletin

This shows the total unfilled vacancies for Scotland only in its 'Main quarterly economic series', quarterly for 11 years.

British Labour Statistics: Historical Abstract 1886–1968

For historical data on vacancies this contains information going back as far as 1948. Unfilled vacancies in Great Britain are given for men, women, total, and young persons, monthly over the period 1948–68. For the same period the placings by both the employment and youth employment services in Great Britain are given annually with men, boys, women and girls shown separately.

A comprehensive occupational analysis of unfilled vacancies for

Great Britain, by sex, is given annually (as at September each year) over the period 1956–68, and finally, there is a breakdown by standard regions of Great Britain plus some sub-regional analysis (mainly counties) of placings by the employment and youth employment services, by sex, all annually over the period 1948–68.

Tertiary sources

Social and Economic Trends in Northern Ireland

A graph plots notified vacancies in Northern Ireland only, monthly for two years, with separate curves for adults and young persons. There is also a graph of the unemployed and vacancies by composition.

Industrial Relations Digest

A table shows notified vacancies unfilled for the latest month plus the change since the previous month, for employment offices (unadjusted and seasonally adjusted) and careers offices separately, all for Great Britain and the UK. There is also usually some commentary on the key trends exhibited in the statistics.

EEC Labour Force Sample Survey

This survey contains information on the methods by which the unemployed seek employment. The methods listed are:

☐ official employment exchange
☐ private employment office
☐ advertising in a newspaper/journal
☐ answering newspaper advertisements
☐ personal contacts
☐ other methods

The results are for the survey year only but are broken down by sex, and with numbers and percentages in each case.

General Household Survey

This contains information gathered annually on how working persons in their present job for less than 12 months first heard about that job, with analyses of the responses on a national, regional and employment status basis (for example, unemployed before taking up their present job).

Age Qualifications in Job Vacancies
(*Employment Gazette*, February 1978, pp166–72)

This was the first of three articles during 1978 dealing with the question of age qualifications and job vacancies, and it analysed the volume of notified vacancies which specified some age limit. There is some industrial and occupational analysis. Subsequent articles considered the reason behind age qualifications (June issue, pp672–81), and the issues surrounding the engagement of professional and executive staff (December issue, pp1377–82).

Engagements and Unfilled Vacancies during 1977
(*Employment Gazette*, November 1978, pp1284–88)

This contains the principal results of a special survey of employers carried out by the ESD during the second quarter of 1977. There are regional, occupational and industrial analyses of engagements and a regional breakdown of the estimated total unfilled vacancies (that is, those notified to ESD offices and those not notified), by manual/non-manual distinctions. The *Gazette* of June 1979 (pp558–63) drew on this survey to provide the basis of its estimates in the article 'Market share of the general employment service'. This looked at the number of vacancies notified to the ESD offices as a proportion of total vacancies.

Fast Service — the Speed with which Vacancies are filled by the Employment Service
(*Employment Gazette*, August 1979, pp753–56)

This article looked at the efficiency of the Employment Service in filling vacancies, with some comparison of job centres with the old-style exchanges. It was a special study by the economics staff of the MSC.

'Hard-to-fill' Vacancies

This had been the subject of special research by the MSC during the later part of 1978 and into 1979, and involved a survey of about one third of ESD district managers. *Employment Gazette* articles appeared in September (pp868–71) and October (pp1004–06) 1979, and an extensive report was published by MSC in September 1979 entitled *Report on Hard-to-fill Vacancies*.

Employment Service in the 1980's
(MSC/ESD, London, 1979)

This looks at the prospects for the future, drawing on past experience;

it contains some statistics on vacancies and placings as they relate to the performance of the Employment Service.

Job Seekers and the Employment Service
(*Employment Gazette*, February 1980, pp124–29, 132)

This article describes some of the results of a survey conducted by MSC in 1979 into the Employment Service and its users. It concentrates on the age of people submitted and placed by the service and the duration of their unemployment. Useful statistics and charts are given.

A Review of Unemployment and Vacancy Statistics
(*Employment Gazette*, May 1980, pp497–508)

The section on vacancy statistics (pp506–08) explains fully the concept, uses and sources of data, outlining some of the problems of measurement. The use of an unemployment/vacancy ratio is also discussed.

Further sources

Department of Employment (Statistics Branch)
Department of Manpower Services (Northern Ireland)
Manpower Services Commission — Employment Services Division
Manpower Services Commission — Employment Service Division or Regional Manpower Intelligence Units
Professional and Executive Register
Federation of Personnel Services (and member employment agencies)

6. Educational Supply: School-leavers

Introduction

The output of the secondary schools in the UK is given varied coverage in the regular statistics. The important elements are the numbers emerging each year (at the end of the academic year — usually July), the age of leavers, and the qualifications held. This section is concerned with information on all school-leavers, with and without formal qualifications, and their destinations — into work, apprenticeship, further education, etc — after they have left school. Unfortunately there are problems in the compilation of the destination statistics because there is no formal mechanism by which they are recorded.

The regular school-leaver statistics are produced by the Department of Education and Science in England and Wales, the Department of Education for Northern Ireland in the province, and the Scottish Education Department for Scotland. In addition separate statistics for Wales come under the Welsh Office. Because of this specialisation by each constituent country of the UK, the statistics produced by each have individual characteristics, which is an advantage when looking at just one particular area but can cause problems when trying to form a more national picture. The separation of Scotland is essential because of its different examination structure (for example, its SCE examinations).

The statistics presented are either based on actual returns (usually from the schools themselves) or samples of varying sizes, ranging up to 20 per cent for some Scottish statistics. The main problem is that many of the data are a few years old by the time they reach publication.

The following breakdown has been applied to the available information:

a) Destination — usually includes the following range of school-leaver destinations:
  □ degree courses
  □ teacher training
  □ other further education

- ☐ courses at other institutions
- ☐ employment (sometimes by broad industry)
- ☐ others.

b) Type of school attended — includes the following types:
  - ☐ maintained by LEA
  - ☐ direct grant
  - ☐ independent (recognised as efficient, ie those which have sought and obtained recognition as efficient after inspection by HM Inspectors of Schools)
  - ☐ other independents.

c) Age.

d) Qualifications gained — shown by CSE, GCE, or SCE (in Scotland only) and by level (ie O, A, H); by grade achieved; by broad subject group (usually arts, social science and science — perhaps by pure and applied, and by individual subjects within these groups). Compatibility is a problem because there are 14 regional examination boards for the CSE and eight for the GCE, which issue their own separate results.

e) Regionally — usually by standard region, but occasionally there is sub-regional analysis.

Points to note

1. Some of the regular statistics are based on samples only, with an average sample size of about ten per cent although the response rates seem to be high in most cases. Nevertheless, some figures are based on no more than the headmasters' best informed guess (particularly in regard to school-leavers' destinations).

2. Most of the statistics are based on an 'academic' year (normally September in one year to July the following year) as opposed to the calendar year.

3. Where a pupil has sat (or obtained a result in) a particular subject examination more than once, then the analysis of passes treats this as a single attempt (or single result) in the particular subject, thereby avoiding some of the problems of double-counting with two examination sessions per academic year.

Primary sources

Statistics of Education, Vol. 2: School Leavers, CSE & GCE

This is the most comprehensive source of data on England and Wales and contains a short summary of the main trends in the statistics for the latest academic year.

Historical tables give school-leavers by destination on leaving (with

6. Educational supply — school-leavers

	Publication / Analysis	Primary					Secondary						
		Statistics of Education Vol. 2	Scottish Education Statistics	Statistics of Education in Wales	Northern Ireland Education Statistics	Education Statistics for the UK	Employment Gazette	Social Trends	Education and Employment 1980	Regional Statistics	Scottish Abstract of Statistics	Digest of Welsh Statistics	Annual Abstract of Statistics
Breakdown	Age	X	X	X	X	X	X	X		X	X	X	
	Destination	X	X	X	X	X	X	X		X			
	Type of school attended	X		X	X		X	X	X				
	Qualifications gained	X		X	X		X	X	X	X	X	X	X
	Examination entries	X											
	Projections			X			X						
Areas covered	United Kingdom					X	X						
	Great Britain												
	Northern Ireland			X	X		X		X			X	
	England	X		X	X		X	X	X	X			
	Scotland		X				X	X	X	X	X		
	Wales			X			X	X	X	X		X	
	Standard region	X					X	X	X	X			
	Sub-regional	X											
Data frequency	Annual	X	X	X	X	X	X	X	X	X	X	X	

NB: See also Tertiary and Further sources

the usual divisions) by sex and by type of school attended (maintained secondary modern, maintained comprehensive, maintained secondary grammar and direct grant grammar) for about 30 academic years. The numbers of entries to external examinations (GCE, CSE and their antecedents) are shown by sex for a long run, with selected years from 1919 to the latest available year (which is usually about two years prior to the year of publication).

Summary tables include analyses of school leavers during the latest available academic year, by destination and by type of school attended (boys and girls separately), plus the numbers of GCE and CSE passes achieved; analysis is also by type of school attended and by sex. Numbers and percentages are given in both cases. There is a comparative table showing the number of leavers by numbers of GCE A-level passes (by subject group) for the past academic year and those of a year earlier.

For the latest year there are analyses of leavers by subject specialisation and destination of those holding A-levels, by age and number/type of qualifications obtained, and by destination from type of school attended with, in addition, a more comprehensive analysis of destinations. CSEs and GCEs obtained, showing the number of subjects, grades and type of school, are also given for England and Wales. The destinations and the level of examination achievements are given full treatment by sex, for each standard region of England and Wales with some sub-regional comparisons within each region.

Analysis is also provided of the number of pupils and students with GCE qualifications over six recent years plus one odd year (about four years previous) by the number of subjects held, but they are based on estimates only. For the latest available summer examinations, a comprehensive breakdown by individual subjects for CSE and GCE (O- and A-levels) is given by sex, number of entries, number of passes and number of passes awarded in each grade. This is supplemented by numbers of passes per subject (but not by grade), by sex, for the latest seven years plus one odd year.

Note: The Scottish Education Department publishes, on a semi-regular a Bulletin issued by the DES and available from their Statistics Branch (address in Part II).

Scottish Educational Statistics

This is the major source of school leavers data for Scotland and contains statistics based on actual returns showing the number of pupils leaving school during the academic year, by sex, by stage of schooling completed, and by qualifications held (if any). The latter two are also given by age (15 to 19 plus) and all these measures by type of school attended. Qualified school leavers by age (15 to 18 plus) and by number of passes held in the SCE are also shown, by sex, for one year only, with an additional table showing the numbers and percentages of all leavers with SCE or GCE qualifications, by sex and number of O and H grades, for five years (from the latest year back).

Based on 20 per cent sample surveys, statistics are given on the number of leavers holding H grades by session of leaving, by qualification level, by destination (the usual ones, plus 'nursing and medical auxiliaries') and by sex, with percentages in each group also given. A similar series also appears for O grades. Leavers entering full-time courses of higher education are given comprehensive treatment, by sex and by subject area of studies (arts, pure science, social science and applied science), by number of H grades achieved and by the type of higher education establishment, with both numbers and percentages shown for the latest year.

Leavers who applied for admission to a university are shown by sex, by H grades obtained, the subject area of study and their destination (numbers and percentages) for the latest year. A similar table shows those who entered employment by four broad occupational groups (building, engineering and manufacturing; clerical; administrative, professional and technical; and others) with the qualification level achieved. A similar analysis covers those leavers entering employment and continuing with part-time education.

Note: The Scottish Education Department publishes, on a semi-regular basis, much of the school leaver details for the previous year in a *Bulletin* which can be available before the annual series. Some projections of leavers are included. The *Bulletins* are available free to users from the Scottish Education Department (for address see Part II).

Statistics of Education in Wales

For Wales the numbers of leavers are shown by sex and by destination and age of leavers (over 15 to 19 plus) for three recent years. The destination and age of leavers is also shown by local authority area for one year only, showing divisions of maintained, direct grant and independent schools, all by sex.

Examinations achieved by Welsh school-leavers (CSE and GCE O- and A-levels) are given for each sex, by numbers of each qualification held (but not by subject) with a more detailed analysis by local authority areas with a similar presentation for one year only. There is also an analysis of examination achievements covering the whole of England and Wales by standard region and sex.

Northern Ireland Education Statistics

This contains data for Northern Ireland on the number of leavers in the age range 14 to 19 plus, with actual figures for about 15 years and projected figures for a further eight years. The destination of leavers by type of school attended is also given for the latest year and this is supplemented by details of the age and qualifications (GCE O- and A-levels) of them, all by sex.

Education Statistics for the United Kingdom

Details of the GCE qualifications and the destination of pupils leaving school during the latest available academic year are given for England and Wales and Northern Ireland only, by sex, with analysis of destinations and numbers of passes at O- and A-level. For the UK, composite details are given of seven years of leavers by highest qualification held, for boys and girls. There are also details of pupils leaving school over seven years, by sex and age (from 14 to 18 plus), again for the UK in total.

Secondary sources

Employment Gazette

There is usually an annual article on young people leaving school, with projections of future output. In 1978 it appeared in the June issue (pp662–71) and covered Great Britain; in 1977 England and Wales were covered in the April issue (pp353–58) and Scotland in the June issue (pp600–02). National details presented include numbers who are in a position to make a decision about staying on at school after the statutory leaving age has been reached; numbers of pupils in school by age and sex; school-leavers by age and sex; school-leavers availability for employment by CSE and GCE qualifications; school-leavers by age and sex; school-leavers by age and sex; school-leavers' availstandard region. Most of the projections in 1978 went as far as 1980–81, although some were shorter than this.

The *Gazette* may also contain occasional articles of relevance (see Tertiary sources below).

Social Trends

There is usually a table showing the destination of school-leavers (with separate tables for England and Wales, Northern Ireland and Scotland) by type of school attended, by sex and by academic qualifications obtained, the destinations being either universities, colleges of education, other full-time further education, and employment. The percentage in each group is shown in most cases for the latest academic year and for one other year about eight years previous. A further table shows the number and percentage of school-leavers by selected qualifications (for the UK) annually for six years, by sex, but the analysis is quite broad. The results of the latest available summer examination for CSE, GCE and SCE are shown for each constituent UK country separately, with numbers and percentage passes for boys and girls separately for about six years.

Finally, the statistics are supported by graphs showing (for England and Wales only) the percentages of each age group with O- and A-level passes over ten years,·and bar charts showing the destination and qualifications mix for two separate years (about eight years apart). There is also a graph showing (by sex) A-level passes by subject area expressed as a percentage of total A-levels taken, but for England and Wales only.

Education and Employment 1980

A table shows the destination of school-leavers in England and Wales by universities, colleges of education, polytechnics, other full-time further education and employment, by sex, with the percentage in each division for the period 1966/67 to 1977/78 annually, plus 1960/61. This is supplemented by a bar chart plotting the details shown in the table and a useful map showing a comparison between the standard regions for 1977/78 (but in total only). For Scotland, leavers are shown by destination for the years 1969/70 to 1976/77 inclusive, with a corresponding bar chart.

The net increases to the total number of students and pupils with either one A-level, two A-levels, or three or more A-levels is shown for England and Wales only, by sex, for the period 1966/67 to 1977/78 annually, plus 1960/61, together with a bar chart for the total of males and females. Also for England and Wales only, the number of school-leavers with two or more A-level passes is given by broad subject group and by sex, for the period 1966/67 to 1977/78 annually, with corresponding bar charts for each sex.

For school-leavers with one A-level or more in England and Wales, the destination (either degree courses, teacher training, other full-time further education, or employment) is given by broad subject area annually for the period 1970/71 to 1977/78. For those school-leavers unemployed (in October each year), the numbers in total for England and Wales, Scotland and Great Britain separately are given for each year between 1968 and 1979.

Projections of the number of school-leavers, by those available for employment, by qualifications and by region, are presented for England and Wales, annually to 1991.

Regional Statistics

This contains details of school-leavers' examination achievements and destinations in England, Wales and Northern Ireland only, for the latest academic year by standard region and by leavers with broad numbers and types of GCE obtained, the percentage of all leavers with a certain number of GCEs, by destination, and by all leavers in each year aged between 16 and 19 plus.

A brief analysis for Scotland only shows, for two years, all leavers by sex and age (16 to 18 plus); all leavers with SCE H and/or O-levels (boys and girls together); and the percentage of all leavers within specific grades.

Scottish Abstract of Statistics

School-leavers are shown by age (15 to 18 plus) and qualifications obtained (O and H grades of the SCE and how many of each) for boys and girls separately for eight recent years and two earlier years.

Digest of Welsh Statistics

This contains details of school-leavers in Wales by sex, age (15 to 18 plus), destination, CSE or GCE (O- and A-level) achievements, and numbers held, all for the four latest academic years.

Annual Abstract of Statistics

For Northern Ireland only, the number of school-leavers is given by selected qualifications, by sex, and by those with GCE O- and A-levels (three divisions), in a short summary for about 11 recent years.

Tertiary sources

Student Numbers in Higher Education in England and Wales
(Education Planning Paper No. 2, HMSO, 1970, price 60p)

This contains some of the main results of a DES survey into the likely demand for places in full-time education up to 1981 and includes some analysis of school-leavers' qualifications obtained (since 1961) and projected (to 1981), with comparative data on other, earlier surveys.

General Household Survey

The education results show the type of school attended, the age of leaving and the qualifications (if any) obtained from the sample taking part in the survey. Not all the same results will appear each year and some years might produce additional relevant information, depending on the questions asked in the survey.

Social Science Students — an Examination of the First Steps in their Careers
(*Employment Gazette*, January 1978, pp41–49)

The first two pages of this article look at school-leavers over the period 1971–75 and examine their destinations, with emphasis on GCE A-level holders and university entrants.

Further sources

Department of Education and Science
Department of Employment
Manpower Services Commission — Regional Manpower Intelligence Units
County and Metropolitan County Councils
Scottish Education Department
Welsh Office
Northern Ireland Department of Education

7. Educational Supply: Further Education

Introduction

The further education (FE) sector has been taken to cover all those institutions providing facilities for after-school study with the exception of universities. Used in this sense FE covers a field of great diversity including GCE/SCE examination courses, first and higher degree courses and vocational courses up to and including some at postgraduate level. The main educational establishments covered are technical colleges, colleges of technology, and the 33 polytechnics in England, Wales and Northern Ireland which provide a whole range of FE courses. In Scotland non-university courses at both first degree and postgraduate level are mainly provided by the 14 central institutions which apart from three are monotechnic, specialising in broad subject areas.

Most of the statistics on the FE sector are produced by the Department of Education and Science in England and Wales, the Department of Education for Northern Ireland, and the Scottish Education Department for Scotland, with additional data supplied for Wales only by the Welsh Office. First destination statistics are compiled by 'Polytechnic careers advisers: statistics working party'; but, as the name suggests, these relate to the output of polytechnics in England and Wales only. Many of the statistics relate to *vocational* courses which can be defined as those that have as their primary aim to prepare students for, or to increase their knowledge of, a particular employment or profession, and include all of the formal qualifications. This leaves *non-vocational* courses to cover the majority of adult education courses pursued for interest and those without a formal qualification at the end.

A distinction must also be made between so-called *advanced* and *non-advanced* courses. The former simply includes all those courses above the level of A-level GCE (or H grade SCE) and OND/ONC, and as such, taken with courses at universities, is commonly referred to as 'higher education'.

The statistics have been broken down as follows:

☐ sex
☐ age — mostly by single years for those students under 21 and

91

then by broader groups

☐ type of establishment — including LEA colleges of further eduction, polytechnics and Central Institutions in Scotland, most of which offer a wide range of courses and teaching programmes

☐ mode of attendance — the most frequent divisions being full-time, sandwich, short full-time (ie of less than 18 weeks duration), block release, day release, part-time day, and evening only

☐ type of course — this covers the qualification or course being pursued, for example, HND, degree, etc

☐ subject area — sometimes broad subject groups or in more detail on three levels as the example below:

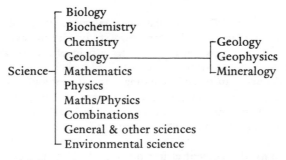

Few of the analyses show the tertiary subject breakdown.

☐ qualifications gained — usually shown as entries and passes in subjects below degree level, while degrees are usually analysed by class or type (honours, ordinary, etc)

☐ first destination — analysis of the known first destination (whether employment, further education or other category) and mostly for graduates only.

Points to note

1. Most of the statistics relate to an academic year (ie September in one year to July the following year) as opposed to the calendar year.

2. Students who sat and were successful in more than one examination in the same period will obviously figure in more than one set of statistics, so student numbers by course may work out to be more in total than the actual student population.

3. There are some differences in the type of establishment and courses offered in the constituent countries of the UK which should be borne in mind when using aggregate data.

4. The destination statistics on polytechnic students should be treated with caution as any trends displayed must be qualified by the large size of the unknown destination categories present in the statistics. In fact

7. Educational supply — further education

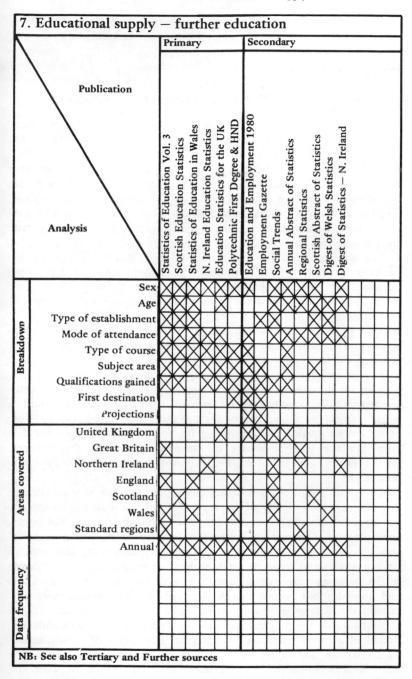

| | Primary | | | | | | Secondary | | | | | | | |
Analysis \ Publication	Statistics of Education Vol. 3	Scottish Education Statistics	Statistics of Education in Wales	N. Ireland Education Statistics	Education Statistics for the UK	Polytechnic First Degree & HND	Education and Employment 1980	Employment Gazette	Social Trends	Annual Abstract of Statistics	Regional Statistics	Scottish Abstract of Statistics	Digest of Welsh Statistics	Digest of Statistics — N. Ireland
Breakdown														
Sex	X	X	X	X	X	X		X	X	X	X			X
Age	X	X	X	X	X	X								
Type of establishment	X							X	X	X	X			
Mode of attendance	X	X	X	X	X	X								
Type of course	X	X	X	X	X	X								
Subject area	X	X	X	X	X	X						X		
Qualifications gained	X	X		X	X	X								
First destination						X								
Projections							X							
Areas covered														
United Kingdom					X		X							
Great Britain	X													
Northern Ireland				X				X	X					X
England	X		X					X	X					
Scotland		X						X				X		
Wales			X			X		X					X	
Standard regions	X										X			
Data frequency														
Annual	X	X	X	X	X	X	X	X	X	X	X	X	X	X

NB: See also Tertiary and Further sources

recent destination figures for polytechnic students displayed twice as many unknowns as the corresponding figures for universities.

Primary sources

Statistics of Education, Vol. 3: Further Education

This volume provides the most comprehensive range of FE statistics on England and Wales and begins with a short historical analysis of students by mode of attendance, annually for the latest 25 years, plus further selected years back to the beginning of the century. Summary tables show student numbers by sex, type of establishment, mode of attendance, some age analysis and type of course pursued, all for England and Wales for the latest available year. Also student numbers by type of course and broad age range are given by sex, annually for the latest seven years.

For each standard region of England and Wales the numbers of students by sex, mode of attendance and whether advanced or non-advanced are given for the latest available year. There are additional tables showing an age analysis by mode of attendance and the number of establishments by type, for each of the standard regions. Numbers by type of qualification sought are given by sex, for a period of about seven years annually, and for just the latest available year the analysis is extended to show qualification by type of establishment, by year of course, and by age, with some separate analyses for advanced and non-advanced courses. Numbers of students by subject area of study are given similar comprehensive treatment with numbers by sex and by broad subject area (separately for advanced and non-advanced) for seven years annually. Further, more detailed analyses, but just for the latest available year, show, for the major qualifications, the numbers on the relevant courses by sex, mode of attendance and detailed subject area of study.

For those students on day and block release courses numbers are given by sex and industry of employer (full SIC) in total and by age, all for England and Wales, and Wales separately, but just for the latest available year. Overseas students are shown by comprehensive subject area, by sex, with Commonwealth students separated, and with a limited analysis by type of establishment attended. The countries of origin are given a more detailed analysis with a breakdown by advanced and non-advanced courses and by the type of course within these categories. All analyses are for the latest available year.

Statistics on the polytechnics are given separate treatment with full details of type of course (CNAA degree, HND, etc) all by sex, mode of attendance and subject area. Also included is a section on professional qualifications. All for the latest available year only. There is further analysis of entrants to CNAA first degree courses for the latest year by sex, mode of attendance and age, with a summary of the highest qualifications held by those admitted to the courses. Finally, there are analyses of results of examinations in total, but by sex and subject for CNAA first degrees, for the latest seven years, and in addition by class for the latest year only. For other qualifications the numbers of entries and passes are given in total, by subject, for a longer run of ten years.

Note: Some of the statistics contained in this volume may appear in a *Bulletin* issued by the DES and available from the Statistics Branch (address in Part II).

Scottish Educational Statistics

For Scotland only there are details of those on vocational FE courses by sex, age group, mode of attendance and broad subject area, all shown separately for advanced and non-advanced courses, annually for the latest five years. A similar analysis is applied to new entrants to the courses joining each year for the latest five. Those on advanced and non-advanced courses are given separate treatment with details annually for the latest five years of numbers by sex, age, mode of attendance and broad subject area. Separate tables for new entrants are also given. Further analyses on the same basis and for the same five years show students by sex, age, mode of attendance and the level of course pursued within the type of establishment; additional analysis is by type of qualification, with separate tables for advanced and non-advanced and all students and new entrants. Overseas students on full-time courses in Scotland are shown by sex, age group, whether advanced or non-advanced, and by broad subject area, all by origin (either Commonwealth or foreign). Another table shows students by type of qualification sought with a more detailed analysis of country of origin. All for one year only.

Also given are those students on day or block release by sex and industry group (full SIC), again for the latest five years, and finally there is a limited analysis of entries and successes in certain examinations, with totals only given but by selected subjects and all for the latest five years.

Note: The Scottish Education Department publishes on a semi-regular basis some of the information outlined above for the latest year in a *Bulletin*, which may be available before the annual series. The *Bulletins* are available to certain users on request from the Department (for address see Part II).

Statistics of Education in Wales

For Wales only the number of enrolments on courses at FE establishments are given in total by mode of attendance and by type of establishment (polytechnics; other major establishments; all students), for five years annually (the latest year being about two years prior to publication). Numbers on advanced and non-advanced courses are shown separately by sex, mode of attendance and type of course, but for the latest year only. Those students on day-release courses are shown by sex, broad age range and by SIC order for the latest year only.

Another useful analysis gives the cross-boundary flows of FE students by broad subject area, showing the number of Welsh students studying in Wales and those studying in England separately, all for one year only (about three years prior to publication). Finally there is some analysis of student numbers on adult education courses by type of course and sex of registrants, all for the latest five years.

Northern Ireland Education Statistics

A summary table lists the number of students at FE establishments in Northern Ireland by sex, mode of attendance, subject area of course and qualifications being pursued. Analyses show total numbers and new entrants to courses, all for the latest three years. Those students attending day, block release, and evening courses are shown by sex, broad occupation and industry, all for the latest year only. There are also details of the numbers of entries and passes in certain examinations for the latest five years and some analysis of adult education students and those on non-vocational courses, by sex and broad subject area of study.

Education Statistics for the United Kingdom

For the UK in total the number of students at FE establishments is shown by sex and age and by type of course for the latest year only, and in total by type of course for the latest eight years annually. A further table covering all courses (advanced and non-advanced) gives numbers by broad subject area, annually for the latest five years. Those on advanced courses are analysed separately with details for those studying for university degrees and CNAA degrees; HNDs andHNCs; other advanced courses; and in total, showing numbers by sex, mode of attendance and comprehensive subject area. All for the latest year only. Day-release students are given by sex and age, and by industry of employer (SIC) for five years annually.

A separate analysis for CNAA first and higher degrees shows results by subject area and class of degree, all by sex, for the latest three years plus a further five years but in total only. Also the number of entries and passes in national diplomas (HND, OND) are given by subject area for the latest five years.

Finally, for those students from overseas attending UK FE

establishments, numbers are given for the latest year only by sex, subject area and whether Commonwealth of foreign, with a more comprehensive list of countries of origin but by type of qualification being pursued.

Polytechnic First Degree and HND Students — Statistical Supplement

This contains details of the first destination of polytechnic first degree and HND students in England and Wales for the latest available year. There is a commentary on the key trends portrayed by the year's statistics, with some basic figures on the number of graduates or diplomates by broad subject area and by sex.

The statistics show, for first degrees and HNDs separately, the first destination by comprehensive subject area, for men and women separately and in total; the employer category by subject area and sex; and the type of work by subject area and sex. Similar analyses are given for degree, HND and CNAA first degrees (separately) and for full-time and sandwich students separately, although the subject areas used are much broader.

Secondary sources

Education and Employment 1980

For UK students undertaking FE courses other than those leading to degrees, numbers are given by sex and mode of attendance for the period 1967 to 1976 annually, with a corresponding graph. Also the number of candidates for City and Guilds final examinations in the UK are given for the period 1967/68 to 1978/79 annually, but in total by broad industry group. Separate tables are given for ONC, OND, HNC and HND passes by broad subject group for the UK and for the period 1967/68 to 1976 annually.

CNAA first degrees awarded in the UK are shown in total by broad subject group and by more detailed subject analysis of three of these groups (engineering and technology; science; and social, administrative and business studies), all for the years 1967 and 1970 to 1977 annually. London University first degrees obtained outside universities are also shown in total by broad subject group, for the years 1966/67 and 1969/70 to 1977/78 annually. The first destination of first degree polytechnic graduates in England and Wales is given comprehensive treatment with analyses by sex for broad destination and in total only for those entering permanent home employment. The latter is further analysed by employment category (in total), by subject group of studies, by sex, and separately for the totals of graduates in engineering, science, and social studies. There is also a table showing the type of work entered. All analyses are for the period 1974/75 to 1978/79 annually. Illustrative charts are given for most of the analyses.

Finally there are details of DES projections of the total number of students in higher education to 1993.

Employment Gazette

Since 1977 there has been a regular feature article in each February issue on graduate supply and demand in the UK. These contain details of a short-term forecast for the year on the likely supply and demand of graduates (as made by AGCAS, CSU and SCOEG) with some separate analyses for polytechnic graduates, although much of the data is presented in total only.

Social Trends

A broad analysis shows the numbers of students in higher education in the UK by sex, age and by type of establishment attended, with separate analyses for full- and part-time. All for the latest four years plus one other. Numbers of students in FE establishments are given by sex and age range, and by mode of attendance and whether advanced or non-advanced courses, all for the latest two years plus a further two. For the latest year only similar analyses are given for England and Wales, Scotland and Northern Ireland separately. Usually a bar chart of the number of A-level GCE passes gained by students in FE establishments in England and Wales is also given for three selected years.

Annual Abstract of Statistics

General statistics on the numbers continuing education beyond 16 years of age in the UK are given, showing those in full-time, sandwich and part-time courses, all by type of course and by age for the latest year only. The percentage of the total UK population in full-time education aged between 15 and 24 years is given by sex and age, and by those in non-advanced FE and those in higher education, all for the latest three years plus one other. The numbers of students at FE establishments in the UK are shown by type of course for the latest seven years, annually, and by broad subject area and whether full- or part-time, for the latest three years.

Examination results are analysed with CNAA first and higher degrees awarded shown by subject area and class of degree, by sex for the latest four years and in total for a further three. HND, HNC, OND and ONC examinations entries and passes are given by subject area for the latest five years.

Regional Statistics

This shows the number of students in FE establishments by sex, age group and mode of attendance with corresponding percentages, for all standard regions of Great Britain, and for the latest year only (about three years prior to publication). For Northern Ireland only, numbers of FE students are given by sex, mode of attendance and whether vocational or non-vocational, for one year.

Scottish Abstract of Statistics

For Scotland the numbers undergoing vocational FE are given by type of establishment (by sex and age), by mode of attendance, and by broad subject group, all for the latest eight years plus a further three over a 20 year period.

Digest of Welsh Statistics

For Wales only the number of FE establishments is given by type, and the numbers of students by mode of attendance with some age group analysis, all for the latest four years plus a further four over a 15 year period.

Digest of Statistics — Northern Ireland

For Northern Ireland the numbers aged 18 and over attending FE establishments full-time are given by sex and age for the latest 13 years. Also, those on vocational courses are analysed by mode of attendance and whether advanced or non-advanced, all for the latest seven years.

Tertiary sources

Employment Prospects for the Highly Qualified
(DE Manpower Paper No 8, 1978)

A report which attempts to estimate the prospects for graduates at all levels up to 1986 in the light of a continuing increase in the number of highly qualified people and the effects of this on their employment. Most of the analysis is concerned with graduates from both universities and polytechnics and there are some useful analyses by subject area. A shorter article appeared in the *Employment Gazette* of May 1978, pp531-39.

The Supply of Potential Engineers
(*Employment Gazette*, December 1978, pp1383-89)

This is an update by the Unit for Manpower Studies of an earlier report by the Engineering ITB on the supply of potential professional engineers from further and higher education to the engineering industry, which concentrates on entrants to and students already on relevant courses at degree, HND and HNC levels. There is also some first destination analysis of graduates in engineering and technology from universities and polytechnics by broad type of employer. Most of the analysis covers the period 1967 to 1977 annually.

The Market for Highly-qualified Manpower: Digest of Information
(*Employment Gazette*, March 1980, pp269–77)

A thorough appraisal of the more important sources of information on graduate supply and demand with details of polytechnic vacancies on courses and CNAA degrees awarded (higher degrees separately). Most of the data range over the period 1973 to 1977.

On the Way Up: an Analysis of First Jobs from the Early Careers Survey of Graduates
(*Employment Gazette*, May 1980, pp472–77)

An article by Lyndsey Whitehead and Peter Williamson of the DE's Unit for Manpower Studies which concentrates on the career aspirations and job changes of graduate students (from polytechnics, universities and other sources) and looks at what methods are used by them to decide on a career.

Further sources

Department of Education and Science
Scottish Education Department
Welsh Office
Department of Employment
Manpower Services Commission – Regional Manpower Intelligence Units

County and Metropolitan Councils
Business Education Council
Technician Education Council
Committee of Directors of Polytechnics
Northern Ireland Department of Education
Industrial Training Boards
Individual colleges

8. Educational Supply: Universities

Introduction

This section covers the available information on UK universities and their output of highly qualified people.* There are 44 universities in the UK if the constituent colleges of the universities of London, Oxford, Cambridge and Wales are not counted separately, and they offer courses not only in first and higher degrees but also in diplomas at postgraduate level in a wide range of subjects. It must be remembered, though, that they are not the only educational institutions offering degree courses. Other educational institutions, most notably polytechnics, account for a significant proportion of the output of highly qualified manpower (see subject heading 7).

Most of the regular statistics on the university sector are compiled by the University Grants Committee (UGC) from information gathered from individual universities throughout the UK. Statistics of the first destinations of students after graduation arc compiled and published by the UGC, although information is sometimes available through other bodies such as the Central Services Unit (CSU). The UGC statistics appear in a wide range of HMSO publications. Survey articles appear from time to time, notably in the *Employment Gazette*, on the future trends in graduate supply and demand. Some of these will be found listed in the Tertiary sources section below.

The Open University does not come within the sphere of the UGC and so publishes its own series of statistics which tend to be different in format to the UGC regular series on UK universities.

The statistics have been broken down by the following main divisions:

☐ sex
☐ age — mostly by single years for those students under 25 and then by broader groups

*Highly qualified is usually taken to include first degrees and other qualifications of a comparable standard, and higher degrees

101

□ level of study — this differentiates between first degrees, higher degrees and diplomas

□ subject area — usually by broad subject groups but occasionally in more detail. Statistics of Education (see Primary sources below) lists nine broad classifications:

    Education

    Medicine, dentistry and health

    Engineering and technology

    Agriculture, forestry and veterinary science

    Science

    Social, administrative and business studies

    Architecture and other professional and vocational subjects

    Language, literature and area studies

    Arts other than languages

□ mode of attendance — whether full- or part-time, or sandwich

□ type of study — indicates for postgraduate courses whether taught or by research

□ qualifications gained — usually by degrees or diplomas awarded and sometimes by class of result

□ first destination — analysis of the first destination of graduates (eg employment, further education or other category as well as sub-divisions of these).

Points to note

1. Most of the statistics relate to an academic year (ie October in one year usually to July the following year) as opposed to the calendar year.

2. The first destination statistics on university students are regarded as a fairly accurate indication of the ways in which they occupy themselves after graduation. However, it must be remembered that the accuracy of this annual assessment relies to a great extent on the responses of the graduates themselves. Furthermore, a first destination may not be indicative of the desired or ultimate occupation of the graduate. These reservations apply with much greater force to the information on the destination of postgraduates.

3. Students who are undergoing a first degree or diploma course but who are already in possession of a first degree (ie they are doing a *second* first degree) are still regarded as undergraduates in their current subject area of study.

4. The UGC statistics on the numbers of degrees and diplomas obtained excludes external degrees and diplomas of the University of London awarded to students outside the university sector (for example, in polytechnics).

8. Educational supply — universities

Analysis / Publication	Primary					Secondary							
	Statistics of Education Vol. 6	Scottish Educational Statistics	Statistics of Education in Wales	Education Statistics for the UK	First Destination/University Graduates	Education and Employment 1980	Employment Gazette	Social Trends	Annual Abstract of Statistics	Scottish Abstract of Statistics	Digest of Welsh Statistics	Digest of Statistics – N. Ireland	Open University Digest of Statistics
Breakdown													
Sex	X	X	X	X	X	X		X	X	X	X		X
Age	X				X								
Level of study	X	X	X	X	X			X		X			
Subject area	X	X	X	X	X								X
Mode of attendance	X				X					X			X
Type of study	X	X	X	X	X								X
Qualifications gained	X	X	X	X	X			X				X	
First destination			X	X	X								
Projections					X	X							
Areas covered													
United Kingdom	X			X	X				X			X	
Great Britain													
Northern Ireland	X		X										
England	X		X										
Scotland	X									X			
Wales	X		X	X							X		
Sub-regional			X										
Data frequency													
Annual	X	X	X	X	X	X	X	X	X	X	X	X	X

NB: See also Tertiary and Further sources

Primary sources

Statistics of Education, Vol. 6: Universities

This volume contains the most thorough review of UK/Great Britain university data. General tables show the number of full-time students by sex (with undergraduates and postgraduates shown separately), by area of origin (either UK or overseas), by qualifications sought and by broad subject area, all for the latest year only, for the UK in total and its constituent countries separately. A similar analysis is given for part-time students and new entrants. UK student numbers are also shown for each individual university by sex, area of origin (UK or overseas), whether full- or part-time, and whether undergraduate or postgraduate, for the latest year only.

Full-time students only are shown by sex, level of study and area of origin for the UK and its constituent countries, annually for the latest 12 years. Undergraduate students on full-time courses are analysed by sex for first time entrants, annually for ten years for each UK country. For Great Britain only (for the latest year) they are shown by subject area and level of study for all universities in total, and by broad subject area for each individual university.

Full-time postgraduate students in the UK are analysed by sex and subject area for each individual university and for Great Britain by subject area and type of study, all for the latest year only. There is an analysis by sex and subject area for the latest year of sandwich course students in Great Britain.

Those students studying part-time are shown in total by sex and level of study for the UK, Great Britain, England and Wales and Scotland separately for the latest 12 years annually, with, except for the latest year, further analysis by subject area. Part-time postgraduate students are analysed by sex and by type of study, for the latest year only.

Qualifications gained are given comprehensive treatment with analyses of UK first degrees and diplomas and higher degrees and diplomas awarded by sex and class of award, annually for 11 years for the UK, Great Britain, England and Wales, and Scotland separately. All degrees (by class) and diplomas awarded in the latest year are given by sex and by individual university in the UK, with first degrees only shown by broad subject area and, for Great Britain, all degrees (by class) and diplomas awarded in the latest year are shown by sex and subject area.

Note: Some of the statistics contained in this volume may appear in a *Bulletin* issued by the DES and available from their Statistics Branch (address in Part II).

Scottish Educational Statistics

For Scotland only, the total number of students at Scottish universities is given by sex and by undergraduate or postgraduate status, annually for the latest 16 years (the latest year corresponding to the year of publication). For the latest year only the numbers are shown by subject area and by individual university. Full-time undergraduates at the Scottish universities are analysed by sex, age, and individual university for the latest year, and by broad subject area (numbers and percentages in each group) for the latest five years annually. First time entrants to the individual universities are also shown by sex, age, and by subject area, for the latest year only.

Postgraduate students at the Scottish universities are analysed by sex, age, and individual university (full-time students only) for the latest year.

Results from the universities are given comprehensive treatment with the numbers of first degrees and diplomas obtained shown by sex and class of result, annually for 14 years, with further analysis by individual university for the latest four years and by broad subject area for the latest academic year, given by level and class for men and women separately and for each university individually.

Broad details of first destination of graduates from Scottish universities are given, with analysis by sex and by broad destination for the latest three years plus one other. Further analyses show these first destinations by whether or not the graduates are staying in or moving out of Scotland, with separate tables for first and higher degrees (the latter in total only). For the latest three years plus one other, first degree graduates entering permanent UK employment are shown by type of employment and whether staying in or moving out of Scotland.

Note: Some of the statistics on universities are first released in a *Statistical Bulletin*. These may be obtained free of charge from the Scottish Education Department (for address see Part II).

Statistics of Education in Wales

There is comprehensive analysis of the numbers of full-time students at the University of Wales by constituent college and area of origin (Wales, rest of UK or abroad) for the latest year. For the University of Wales in total, student numbers on full-time courses are shown by county of origin within Wales, with the corresponding proportions these numbers represent per 10,000 population, annually for the latest four years. Also shown for the University of Wales (in total) is the number of full-time students by sex and level of study for the latest six years annually and with a similar analysis for part-time students. Separate analyses for full-time undergraduates, full-time postgraduates and corresponding part-time students show numbers by sex, age, qualifications aimed for and broad subject area, all for the latest three years.

Welsh students undertaking first degree courses and (given separately) higher degree courses in UK universities are shown by broad subject area, with the numbers of Welsh students expressed as a percentage of all UK students. Latest year only. This is supplemented by analysis of cross-boundary flows of undergraduates by broad subject area, showing the number of Welsh students in Wales and those in England, and the number of English students in Wales and in England for one year only (about three years prior to publication). There is also a brief analysis of degrees and diplomas awarded from the University of Wales, annually for the latest five years, showing the class and broad subject area.

Lastly, for the latest year only, the occupations taken up by first degree graduates normally resident in Wales are shown by broad subject area and destination.

Education Statistics for the United Kingdom

Detailed analyses of student numbers in UK universities are given, showing separately those pursuing undergraduate or postgraduate courses, by sex, and whether full- or part-time, all annually for the latest 15 years. Whether these students are from the UK or overseas is shown in a further table for the same years.

Separate analyses of full-time undergraduates and postgraduates show the number of students by sex and subject area (full-time only). For full-time and part-time students separately, the numbers and percentages are shown by broad subject area for the UK, with full-time students only shown also by England and Wales, Scotland and Northern Ireland. All for the latest year. Degrees and diplomas obtained from UK universities are shown by sex and area of study, with first degrees and higher degrees given separately.

First Destination of University Graduates

A summary analysis at the beginning of each volume shows the trend in numbers of UK graduates by sex, the subject area and type of degree for the latest year in detail plus a few other years, with commentary on the major points of interest.

For the latest year (that is, the year of the volume) separate analyses for first degree and higher degree graduates show, by sex, the first destination (comprehensive breakdown of employment groups, types of further education or training) by comprehensive subject area; the employment categories of those graduates who entered home employment, by subject area; and the destination (country or broad area) of those graduates going overseas for further study or employment, by subject area.

Secondary sources

Education and Employment 1980

A section on applications and admissions to universities in the UK shows the number of applications in total, the percentage represented by each broad subject group for home students and the applicants per admission (ratios) by broad subject group, annually for the years 1968 and 1970–78 (inclusive). For the same years, admissions are shown by broad subject area with percentages of the total in each, with separate tables for men and women. Numbers of admissions in total are given further analysis with separate tables for courses in engineering and technology, science, and social, administrative and business studies, by subjects within these broad groups. All tables are supplemented by graphs or charts.

For Great Britain, first degrees obtained in universities are shown for each sex by broad subject group and more detailed subject analyses for degrees in engineering and technology, science, and social, administrative and business studies, but in total only. All for the years 1966/67 and 1969/70 to 1977/78 inclusive. There is also a short analysis of graduates from the Open University by broad subject area, annually from 1973 to 1978.

The destinations of first and higher degree graduates in Great Britain are treated separately with tables showing, by sex, broad destination; those entering permanent home employment by employment category; those entering permanent home employment by subject area of studies; and by type of work (general management, legal work, teaching and lecturing, etc), the latter in total only. Most of the tables cover the years 1967/68 to 1977/78 annually.

The projected output of university first degree graduates in the UK is given by broad subject area for the years 1979 to 1982 annually with corresponding graph and some longer alternative projections up to 1993 based on information from the DES.

Employment Gazette

Since 1977, the February issue has contained an article on graduate supply and demand for the coming year. Estimates are made on the likely number of graduates from both universities and polytechnics, with most of the analysis presented in a composite form. The analysis details subject area (supply side) and likely destination (demand side) and covers the UK. There is extensive commentary on the key trends forecast. The latest estimate, that for 1980, appeared in the February issue, pp133–35.

Social Trends

This usually contains details of the destination of home (UK) graduates from universities in Great Britain for the latest three years plus one other, showing, by sex, the broad divisions of teacher training; other FE or training; already in employment; gained UK employment (in public service, education, other); employment overseas; and other.

Annual Abstract of Statistics

The number of students at UK universities is shown by sex and whether from the UK or overseas, with separate analyses for full- and part-time, and undergraduates and postgraduates, annually for the latest 11 years. For the same years new admissions to UK universities are given in total and by country of origin (UK, Commonwealth or foreign) and by type of residence whilst at university (eg hostel, living at home, etc). There is some analysis of numbers by broad subject area and by sex, for the latest ten years annually, and an analysis of degrees (by class) and diplomas is given, by sex, for the latest 11 years annually.

Scottish Abstract of Statistics

The numbers of students at the individual Scottish universities are given, with the totals by sex, and those on full-time or part-time courses separately (but in total only). Also full-time new entrants are given by broad subject area and in total only, by sex, all for the latest ten years annually.

Digest of Welsh Statistics

The number of students at the University of Wales is shown for each individual college, by full- or part-time attendance, subject area, and type of study, for the latest four years annually plus four other selected years. Separate tables for undergraduates and postgraduates show the numbers of Welsh students pursuing courses at UK universities by sex and broad subject group, together with the percentage of total UK students represented by the Welsh numbers. For the latest year only.

Digest of Statistics — Northern Ireland

New entrants to full-time courses at the two Ulster universities are shown by sex, for the latest 12 years annually. For each university full-time students are shown by sex and by level of study, for the latest six years annually, with further analysis by broad subject area for the same years. Also the degrees and diplomas obtained at the two Ulster universities are given by sex and class for the latest seven years.

Open University Digest of Statistics: Vol. 1: Students and Courses

This contains comprehensive details of students at the Open University including numbers of applicants by sex, region of study, occupation of applicant, level of highest educational qualification of applicant and course applied for, mostly for the latest eight years annually. Registered students are broken down in a similar way but with additional information on the student's age on completion of full-time education and experience of part-time education.

Detailed analyses of results show first degree graduates by type of qualification (ordinary or honours), region of study, sex and date of birth, occupation at commencement of studies, level of highest educational qualification attained, and student's age on completion of full-time education. All this for the latest eight years. (The first graduates date from 1972.) There is also a briefer analysis of higher degree students.

Tertiary sources

Social and Economic Trends in Northern Ireland

This contains a bar chart showing the number of full-time students in the Northern Ireland universities, by broad subject area for the latest six years annually.

Employment Prospects for the Higher Qualified 1971–1986
(DE Manpower Paper No 8, 1978)

A report which attempts to estimate the prospects for graduates at all levels up to 1986 in the light of a continuing increase in the number of highly qualified people, and the effects of this on their employment. Most of the analysis is concerned with graduates from both universities and polytechnics and there are some useful analyses by subject area. A shorter article appeared in the *Employment Gazette* of May 1978, pp531–39.

The Supply of Potential Engineers
(*Employment Gazette*, December 1978, pp1383–89)

An examination of the numbers of people studying on courses in engineering and technology in the UK. Analyses for universities show admissions by broad subject area, and first destination of graduates in engineering and technology, annually for the period 1967 to 1977.

Higher Education into the 1990s
(DES, February 1978)

A discussion document which sets out alternative policy options for higher education into the 1990s to take account of anticipated demographic changes. It includes statistics on total student numbers since 1960/61, with projections to 1995, with more detail given by type of institution. Also contains details of age participation rates. A further paper by DES on this subject appeared in 1979.

Education to Employment: The Mix and the Market
(Richard Pearson, *Personnel Management*, June 1979, pp24–27, 35)

A survey article looking at the main trends in graduates which examines the possible developments over a ten year period, with an assessment of the implications for the personnel manager.

Career Attitudes of Final Year Undergraduates
(*Employment Gazette*, January 1980, pp13–15, 22)

An article highlighting the main results from a survey of final year undergraduates carried out in March 1979. It discusses their career expectations, factors influencing career choice and the source of advice on possible careers. There are some statistics on other years' surveys.

The Market for Highly-qualified Manpower: Digest of Information
(*Employment Gazette*, March 1980, pp269–77)

An appraisal of the more important sources of information on graduate supply and demand, with comprehensive statistics given for periods up to 1978. These show admissions to universities by qualifications and broad subject area, degrees awarded by subject area and first destination. All with commentary on the key trends.

Further sources

Department of Education and Science
Scottish Education Department
Welsh Office
Department of Employment — Unit for Manpower Studies
Individual universities and their career services
Standing Conference on the Employment of Graduates
Central Services Unit
Institute of Manpower Studies
University Grants Committee

9. Training

Introduction

This section is concerned with the amount, nature and cost of training and covers both training which is carried out wholly within the firm and that which is carried out in other establishments such as colleges and training centres. So the area is fairly well-defined but includes wide-ranging types of training within its boundaries.

Regular statistics on training are scarce, with perhaps the best sources being the reports and statistics produced by the Industrial Training Boards.* However these cover only the industries in scope and tend moreover to concentrate on formal apprenticeships or areas where specific financial incentives (grants) are involved. Some of the sectors not covered by an ITB may have their own industry training body, for example the Electricity Supply Industry Training Board or the Insurance Industry Training Council. The nationalised industries each have responsibility for their own training. Each of these non-ITB sectors may produce data on their industry's training. The decennial census provides a benchmark source of information on the numbers undergoing training and of what type, but the information suffers from being relatively out-of-date by the time it is published.

Government finance for training, mainly through the provision of places at skillcentres and the Training Opportunities Scheme (TOPS), is quite well documented, but represents only a part of the total training being done. The most serious omissions seem to be in information relating to professional training within the firm, for example, that for accountants and managers, which may be covered to some extent by regular statistics from the ITBs, but very seldom elsewhere.

The following breakdown has been applied to the available statistics:

- ☐ sex
- ☐ age

*There are 24 boards and one statutory committee; for names and addresses, see Part II

111

☐ industrial – mostly by broad groups in the official statistical series, but obviously by much more detailed analysis within each industry for the ITB statistics

☐ occupational – again the best analyses are those from the ITBs, with specific skills usually given

☐ type of training – whether apprenticeship, professional, etc

☐ training finance – covers both ITBs and the government training schemes

☐ government schemes – the type and throughput of government supported training schemes such as TOPS.

Points to note

1. The regional breakdowns used by the ITBs in their statistics may not correspond with the standard regions of Great Britain but rather represent their own regional structure. This may also be said of statistics emanating from the Training Services Division.

2. ITB statistics are usually based on the information gathered from firms as a basis for calculating levy and grants. Since smaller firms are often excluded from levy, the statistics may relate to only part of the industry concerned.

3. Not all types of training in industry can be identified by the available statistics, and this is particularly true of short duration and safety and induction training. Again the ITBs offer the best and in some cases the only regular information on these kinds of training.

Primary sources

Industrial Training Boards – Annual Reports

Each of the 24 ITBs and the Foundry Industry Training Committee (FITC) are required under the terms of the present legislation on industrial training* to submit to MSC an annual report of their operations. In addition to the financial information given on the balance sheet, the apportionment of income to specific training projects is also shown. There is usually extensive commentary on the performance of both the board and training within the industry which is quite useful in presenting an overall picture.

The level of detail and range of information contained in each report will vary slightly from board to board, but as a rule there are statistics on employment in the industry, numbers of people undergoing training and of what type, together with details of numbers of establishments and the relative size of these as measured by numbers of employees.

* Embodied in the 1964 Industrial Training Act and the 1973 Employment and Training Act

9. Training

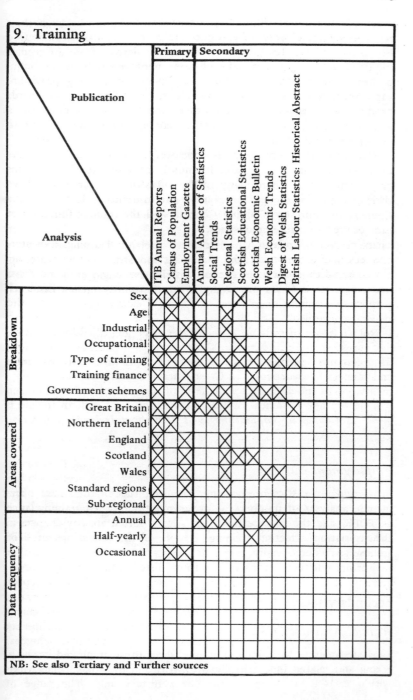

Breakdown / Areas covered / Data frequency	Analysis	Primary			Secondary								
		ITB Annual Reports	Census of Population	Employment Gazette	Annual Abstract of Statistics	Social Trends	Regional Statistics	Scottish Educational Statistics	Scottish Economic Bulletin	Welsh Economic Trends	Digest of Welsh Statistics	British Labour Statistics: Historical Abstract	
Breakdown	Sex	☒	☒	☒	☒		☒		☒			☒	
	Age		☒				☒						
	Industrial	☒					☒						
	Occupational	☒	☒	☒			☒						
	Type of training	☒	☒	☒					☒				
	Training finance	☒											
	Government schemes	☒			☒	☒	☒						
Areas covered	Great Britain	☒	☒	☒	☒	☒	☒						
	Northern Ireland	☒	☒										
	England	☒					☒						
	Scotland	☒					☒	☒					
	Wales	☒					☒			☒	☒		
	Standard regions	☒											
	Sub-regional												
Data frequency	Annual	☒			☒	☒	☒	☒		☒	☒		
	Half-yearly								☒				
	Occasional		☒	☒									

NB: See also Tertiary and Further sources

Most of the boards show their statistics by region, although their regional structures may vary slightly from the standard regions (see Points to note 1). Most of the information is derived from the regular inquiries for the purposes of levy assessment and so there are comprehensive analyses of the financial aspects of training provision, supplemented on occasions by *ad hoc* surveys. Some of the boards produce other regular statistics on their industries, but output varies a great deal, and some of the statistics may not be readily available to people outside the ITB itself.

Currently the ITBs have within scope over half of the total employees in employment in Great Britain. The non-ITB sector, therefore, remains very significant and here many of the industries and services do have their own training bodies, for example the Insurance Industry Training Council, the Forestry Training Council, and the training functions of each of the nationalised industries.

In Northern Ireland, the Northern Ireland Training Executive oversees the activities of the following industrial sectors: catering, clothing and footwear, construction, distributive, engineering, food and drink man-made fibres producing, road transport, and textiles, each with its own training board.

Census 1971: Great Britain: Qualified Manpower Tables

This contains statistics on the number of apprentices, articled clerks and trainees by occupation in Great Britain, and of persons in employment aged 18 and over, by sex, by level of educational qualification and whether or not a trainee. Similar information for Northern Ireland is given in *Census of Population 1971 (Northern Ireland): Education Tables*.

Employment Gazette

Semi-regular statistics on training are given first in the *Gazette* and include analyses of numbers on government sponsored training (such as TOPS) and the finance for these. Also reported are any changes in the legislation affecting training. Details of the operations of ITBs are also given occasionally.

Further relevant articles will be found listed in the Tertiary sources.

Secondary sources

Annual Abstract of Statistics

Separate analyses for men and women show those employed in engineering and related industries by SIC/MLH and by broad occupations within each industry group for Great Britain only. The range of occupations includes the categories of operative apprentices, other trainees, and the total of the two. All for the latest year only which is usually the year prior to the publication year.

Social Trends

Details are usually given of the training under government schemes, with graphs showing for Great Britain the total number of people aged over 14 years undergoing government supported training, and those in skillcentres over the period since 1968, the year TOPS was introduced.

Regional Statistics

The numbers of apprentices and full-time trainees are shown, by sex, in each of the industry groups of: coal and petroleum products, chemicals and allied industries, metals manufacture; mechanical, instrument and electrical engineering, shipbuilding and marine engineering, vehicles, metal goods not elsewhere specified; and other manufacturing industries, all by standard region of Great Britain, for one year only (about four years back from publication year).

There are also details of TOPS, showing the number of applicants for the scheme, the employment status of applicants (that is, employed, unemployed, or non-employed), the number of entrants to training (those aged under 19 and those aged 19 and over), and the number completing their training (under and over 19), all by TSD regions, for the latest year only.

Scottish Educational Statistics

This contains details of qualified school-leavers entering employment and continuing part-time education. The figures are for Scotland and show numbers and percentages, by sex, and by the number of O or H grade SCEs, for the two latest years.

There is also extensive analysis of the numbers of students undergoing vocational further education by type of course, etc. Fuller details can be found by reference to Chapter 7, Primary sources.

Scottish Economic Bulletin

The 'Charts and Statistics' section contains details of the number of people covered by government training measures with the total number of training places supported and the special provisions made for young people given separately. All are half-yearly for the latest four years for Scotland only, together with the percentage that Scotland represents of the total outlay on such measures in Great Britain.

Welsh Economic Trends

This contains an analysis of the TOPS programme in Wales showing separately the number of skillcentres, the number of annexes, the capacity of the skillcentres, the number of instructors, the number of TOPS completions at skillcentres, and the number of completions at colleges and employers' establishments. All annually for five years (from the year prior to publication back).

Digest of Welsh Statistics

Details of the TOPS programme in Wales are given, showing the number of skillcentres, the number of annexes, the capacity of skillcentres and annexes, the number of instructors, the throughput of trainees in skillcentres and annexes, and the numbers trained at colleges and employers' establishments. All annually for the latest six years (the latest being the previous year to publication).

British Labour Statistics: Historical Abstract 1886-1968

Shows the numbers of young people entering employment in Great Britain in the following categories: apprenticeships to skilled occupations; employment leading to recognised professional qualifications; and other types of planned training. All are shown by sex, annually for the period 1950-68.

Tertiary sources

IDS Study (Numbers 135 and 198)

Study Number 135 (December 1976), *Training*, examined the government's plans for training as embodied in the consultative document 'Training for vital skills', which was particularly concerned with training as a method of alleviating serious skill shortages in certain industries. Study Number 198 (July 1979), *Apprentices' Pay*, concentrated on the remuneration of apprentices during their training and explored the possible link between this and skill shortages in certain industries. The record section contains useful details for selected employers of relative pay for apprentices at varying ages and stages in their training.

Recent Surveys of Engineering Craftsmen
(*Employment Gazette*, April 1977, pp345-52)

A lengthy article which attempts to draw together the factors and statistics surrounding skilled labour shortages in engineering. A section on training in the industry contains useful commentary and statistics on numbers trained and being trained over a number of years (the latest being 1975), with analysis of losses of craft trainees by reason for leaving.

Training for Skills — A Programme for Action
(MSC, London, 1978)

A report from MSC which draws together many of the sources of data on apprentices and trainees to present a composite picture, together with an assessment of the performance by the ITB sector and a programme for future action and development.

Skill Shortages in British Industry
(*Employment Gazette*, May 1979, pp433–36)

This was the first in a series of articles on skill shortages in British industry based on the quarterly surveys carried out by the DE and MSC, and was concerned with looking at the results of the surveys and the causes and possible remedies that could be applied. Subsequent articles have appeared in the July 1979 issue (pp645–47), and the October 1979 issue (pp1004–06), each looking in detail at the relevant quarterly results.

Studying for Professional Qualifications
(*Industrial Relations Review and Report*, No. 210, October 1979, pp9–12 and No. 211, November 1979, pp2–6)

A survey article examining what study incentives are given to employees pursuing professional qualifications, with the second part (November) looking at the rewards for success in examinations. Examples of schemes in operation with specific employers are given.

National Training Survey

This was a special survey commissioned by the Training Services Agency (the forerunner of TSD) in 1975 to obtain information about the types of training undergone by individuals in Great Britain as well as details of the background and status of the respondents. The initial report is due for publication in 1980 to be followed by more detailed analyses of specific topics.

Further sources

Department of Employment
Manpower Services Commission — Training Services Division
Industrial Training Boards

The nationalised industries
Northern Ireland Training Executive
British Association for Commercial and Industrial Education
Local Further Education Colleges

10. Travel-to-work Areas

Introduction

Travel-to-work areas (TTWA) can be generally defined as areas within which the employed resident population travel to their normal place of work. Most people travel short distances to their daily work but some go beyond the local area and a TTWA would be delineated to catch as many of these people as possible, although it becomes an unwieldy exercise to keep extending the boundaries of the TTWA in an attempt to catch everybody. The important measure for a TTWA is to assess what is a reasonably self-contained area, that is, an area beyond which few of the employed residents travel to work. No area of reasonable size can be completely self-contained (sometimes called 100 per cent self-containment), and commonly if over 80 per cent of the employed residents of the defined area work within that area then this is regarded as being satisfactory.

Most areas of the UK can be subjected to a reasonable analysis by TTWAs, but London presents a particular problem in that travel-to-work journeys are sometimes exceptionally long-distance, so complicating any assessment.

The DE defines its TTWAs in terms of the local employment office areas and for each office the TTWA is derived from information gathered in the latest Census of Population. If one local office does not cover a sufficiently self-contained area, then a number of local office areas are formed together until a high level of self-containment (at least 80 per cent) has been achieved. Naturally some areas present particular difficulties in measurement and so a lower level has to be accepted.

Apart from data contained in the Census of Population, there is little comprehensive analysis of TTWAs in published form, although some statistical series do contain relevant information which can be of use in forming an idea of particular TTW patterns. The census information, however, takes a long time to reach publication, which means that much of the information is out-of-date by the time it becomes available.

The other primary source of data on TTW patterns is that contained in the publications of the Department of Transport. There are statistics

119

on the journeys made to and from work which give the mode of transport used, the average mileage, the length of journey (in minutes) and other useful information which can be assembled to form a picture of the TTW patterns. A large proportion of this data is based on an occasional sample survey — the National Travel Survey — the latest recorded results being for the 1975/76 survey. The sample is relatively small (about 11,000 households) and relates to just one week, but nevertheless is a useful and important source of data on TTW patterns.

Many of the regular publications listed in Secondary sources below draw upon the results of the National Travel Survey and report them in an annotated form

The TTW data has been broken down into the following analyses:

- ☐ sex — displaying the different TTW patterns of males and females
- ☐ age — with either bands or specific ages given
- ☐ main mode of transport to and from work
- ☐ travel mileage to and from work
- ☐ journey time to and from work
- ☐ occupational — analysis of workplace movements
- ☐ industrial — analysis of workplace movements
- ☐ delineation of TTWAs — containing information which can be of use in defining a particular TTWA.

Points to note

1. TTWAs may not include *all* the workplace movements of the employed residents in a defined area. Most, however, would claim to represent a very high percentage.

2. TTWAs can change quickly. In some cases this may be due to factors such as industrial development, a new motorway/major road, a new town or the emergence of a new housing estate. This is why the Census of Population results — although probably the best data available — must be treated with caution because of the long gap between the actual census taking place and publication of the results.

3. The latest Census of Population was carried out *before* the changes in county and local authority boundaries were introduced consequent upon the 1972 Local Government Act. However, some of the data can be arranged to take account of these changes by special request to OPCS, from whom further details should be sought (address in Part II). Comparisons of areas before and after the act can be made by reference to the booklet *Reorganisation of Local Government Areas: Correlation of New and Old Areas* (HMSO, 1975, price 48p).

10. Travel-to-work areas

Analysis \ Publication	Primary		Secondary				
	Census of Population	National Travel Survey	Transport Statistics: Great Britain	Regional Statistics	Social Trends	Welsh Economic Trends	Digest of Welsh Statistics
Breakdown							
Sex	X	X	X		X		
Age		X	X				
Mode of transport	X	X		X	X		
Travel mileage		X			X		
Journey time		X			X		
Occupational	X	X					
Industrial	X						
Delineation of TTWA	X	X	X				
Areas covered							
Great Britain		X	X	X	X		
Northern Ireland	X						
England	X	X		X	X		
Scotland	X	X		X	X		
Wales	X	X		X	X	X	X
Standard regions	X	X		X			
Sub-regional	X	X				X	
Data frequency							
Annual			X			X	
Occasional	X	X		X	X	X	

NB: See also Tertiary and Further sources

Primary sources

Census of Population

The 1971 census information on TTWAs was published in the following:

- ☐ *Census 1971: England and Wales: Workplace and Transport to Work Tables (Parts I and II)*
- ☐ *Census 1971: Scotland: Workplace and Transport to Work Tables*
- ☐ *Census of Population 1971 (Northern Ireland); Workplace and Transport to Work Tables*

For England and Wales (in Part I) and for Scotland there are details of persons by area of usual residence and workplace both by country, standard regions, sub-regional areas, conurbations, counties, and local authority areas. There is also some analysis of Scottish new towns. It must be remembered that the analysis by these areas was carried out before the changes brought about by the Local Government Act of 1972. There are also details of the resident population by area of workplace and working population by usual residence for each local authority area, conurbation centres and for Scottish new towns. For the conurbations only, there are details of areas of workplace and usual residence of the population by social class and socio-economic group, and by broad occupation and industry.

Also for England and Wales (Part II) and for Scotland, analyses of transport to work include data on the mode of transport used by residents in each local authority area. The means of transport to work by area of usual residence and workplace is given, for the conurbations and their centres separately.

In the Northern Ireland volume there is analysis of the resident population by area of workplace and, for those in employment, by area of residence and workplace. There is also analysis of those working by mode of transport to work for each local authority area together with some brief analysis by socio-economic group.

National Travel Survey

The National Travel Survey was first carried out in 1965 and repeated in 1972/73. The latest, relating to 1975/76, was carried out over a 12 month period and involved the sampling of around 11,000 households on their travel patterns during one week. The survey covers Great Britain only.

A section on comparisons with the previous surveys includes useful analysis of journeys to and from work showing them by main mode of transport for the socio-economic group of the respondent, by travel mileage (including some analysis by standard region and London separately) and by category of distance.

Journeys to and from work are shown by the main mode of transport used, with analyses by age and sex of the respondent; the average length of journey (also by age and sex); the overall journey time; household vehicle availability; gross annual income of the individual; socio-economic group of the individual; and the mode by economic planning regions and the type of area (urban, rural, etc). There are further analyses which concentrate on the length of journey between home and work, the average journey speed and the time spent in travelling. Finally, a graph links the journey start time for journeys to work to the working status of the individual in order to demonstrate any connection between the two factors.

Secondary sources

Transport Statistics: Great Britain

For Great Britain only the number of journeys to and from work per person per week are given by sex and age group. For journeys to and from work, the main mode of transport is given by the respondent's socio-economic group, the travel mileage by main mode of transport and the average length of journey (in minutes). These all cover the three National Travel Surveys (see above).

For Great Britain, and for just the year of the latest National Travel Survey, the length of journey to and from work is analysed into six divisions of length with the percentage of journeys falling in each one. Long distance journeys (which include some to and from work), are shown by sex and age of the traveller and by journey length (in miles). These long distance journeys are further shown by type of area of residence of the traveller (urban, rural, etc) and by main mode of travel used. The frequency of journeys to and from work, expressed as journeys per head per annum, is given by constituent country of Great Britain and by standard region, together with the main mode of transport used.

Regional Statistics

Drawing upon the latest *National Travel Survey*, results for each standard region of Great Britain are given showing the average mileage travelled per person per week going to and from work or school (not shown separately). There is also some broad analysis of mode of transport used. For longer journeys of more than 25 miles by residents of Great Britain over 16 years of age, there is a regional breakdown for the number of journeys per head per year to and from work or education.

Social Trends

This contains an analysis showing the percentage of journeys to work taking a certain number of minutes within four time ranges (under 15; 15–30; 30–60; over 60 minutes) by areas of residence (urban/non-urban, with broad size bands of population in the urban divisions). All are for Great Britain and are based on the latest National Travel Survey results (usually giving the results of another year's survey as well). Sometimes a bar chart also shows for the same years the distribution of journeys by means of transport, but for England and Wales only.

Welsh Economic Trends

This publication gives extensive analysis of Wales and Great Britain separately showing, for males, married females, all females and all persons separately, the time taken to get to work and the percentage of journeys in each of seven categories of journey time. The distance travelled to work (by seven divisions) and the means of transport used are also given by the same breakdown. Also, in the appendices section, maps show the constituent ESD offices of Welsh TTWAs.

Digest of Welsh Statistics

The appendices list the constituent employment office areas considered to constitute the TTWAs in Wales, giving the employment and unemployment levels for each one.

Tertiary sources

Employment and Unemployment in the English Inner Cities
(*Employment Gazette*, August 1979, pp746–49)

This article presents both maps and descriptive detail of TTWAs in the five cities of London, Birmingham, Liverpool, Manchester and Newcastle-upon-Tyne, together with statistics on employment and un-employment levels.

Office of Population Censuses and Surveys: 1971
Information Paper 3
(free from OPCS)

The OPCS produces a great deal of information that is not published — most of it relating to the 1971 Census. Brief details are given in this booklet. Reference to their office will give details of what is available on request and at what cost.

Further sources

Department of Employment
Manpower Services Commission — Employment Service Division
Department of Manpower Services (NI)
Department of Transport
Office of Population Censuses and Surveys
CACI Inc. International (the SITE programme)

11. Labour Mobility

Introduction

Two aspects of labour mobility need to be defined in order to clarify the concept, although they may operate independently of each other or together.

Occupational mobility is concerned with changes of job across occupations, for example from bus driver to window cleaner, and within this category the term *industrial* mobility indicates that the move has involved a distinct change of industry. Clearly such a move may not involve an occupational change as such, as in the case, for example, of an electrician working for a house-building company who moves to an electrician's job in a firm of vehicle manufacturers. *Geographical* mobility is somewhat more straightforward in that it is concerned with movement that involves a significant change of residence because of a change of job or prospects for a new job in the future.

Either way the amount of published information on labour mobility is very small indeed and many of the sources listed below only hint at where data might be found. In short, there is no easy source of information. The decennial Census of Population provides some published details of geographical movement and can be linked to change of occupation data, but only a small proportion of the total information gathered is published. One-off studies on mobility are useful despite the rather specialised coverage of most of them, and some are listed in the Tertiary sources below.

The limited range of published information has been broken down as follows:

- ☐ sex
- ☐ age — usually broad groups
- ☐ occupational mobility — usually very unspecific
- ☐ geographical mobility — again largely using broad areas

Points to note

1. The General Household Survey results tend to vary in content from year to year, and in all cases are based on a small sample of households.
2. Geographical mobility within sub-regions is much more difficult to detect than that which goes on across regions, especially where the detection is on the basis of a questionnaire. For example, people may be less inclined to think that a short move across town implies geographical mobility.
3. Some types of mobility may be labelled 'internal' mobility, and involve the movement of workers — either across occupations or regions — within the same organisation. Bank managers provide a good example of where a high degree of geographical mobility is practised internally. This type of movement is extremely difficult to detect, however, unless the employers themselves come forward with the information.

Primary sources

Census 1971: Great Britain: Migration Tables

This contains details of the geographical mobility of enumerated persons through analysis of where they lived one year and five years prior to the census date, with the statistics given by usual residence, former usual residence, sex, age group and marital condition. All this for standard regions of Great Britain (England separately) and the conurbations.

For more localised but detailed information (usually down to small urban areas), the following should be consulted: Census 1971: England and Wales: Migration Regional Reports, and Census 1971: Scotland: Migration Tables. The information on labour mobility in the census is implicit rather than explicit, and the record of people's movements over a five year period has to be linked to information about occupation and industry to gain a useful picture. Also, it can be useful to compare census data (the 1966 interim census being particularly useful in this respect) to establish movement over a long period.

The data gathered during the census included (in 1971) analysis of a person's occupation one year before the census date, but details have not been published of what could prove to be a good reflection of patterns of occupational mobility. However, much of the census data is not published and so the OPCS remains a primary point of contact for further information (see Further sources below).

General Household Survey

This contains details of the reasons for moving given by the sample of households that reported moving recently, categorised by distance of

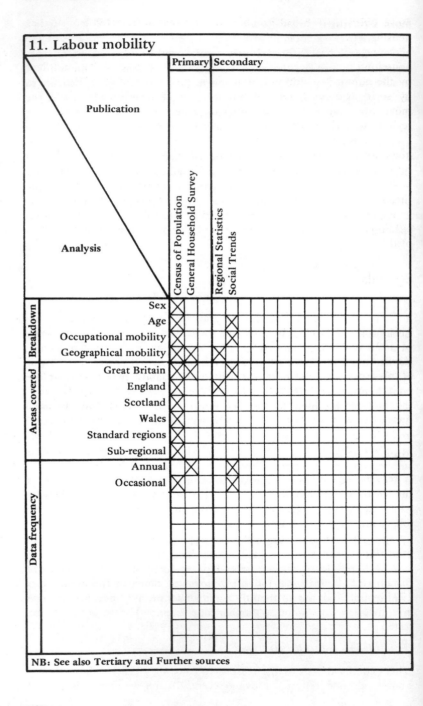

move (with three broad groups), and by reason (selected from either housing, environmental, job/study, personal, or other reasons), with the percentage of movers in each case. Further analysis shows the head of household by socio-economic group (professional, semi-skilled, etc) and by the number of moves of residence in the past five years. Households by socio-economic group of the head are further shown by type of move over the five years, identifying moves between regions, sub-regions, within sub-regions or those where there was no movement.

There is usually analysis of those who moved compared to all households (movers and non-movers), with divisions by household type (ie number of people), tenure, bedroom standard (number of bedrooms), amenities (bathroom, etc), annual income of the head of the household, and the socio-economic group of the head.

From year to year the range of questions asked and information published on mobility might vary, but usually there is some content of the type listed above.

Secondary sources

Regional Statistics

This contains results from the National Dwelling and Housing Survey of 1977 (commissioned by the Department of the Environment) and shows the percentage of heads of households in six categories of length of residence (in years) for each English standard region and metropolitan county. There is also an analysis for the same areas showing the movers over the previous 12 months with the current address/ previous address by region and the percentage of moves within each

Social Trends

A regular feature of this publication is a summary analysis (based on the GHS) of job mobility in Great Britain over a 12 month period, which shows the percentage who changed jobs, the average number of job changes (per person in the sample), and the total sample size, all by age group. Usually two years are given, the latest being two years prior to publication.

An occasional series has analysed occupational change in Great Britain (based on the census results) showing males in employment in 1971 by full SIC industry breakdown — whether in the same occupation, in a different occupation, with no occupation, or their occupation not stated — compared to their position in 1970. The latest analysis appeared in the 1976 edition.

Tertiary sources

A Case Study in Labour Mobility
(Jones, R M, in the *Manchester School of Economic and Social Studies*, Vol. 37, No. 2, June 1969, pp169–74)

This is rather a dated article but nevertheless useful as it is based on a case study of the Ford Motor Company's expansion in Swansea in the late 1960s. It is mainly concerned with occupational and industrial mobility and the effects that the new plant had on inducing these in the local workforce.

Recruitment and Mobility of Labour
(Atkinson, G and Purkiss, C, in Ungerson, B (ed), *Recruitment Handbook*, Gower, 1975)

This looks at the importance of labour mobility in the context of the recruitment policies of employers.

An Analysis of Graduate Job Mobility
(Kuhn, A *et al*, in *British Journal of Industrial Relations*, Vol. 11, No. 1, March 1973, pp124–42)

An analysis of occupational mobility amongst graduates with different employment sectors proving to display different mobility characteristics.

You get more out of life ... Out of town
(Jones, D and Lawrence, S, in *Personnel Management*, Vol. 5, No. 2, February 1973, pp37–39, 42)

A look at the case for and against employees moving from London, based on a case study of a firm's move from Wembley to Plymouth.

Labour Mobility and the 'Net Advantage' Theory
(Perline, M M and Presley, R W, in *Personnel Journal*, Vol. 52, No. 12, December 1973, pp1040–45)

This article pursues the fortunes of 599 engineers and technical workers laid off by an aerospace company in the USA city of Wichita over the period January 1969 to March 1971 and attempts to examine the 'net advantage' of those who migrated in search of work compared to those who decided to stay put.

IDS Study (Number 132)

Study Number 132 (October 1976), *Housing Assistance*, examined, through the usual range of examples, the provisions made by employers for transferred staff and for mortgages on property in the new areas.

Interrelatedness of Occupational and Geographical Labour Mobility

(Schroeder, L D, in *Industrial and Labour Relations Review*, Vol. 29, No. 3, April 1976, pp405–11)

This looks at the case for assuming some degree of interrelatedness between the types of mobility with a view to highlighting the policy implications.

Assessing the Performance of Assisted Labour Mobility Policy in Britain

(Beaumont, P B, in *Scottish Journal of Political Economy*, Vol. 24, February 1977, pp55–65)

A useful and interesting article which attempts to evaluate the success of assisted labour mobility policy in Great Britain (and specifically the Employment Transfer Scheme) in achieving the desired aim of persuading workers to move who would not have done so without the assistance of specific policy measures. A model is set up with some interesting conclusions.

The British Manager: Careers and Mobility

(Guerrier, Y and Philpott, N, BIM, 1978)

This is concerned with the mobility of management in Britain and examines the reasons for and types of mobility, drawing on the results of a sample of over 1000 managers.

Occupational Change

(Townsend, C and Hayes, C, in *BACIE Journal*, July 1978, pp114–16)

This looks at the (alleged) increasing amount of occupational change and mobility within the labour force and examines the effects this might have and how it should be accommodated in work and education.

Job Choice and the Manual Worker

(Curran, J and Stanworth, J, in *Personnel Management*, September 1978, pp41–45)

This looks at the implications of change in the occupational mobility of manual workers, highlighting the differences between technologies and firm size.

Motivating Managers to Move On
(Rozier, B, in *Personnel Management*, May 1980 pp30–33)

This article examines the problems of enforcing mobility clauses in contracts of employment and looks at methods used to persuade managers to move on.

Moving around in the Room at the Top
(*Employment Gazette*, December 1979, pp1220–1228)

This article by Peter Williamson of the DE's Unit for Manpower Studies looks at some of the first results from a special survey carried out to examine the early careers of graduates. The survey covered the period 1970–77 and looked at graduates from all sources. A further article appeared in the *Gazette* of May 1980, 'On the way up: an analysis of first jobs from the Early Careers Survey of Graduates', (by Lyndsey Whitehead and Peter Williamson), pp472–77.

Further sources

Department of Employment
Manpower Services Commission
Department of Manpower Services
Office of Population Censuses and Surveys
Board of Inland Revenue
Department of the Environment

12. Absence from Work

Introduction

Absence from work includes all time lost through unavoidable and avoidable reason. The former involves mainly absence through sickness or injury, for example, while the latter covers absence without obvious reason, where the explanation may not be genuine.

Generally, information on absence levels is poor; most of what is available either relates to unavoidable absence through sickness or injury specifically, or is arranged in broad categories of reason for absence, and it emanates largely from government sources. Most of the regular official data are on unavoidable absence, and the Department of Health and Social Security provides detailed analysis of days of absence per person, but this is limited to those claiming benefit. The annual General Household Survey provides the widest and most regular analysis of absenteeism by reason, although the questions asked are of necessity broadly based and relate to the week of the survey only.

The Tertiary sources below list some of the articles that have been written on the subject, but they are noticeably short of detailed statistics which is the main problem in this subject area.

The available data have been broken down as follows:

☐ sex
☐ age
☐ reasons for absence — usually those given by the absentee
☐ industrial
☐ occupational.

Points to note

1. The statistics on days lost through sickness and injury only include those absentees who are notified to the DHSS (usually those in need of financial assistance); this will obviously preclude large numbers of people who are not notified, being especially the case for non-manual workers.

2. The GHS results on the reasons for absence from work are based on a sample of households and relate to one week only. Such limitations should be remembered when using the statistics.

3. There is a clear distinction between avoidable and unavoidable absence; the former is sometimes called 'absenteeism' in a few publications at the exclusion of the latter.

4. Some of the sickness/invalidity statistics are expressed as a rate of the 'population at risk' which, broadly defined, is the working population with the exclusion of the following:

- ☐ men aged 65–69 and women aged 60–64 who are retirement pensioners and all men aged over 70 and women over 65
- ☐ members of the armed forces
- ☐ mariners while at sea
- ☐ most non-industrial civil servants/Post Office employees who do not normally claim benefit until an illness has lasted six months
- ☐ married women and certain widows who have chosen not to be insured for benefit.

Primary sources

General Household Survey

Included in this annual survey are questions on reasons for absence from work during the week of the survey. The reasons are rationalised into the three categories of: own illness or accident; strike/short-time/lay-off; and personal and other reasons (excluding holidays). The total is also shown in most cases. Analyses by these reasons for absence show the percentage in each category by sex and age group for all persons aged 16 and over. Males and females together are analysed by reason and socio-economic group, and by reason and SIC industry group. All the analyses are for Great Britain only.

OPCS Monitor – Infectious Diseases (Ref MB2)

This contains details of the number of insured persons absent from work on the first Tuesday in the month as a result of certified* sickness, invalidity or injury, for the standard regions of England and Wales. The data is presented quarterly usually for the latest eight quarters.

OPCS monitors can be obtained free of charge from OPCS Information Branch (for address see Part II).

---

* 'Certified' in this sense is usually taken to mean sickness, invalidity or injury supported by a certificate from a medical practitioner

12. Absence from work

Analysis \ Publication	Primary		Secondary						
	General Household Survey	OPCS Monitor	Health & Personal Social Service Statistics	Annual Abstract of Statistics	Regional Statistics	Scottish Abstract of Statistics	Welsh Economic Trends	IDS Study	Compendium of Health Statistics
Breakdown									
Sex	X		X	X	X	X		X	X
Age			X						
Reasons for absence	X	X	X	X	X	X	X	X	X
Industrial						X		X	
Occupational	X							X	
Areas covered									
United Kingdom				X			X		
Great Britain	X		X	X			X		
Northern Ireland									
England		X		X					
Scotland					X	X			
Wales		X					X		
Standard regions					X			X	
Data frequency									
Annual	X		X	X	X	X	X		X
Quarterly		X							
Occasional							X		

NB: See also Tertiary and Further sources

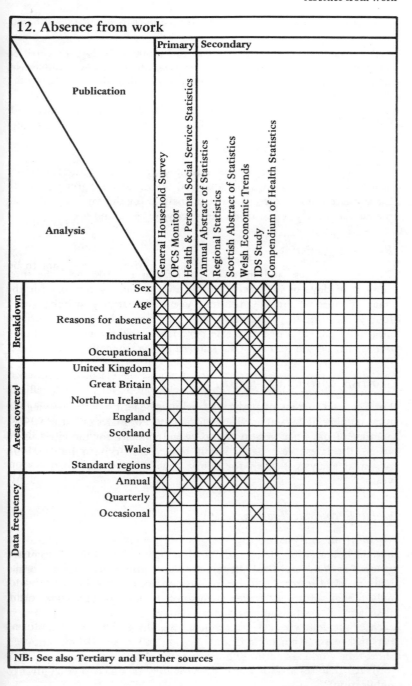

135

Health and Personal Social Service Statistics for England

This contains details of new spells and number of days of certified incapacity and the rate per 1000 persons at risk, by sex and cause, annually for seven years and for Great Britain only.

Secondary sources

Annual Abstract of Statistics

This shows details of sickness benefit in Great Britain with the number of days of certified incapacity analysed by sex and age group annually for the latest nine years. A further analysis for the same years shows the number of days of certified incapacity by cause and sex.

Regional Statistics

Details of sickness and invalidity benefit in the UK show the total number of days of incapacity during the period, by sex and for the standard regions, annually for four years (the latest year being about four years prior to publication). Also, for men only, days of certified incapacity are expressed as a rate per man at risk, showing the number of days per person for each UK standard region, annually for five years.

Scottish Abstract of Statistics

For Scotland there is an analysis of sickness benefit by sex, showing the total number of days of certified incapacity. For males only the average number of days per person is also given, annually for the latest seven years (the latest year being about two years prior to publication). A similar analysis is given for injury benefit by sex and for the same years.

Welsh Economic Trends

There is an analysis of the reasons for people working other than normal hours (with males and females together) by full SIC industry group. For Wales and Great Britain separately, the percentage of normal hours worked in total is given for all industries and services. For Wales only there is a further detailed analysis of the reasons for working other than normal hours, showing the percentage of hours lost or gained in each of the following categories: overtime; illness or accident; holidays; personal reasons (including flexible hours); and 'other' (labour disputes, short-time working and those hours worked at the beginning or end of a job). All analyses are for the latest year only (about two years prior to publication).

IDS Study (Number 169)

IDS Study Number 169 (May 1978), *Absenteeism*, contains details of rates of absence, the type of controls imposed by companies and the incentives given for low absenteeism in individual employees, in selected organisations. Most of the analyses relate to manual workers but there are useful comparative data.

Compendium of Health Statistics

This contains comprehensive details of days lost and numbers (spells) of sickness/invalidity claims for Great Britain. Days lost and spells are analysed by sex, annually for 22 years (the latest year being about two years prior to publication), with expenditure from National Insurance funds on sickness benefit given for a similar period. The number of days and spells of male certified incapacity/sickness for each standard region of Great Britain are given, with the numbers and rate per person at risk, for the latest year only. The tables are supplemented by graphs and bar charts on the key indicators, with a useful graph showing the average number of days of certified incapacity per person at risk by sex and age group over an 11 year period.

Tertiary sources

Dealing with Absenteeism
(*Industrial Relations Review and Report*, No. 160, September 1977, pp5–10)

This article looks at the more important factors which influence levels of absenteeism and examines the efforts of selected companies in monitoring, controlling and improving their own levels of absenteeism. Some comparative statistics are given. Also in the 'Legal Information Bulletin' (in the same issue) there is an examination of the law surrounding absenteeism and the grounds for dismissal.

The Absenteeism Culture: Becoming Attendance Orientated
(Allen, R F and Higgins, M, *Personnel*, Vol. 56, No. 1, January/ February 1979, pp30–39)

A useful article which argues that levels of absence (most of it avoidable) have come to be accepted as the norm in the majority of industry, yet the costs remain high. The authors argue for a change in attitude by management (and also by the employees) to become less complacent about absenteeism. Ways of progressing towards this goal are given.

Further sources

Department of Employment
Department of Health and Social Security
Department of Industry
Health and Safety Executive
Institute of Manpower Studies (Absence Workshop)

13. Hours of Work

Introduction

This section covers the broad area of hours of work with the main divisions being normal hours, overtime hours, shiftworking, part-time working, and holidays. It is important that the distinctions between different definitions of hours are clarified as the statistics can sometimes convey a confused picture through their terminology. *Normal* hours of work are those hours which constitute the *basic* work week and with the addition of overtime hours represent the *actual* hours worked. Overtime hours are not normally equivalent to normal hours in terms of pay, since most overtime is paid for at a premium rate.

Further distinctions need to be made between what is meant by *full-time* and *part-time* work. Unfortunately definitions of part-time work vary considerably, but for the benefit of the regular statistics on the subject the DE has tended to adopt an upper limit of 30 hours per week excluding meal breaks and overtime; hours of 30 or below would therefore be classified as part-time. Needless to say, this limit has been in existence for some time, and with normal full-time weekly hours generally on a downward path, 30 hours must soon become due for revision downwards. In fact most of the part-time work done in Great Britain has a weekly hours total of around half the normal week. In 1971 the Census of Population revealed that about two-thirds of part-time women worked less than 22 hours a week.

The major series of regular statistics on hours of work is compiled by the DE and is based on either monthly or annual inquiries into the prevailing hours in certain industries. More detailed analyses are made annually for certain key industrial sectors and these are reported (as regular articles) in the *Employment Gazette*. The annual New Earnings Survey is another useful source of information on hours of work in all industries and services, and includes hours data on overtime working in both normal and shiftworking situations, but, of course, is based on a small (one per cent) sample of employees. The now well-established EEC Labour Force Sample Survey is an extremely useful source of data on hours worked, and it contains the only regular source of information on the part-time hours of males.

The statistics have been broken down as follows:

- □ sex — usually for youths and boys, and girls, in addition to male and female adults
- □ manual/non-manual — an important distinction in hours data, although many of the regular series are presented in aggregate form
- □ overtime hours — those hours worked over and above normal hours
- □ shiftworking hours — containing some details of normal and/or overtime hours of those on shiftworking, sometimes defined as those in receipt of shift premia
- □ part-time hours — mostly presented for women only with few analyses covering men
- □ holidays — usually referring to basic holiday entitlement per year, and sometimes public holidays are given
- □ industrial — many of the analyses being by MLH in addition to SIC groups
- □ occupational — this is in addition to simply manual or non-manual and can be quite detailed.

These are the main divisions used to describe the range of information available, but others may be found in some of the statistical series mentioned below.

Points to note

1. In many of the regular statistical series on hours of work, the term *average* hours is used which should be regarded as being synonymous with the term *actual* hours, defined in the Introduction to this section.

2. The statistics often limit their analysis to operatives (particularly in those relating to overtime), and this group can be taken to include all workers except administrative, technical, professional and clerical workers.

3. The distinction between adults and youths, boys and girls is usually quite clear in the statistics. Adults are men aged 21 and over and women aged 18 and over, and young people come below these age limits.

4. The difference between national and local hours of work can be a significant one, and it must be remembered that national statistics on hours — usually combining local figures and averaging the total — may not accurately reflect the number of hours worked in a particular area. This may be less of a problem with nationally-negotiated normal hours which usually apply to all sub-regions.

13. Hours of work

Analysis \ Publication	Primary				Secondary										
	Employment Gazette	Time Rates of Wages and Hours of Work	New Earnings Survey	EEC Labour Force Sample Survey	British Labour Statistics: Yearbook	Monthly Digest of Statistics	Economic Trends	Annual Abstract of Statistics	Social Trends	Regional Statistics	Scottish Abstract of Statistics	Digest of Statistics – N. Ireland	Digest of Welsh Statistics	Welsh Economic Trends	British Labour Statistics: Historical Abstract
Breakdown															
Sex	X	X	X	X	X		X		X	X		X	X		
Manual/non-manual	X	X	X		X			X		X					
Overtime hours	X	X	X		X					X					
Shiftworking hours		X	X												
Part-time hours	X	X	X	X										X	
Holidays		X						X							
Industrial	X	X	X		X	X	X	X	X	X					
Occupational	X	X	X												
Areas covered															
United Kingdom	X	X			X	X	X	X	X	X					X
Great Britain	X		X		X	X	X	X							
Northern Ireland	X	X										X			
England	X		X							X					
Scotland	X	X								X	X				
Wales	X	X								X			X	X	
Standard regions	X	X								X					
Sub-regional	X									X					
Data frequency															
Annual	X	X	X	X	X	X	X	X	X	X	X	X	X	X	X
Half-yearly	X			X											
Quarterly						X									
Monthly	X					X									
Weekly	X		X		X				X	X				X	
Occasional	X														

NB: See also Tertiary and Further sources

Primary sources

Employment Gazette

Monthly tables show the normal weekly hours of manual workers for all industries and services in Great Britain, with a corresponding index and analysis of the numbers of workers affected by any reductions in normal weekly hours for each SIC industry group, for the latest month. Also the UK annual averages of normal weekly hours worked are shown for the latest four years by SIC industry group. Actual hours of work are given more extensive treatment each month with, for Great Britain, an index of actual weekly hours worked in manufacturing industry (actual and seasonally adjusted) and in four broad industry groups, with hours worked per operative, monthly for four years and annually for the latest 22 years.

For the UK, average actual hours worked are shown by sex and by SIC, annually for the latest four years, and for full-time men, women, boys, girls, and part-time women, annually for the latest three years, all separately for manufacturing industry only and all industries. The monthly series also contains details of overtime worked in manufacturing industry in Great Britain, showing the percentage of all operatives working some overtime and the hours of overtime worked (in thousands and the average per operative), all by comprehensive MLH for the latest month (about two months prior to the publication month) and a longer run of four or five years monthly. Annually (usually in the February issue), the results of the October survey of earnings and hours in the UK are given, showing average actual hours worked by SIC industry group, with separate analyses for full-time men, youths and boys, women, girls, and part-time women. Manual workers only are shown by SIC and by UK standard region, by sex. The results of the special April survey appear in the August issue and show average actual hours worked in selected industries (MLH) by sex and type of work. Regular surveys of hours of work are also taken in certain industries. For the June survey in engineering, shipbuilding and chemicals (appearing in the November issue), average actual hours and overtime hours are shown separately, by broad skill and MLH and by standard region of Great Britain for the latest survey year. For agriculture, surveys are taken in April and September each year with results published in the October and March issues respectively, showing the average actual hours worked for men, youths, women and girls (separately) for the latest three years at half-yearly intervals.

Finally, the summary results of the April New Earnings Survey (see below), which includes extensive analysis of hours of work, are published in the October issue.

Time Rates of Wages and Hours of Work

This annual publication sets out the latest agreed normal weekly hours of work (exclusive of overtime hours or main meal breaks) reached through national collective agreements, organisations of employers, statutory wage boards or councils and the like, for the industry concerned (MLH), and covers the UK. Also details of the appropriate wage rates based on multiples of normal hours are given for shiftworking, night duty, and some forms of overtime working. The appendices list the number of days or weeks holiday entitlement of workers by comprehensive MLH and standard UK region or sub-region, including separate details of basic entitlement and 'public or customary' holidays.

The month by month changes in the factors outlined above first appear in the monthly publication *Changes in Wage Rates and Hours of Work*.

New Earnings Survey

The annual NES contains comprehensive details of hours of work in Great Britain based on the regular April survey. The individual parts are summarised as follows:

Part A contains a summary analysis of the main findings of the year's survey, including broad details of hours of work, by sex and whether manual or non-manual. Actual and overtime hours worked are shown separately for all industries and services, for national agreements, for a comprehensive selection of MLH industries and for occupations. Further analyses show the actual and overtime hours (separately) for each standard region of Great Britain, by sex and whether manual or non-manual, in total for all industries and services.

Subsequent parts concentrate on an analysis of normal hours and overtime hours (separately) for all workers, for those receiving overtime pay, and for those receiving shift premia, by sex and whether manual or non-manual, with Part B as reached by collective agreement; Part C broken down by industry; and Part D by a comprehensive occupational breakdown.

Part E shows actual and overtime hours separately, by sex and whether manual or non-manual, for each standard region of Great Britain and each county within those regions, with the GLC also shown by boroughs. Basic normal hours and overtime hours are shown separately by sex and whether manual or non-manual, and by age group, with separate analyses for those receiving overtime pay and those receiving shift premia.

Part F contains a thorough analysis of hours showing normal basic hours per week with the distribution (showing the percentage of the sample within ranges of weekly hours) for manuals and non-manuals, given by sex. Similar analyses cover overtime hours and actual hours worked, and all are presented by industry (SIC), occupation, age group and standard region of Great Britain, plus Greater London. Further tables show the distribution of total hours, normal hours, and overtime hours by sex and whether manual or non-manual, for those with earnings within specified ranges. Lastly in this part, the hours of part-time women workers in Great Britain are shown, with normal and actual hours given by whether manual or non-manual, by collective agreement, industry (SIC with some MLH), occupation, age group, and standard region of Great Britain, plus Greater London separately.

EEC Labour Force Sample Survey

For each EEC nation and the total of the nine, the average number of actual hours worked by persons who worked during the reference week are shown by sex, and whether full- or part-time, separately for those with a main occupation and those with an occasional occupation. Those with a main occupation are further analysed by sex, professional status, and sector of activity, with actual hours per week shown in each category of employers and self-employed, employees, family workers (not available for the UK), and total.

Industrial analyses by broad groups are given for all persons with a main occupation, by sex, professional status and sector of activity, and for employees separately. The analyses are for the year of the survey only.

Secondary sources

British Labour Statistics Yearbook

This contains a comprehensive selection of statistics on hours of work, including summary analyses from the New Earnings Survey. There are indices of normal weekly hours of work for the UK in total by SIC industry group, given monthly (for the year of the yearbook) and with annual averages of the latest two years. For the same periods the index is shown for men, women, juveniles and all workers separately, but for all industries and services in total only. For manual workers only, the annual changes in these indices are given annually for the latest ten years for all industries and services, with manufacturing separately.

Average actual hours worked in the UK are analysed by sex (with separate analyses for adults and young people), and by SIC industry groups, for the latest six years annually, and by MLH for the latest year only (the latter also including an analysis of part-time women workers). A UK regional analysis of actual hours worked is given for full-time manual men in total for three years annually, and by SIC industry group for the latest year. An index of average actual weekly hours worked per operative in manufacturing industry is also given, monthly for the latest three years and annually for the latest 14 years. Average actual hours and average overtime hours worked per week in selected industries in Great Britain are shown, all based on the regular annual or half-yearly inquiries first recorded in the *Employment Gazette*. The engineering sector is analysed by selected industry groups within that sector, by occupation and skill and with the latter by standard region of Great Britain. For the sectors of shipbuilding and ship-repairing, and chemicals, the figures relate to full-time manual men only, but are half-yearly.

Overtime hours worked per week in Great Britain are analysed separately for manufacturing industry, monthly for the latest three years and annually for the latest ten years, and by selected SIC/MLH industry groups monthly for the latest year only.

In addition to the series of statistics listed above, there are comprehensive results from the New Earnings Survey including most of the main summary analyses appearing in the regular *NES*, Part A (see Primary sources above).

Finally, the basic holiday entitlement of UK manual workers as set out in national collective agreements and the like, is shown for about 15 years annually, with the percentage of all workers having an annual entitlement given within certain numbers of weeks and days.

Monthly Digest of Statistics

This contains analysis of average weekly hours worked in Great Britain for manufacturing industries only and for manufacturing and certain other industries, with separate figures for men, women, youths and boys, full-time women, part-time women, and girls, annually for the latest nine years. Overtime worked in manufacturing industry only is shown by the number of operatives involved, total overtime hours worked, and the average per operative, monthly for the latest three to five years.

Economic Trends

An index of average actual hours worked (per operative) in Great Britain in manufacturing industry is given, monthly for about 21 months, quarterly for the latest five years, and annually for the latest 12. A longer series annually and quarterly for about 16 years can be found in *Economic Trends Annual Supplement*, showing the index of average hours worked per operative in manufacturing industry, with some seasonally adjusted rates also given.

Annual Abstract of Statistics

This shows the average weekly actual hours worked in Great Britain, separately for manufacturing industry only and for manufacturing and certain other industries, by sex, annually for the latest ten years.

Social Trends

This usually contains details of normal and actual weekly hours worked by UK male manual workers, together with the annual holiday entitlement in weeks (the percentage in each range of weeks), annually for the latest five years plus a further two. A graph over a long period of about 20 years occasionally supplements the analysis. There is also usually an international comparison of hours of work showing, for about 12 selected countries plus the UK, the actual hours per week in manufacturing industry, all for the latest three years plus one other.

Regional Statistics

Some of the results from the annual New Earnings Survey are presented by UK standard region. Usually the average weekly actual hours of full-time male manuals are given by broad industry group (SIC), for two years annually. Also the average weekly actual hours and overtime are shown separately for full-time men and women but by manual or non-manual, and for the metropolitan counties in addition to standard regions for the latest year.

Apart from the NES results, there is an analysis of overtime working in each standard region of Great Britain, showing the number of operatives working overtime, the percentage this represents of all operatives, and the total overtime hours worked, all for manufacturing industry only and for the latest two years.

Scottish Abstract of Statistics

Average weekly actual hours worked by male manuals in manufacturing industries and all industries covered by the DE (October) survey are shown for Scotland and the UK separately, annually for the latest nine years. Another analysis (based on the NES) shows the overtime working of manuals by sex, for Scotland and Great Britain separately, but just for the latest year.

Digest of Statistics — Northern Ireland

For Northern Ireland only, the average weekly actual hours of male manual workers are given by broad industry groups, annually for the latest 11 years (the latest being about two years prior to publication).

Digest of Welsh Statistics

The average actual hours of male manual workers for the latest year (in October) are shown for Wales and the UK separately. Overtime hours of full-time manual workers by sex are also given for Wales and Great Britain separately, all for the latest five years annually.

Welsh Economic Trends

This shows the average normal and overtime hours worked per week by full-time manual workers, by sex, for Wales and Great Britain separately, annually for the latest five years.

British Labour Statistics: Historical Abstract 1886–1968

This contains a wide selection of data on hours of work including some analyses of selected occupations/industries covering normal weekly hours worked each year from the beginning of the last century to 1968. Indices of normal and actual weekly hours worked mostly cover manual workers in manufacturing industries, and most are post-1950.

Overtime hours are also given comprehensive treatment with an analysis of numbers and average hours worked in manufacturing industries given monthly for the period mid-1961 to 1968 and quarterly from 1950 to mid-1961.

Paid holidays of manual workers, showing the percentage of all workers within each band of weeks, are given annually for the period 1951 to 1968.

Most of the analyses relate to the UK or Great Britain, although there are some regional breakdowns.

Tertiary sources

Incomes Data Report

This twice monthly report lists a selection of the major settlements recently reached by selected industries/occupations on matters of pay, hours, holiday entitlement and rates of pay for overtime and shiftworking. Some of the reports give quite detailed information.

Part-time working in Great Britain
(Robertson, J A S and Briggs, J M, *Employment Gazette*, July 1979, pp671–75, 677)

This contains details of the sources of data on part-time working in Great Britain and analyses the range of data that is available. Statistics are presented on numbers and hours worked, by sex, together with details of earnings.

IDS Study (Numbers 206 and 211)

Study Number 206 (November 1979), *Holidays 1979*, is that year's issue of a regular annual publication looking at basic holiday entitlements and holiday pay, together with analysis of such features as service-related holidays and special leave. There are records of company schemes listed in detail. Study Number 211 (February 1980), *Hours of Work*, looked at the trends in basic normal and actual hours worked with the usual range of case studies to illustrate these trends.

IDS Guide to Shiftwork
(September 1979, Incomes Data Services Ltd, London)

This gives a comprehensive survey of the reasons for working shifts, the types of shift that are used, the range of extra facilities needed and the comparative costs and benefits in use. All are supported by examples of shiftworking in practice with major employers. An extremely useful guide to all aspects of shiftworking.

Recent Changes in Normal Weekly Hours and Holiday Entitlements of Manual Employees
(*Employment Gazette*, May 1980, pp519-20)

A review of the significant changes in the normal hours and holiday entitlement of UK manual workers, with useful statistics over the ten years 1970–79, with commentary on the key trends displayed.

Further sources

Department of Employment
Department of Manpower Services
Manpower Services Commission
EEC Commission
International Labour Organisation
Trades Union Congress (and trade unions themselves)

14. Redundancy, Temporary Stoppages and Short-time Work

Introduction

This section covers three distinct areas yet all have a common link in that they are usually the result of management action on the workforce, although the reasons persuading management to take these measures may vary widely. Brief definitions of each of these areas are given below.

Redundancies are job losses due in the main to reductions in business activity. The statistics available on redundancies are generally scant and the official figures that do exist only record those involving ten or more persons (prior to March 1976 it was 20 or more persons) which have to be notified to the Department of Employment. Redundancies usually involve compensation to workers made redundant under the terms of the Redundancy Payments Act of 1965 with subsequent amendments, and more details of the conditions for both employers and employees are given general coverage in a DE booklet entitled *The Redundancy Payments Scheme* (HMSO, London, 1977).

Temporary stoppages of work are those stoppages which are the result of a mangement decision temporarily to suspend employees on the understanding that they will shortly resume normal working. The official statistics from the DE only show those registered at local DE offices for benefit claims, and they are not included in the unemployment figures.

Short-time working arrangements are those made by an employer for employees to work less than their normal hours. This does not include any time lost through sickness, absenteeism, holidays or the direct effects of industrial action.

The main statistics on temporary stoppages and short-time working are compiled by the DE through its regional offices on a monthly basis, supplemented with occasional studies on such aspects as the levels of compensation paid to employees when such restrictions on working are imposed upon them.

The range of published information has been analysed as follows:

☐ sex
☐ redundancies
☐ temporary stoppages
☐ short-time working
☐ industrial — usually by SIC group for redundancies and more comprehensive MLH for short-time working
☐ finance — details of redundancy payments or financial help through, for example, the Temporary Employment Subsidy (TES) scheme of the DE

Points to note

1. Redundancies, temporary stoppages and short-time working are initiated by employers on employees and are quite distinct from employee-initiated reductions in normal working such as strikes.
2. Those recorded by the DE as being temporarily stopped include only those who register with their local office in order to claim benefit. This will obviously preclude many who are not eligible or who do not register for benefit claims but are nevertheless temporarily stopped.

Primary sources

Employment Gazette

A monthly series gives the incidence of short-time working in manufacturing in Great Britain by selected industries (MLH) and by standard regions, showing those stood off for a whole week, those working part of a week and the total of both analysed by number of operatives, total hours lost and the average loss per operative. There is an analysis for the latest month (usually two months prior to the publication month), and a longer analysis monthly for about four to five years.

Those temporarily stopped are shown by sex for each standard region of Great Britain, for the latest available month (previous month to publication). The figures are based on those claiming benefit.

Also, the *Gazette* occasionally contains details of redundancies (usually in the 'Employment brief' section) on a semi-regular basis, including details of payments made under the Redundancy Payments Act.

Welsh Economic Trends

Redundancies in Wales are shown by the number of jobs lost in broad industry groups, annually for the latest eight years (the latest being the previous year to publication). There is also a pie chart (latest year only) showing the percentage of total redundancies by sector of activity.

There are details of the TES and STEP schemes showing the approved

14. Redundancy, temporary stoppages, and short-time working

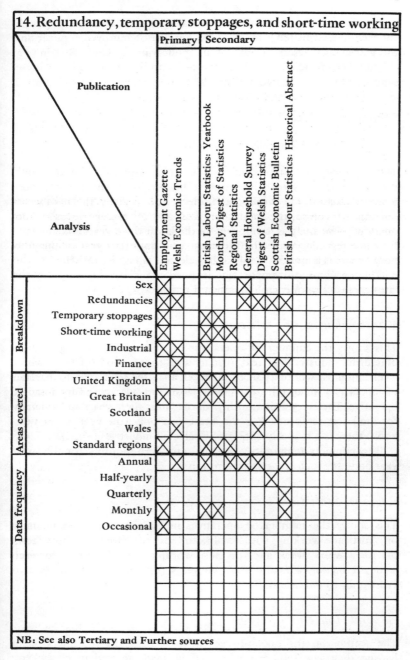

Analysis	Primary		Secondary									
	Employment Gazette	Welsh Economic Trends	British Labour Statistics: Yearbook	Monthly Digest of Statistics	Regional Statistics	General Household Survey	Digest of Welsh Statistics	Scottish Economic Bulletin	British Labour Statistics: Historical Abstract			
Breakdown												
Sex	✕					✕						
Redundancies	✕					✕	✕					
Temporary stoppages			✕	✕								
Short-time working	✕		✕					✕				
Industrial	✕	✕	✕			✕						
Finance		✕					✕					
Areas covered												
United Kingdom			✕	✕								
Great Britain	✕		✕	✕		✕		✕				
Scotland								✕				
Wales		✕					✕					
Standard regions	✕		✕	✕	✕							
Data frequency												
Annual		✕	✕	✕	✕	✕						
Half-yearly								✕				
Quarterly								✕				
Monthly	✕		✕	✕								
Occasional	✕											

NB: See also Tertiary and Further sources

applications at the end of the latest year by broad industry group with, for each, the estimated gross cost, the number of approved applications, the percentage these represent of all applications in Great Britain, and the number of individual jobs supported with the percentage this represents of all jobs supported in Great Britain.

Secondary sources

British Labour Statistics: Yearbook

The numbers in manufacturing industry in Great Britain on short-time working are shown by those stood off for a whole week, those working part of the week and both in total, all by the number of operatives involved, the total hours lost, and the average hours lost per operative. The analysis is monthly for the latest three years and annually for the latest ten years. For the latest year only (the year of the year-book) there is a monthly analysis by selected industries (MLH).

The numbers of temporarily stopped are given monthly for the latest year only, for each UK standard region.

Monthly Digest of Statistics

This shows the number of operatives on short-time working in manufacturing industry in Great Britain with those stood off for a whole week and those working part of the week analysed separately by number of operatives involved, total hours lost and average hours lost per operative. The analysis is monthly for the latest three years and annually for the latest ten years. For the latest year only (the year of the year-book) there is a monthly analysis by selected industries (MLH).

The numbers temporarily stopped are given monthly for the latest year only, for each UK standard region.

Regional Statistics

This shows the number of operatives in UK manufacturing industry on short-time working, with total hours lost separately for those stood off for a whole week and for those working part of a week, for each standard region, annually for two years (the latest being about two years prior to publication).

General Household Survey

The section on the unemployed shows six reasons for interviewees leaving their last job, one of which is 'made redundant or sacked'. Results are given by sex for all those classed as unemployed aged 16 and over who have ever worked, for Great Britain only.

Digest of Welsh Statistics

The number of workers made redundant in Wales each year for the latest five, are analysed by broad industry group (ie extractive, metal manufacture, engineering and allied industries, textiles, other manufacturing, construction, and services). For the latest year only the percentage of total redundancies represented by each industry group is also given.

Scottish Economic Bulletin

This shows the number of people in Scotland covered by TES, with the Scottish portion as a percentage of the total TES payments in Great Britain. The figures are half-yearly for the latest four and a half years.

British Labour Statistics: Historical Abstract 1886-1968

Short-time working in manufacturing industry in Great Britain is analysed for those stood off for a week and for those working part of a week separately, showing the number of operatives, total hours lost and the average hours lost per operative (the latter for those working part of a week only), all quarterly for the period 1950 to mid-1961, and monthly from mid-1961 to 1968.

The expenditure in Great Britain on redundancy payments is shown annually for the years 1966-68, with the amounts borne by fund and paid by employers shown separately in addition to the total of the two.

Tertiary sources

IDS Study (Numbers 175 and 178)

IDS Study Number 175, (August 1978), *Redundancy Schemes*, looked at the range of such schemes in practice and those being negotiated, with details of levels of redundancy and payments made and agreed. Study Number 178 (September 1978), *Redundancy in Practice*, was mainly concerned with how companies deal with redundancies in terms of procedure and payments, with details from about a dozen organisations.

IDS Study (Number 192)

IDS Study Number 192 (April 1979), *Guaranteed Week and Lay-Off*, discusses the rights of workers to pay when temporarily laid off and the legislation surrounding this issue. This is supported by analysis of specific agreements in over 30 organisations or industrial sectors.

153

Age and Redundancy
(*Employment Gazette*, September 1978, pp1032–39)

A useful article which explores the relationship between age and redundancies notified under the Redundancy Payments Acts. There is analysis of numbers made redundant by age and selected industry group, with further breakdowns by length of service and earnings levels. Most of the more comprehensive data relate to 1976.

An Employers' Guide to Redundancy Procedures
(Armstrong, M and Robertson, M D, Kogan Page, London, 1977)

A comprehensive volume giving details of the legislation and problems involved with the actual implementation of redundancies.

Temporary Short-time Working Compensation Scheme
(*Employment Gazette*, May 1980, pp478–81)

This article looks at the results of the temporary short-time working compensation scheme since its introduction in April 1979. The application process, use and effects of the scheme are discussed in detail.

Further sources

Department of Employment
Manpower Services Commission — Employment Service Division
Department of Manpower Services (Northern Ireland)

15. Labour Turnover

Introduction

Readily accessible information on labour turnover is scant and what is available usually relates to the aggregate national picture, with few exceptions. Many employers do assemble such information for internal use only which, of course, does not help in making comparisons outside the organisation to establish an idea of its relative position. The Department of Employment compiles national turnover data but in manufacturing industry only. This, despite its limitations, is the best source generally available and is given quarterly (in March, June, September and December) being based on information provided by a sample of employers. The official figures on the number of engagements, discharges and other losses are expressed per 100 employed at the beginning of the period.

Some data on the turnover for specific employers can be found in Tertiary sources below, but naturally this is limited because of the reluctance of many employers to release such information to outside users.

The lack of published data on turnover means that in many cases it will be necessary to approach alternative unpublished sources and here the DE local offices are perhaps the best prospect, although there will be some variation in the amount of information available from office to office.

The regular statistics that do exist have been broken down as follows:

- ☐ sex
- ☐ industry — the DE official data only covers manufacturing
- ☐ occupation — usually broad groups
- ☐ specific employers — occasional studies and usually of the larger organisations
- ☐ reasons for leaving job — analysis of ostensible reasons
- ☐ source of job information — how new employees learnt about their present job

155

Points to note

1. In the official DE figures, the number of discharges and other losses is derived by adding the engagements during a period (usually four or five weeks) to the numbers on the payroll at the beginning of the period and then subtracting the total on the payroll at the end of the period. This means that people who joined and left the firm within the period are excluded from the count, so there will inevitably be a degree of underestimation.

2. When using turnover data from individual employers, it must be remembered that there may be some inconsistencies in the way they are compiled.

3. In the GHS analysis of reasons for leaving last job, the responses given represent the ostensible reason for quitting as given in the interview and may conceal other reasons. For example, an interviewee may be reluctant to admit that he or she was sacked.

Primary sources

Employment Gazette

A quarterly analysis of labour turnover in Great Britain's manufacturing industry appears in the February, May, August and November issues covering the months of December, March, June and September respectively. It shows the number of engagements per 100 employed at the beginning of the period and, separately, the number of discharges and other losses per 100 employees. All this is shown for males, females and total separately and by a comprehensive MLH breakdown.

There is also a table showing a four-quarter moving average of total engagements and discharges (and other losses) for the same industries, giving, for five quarters, the total engagements and discharges (and other losses). These are also plotted on a graph covering about 14 years (with engagements and discharges having separate curves).

Secondary sources

British Labour Statistics Yearbook

Separate tables for males and females show the distribution of employees by length of service with their current employer broken down by occupation (comprehensive CODOT). They show the percentage of the sample in service by 11 periods of yearly gradations. All this is for Great Britain only and is usually about one year old. Also, the number of engagements and discharges per 100 persons employed at the beginning of each period is given by sex for manufacturing industry only, but by comprehensive MLH. The figures are for Great Britain only and cover one year quarterly.

15. Labour turnover

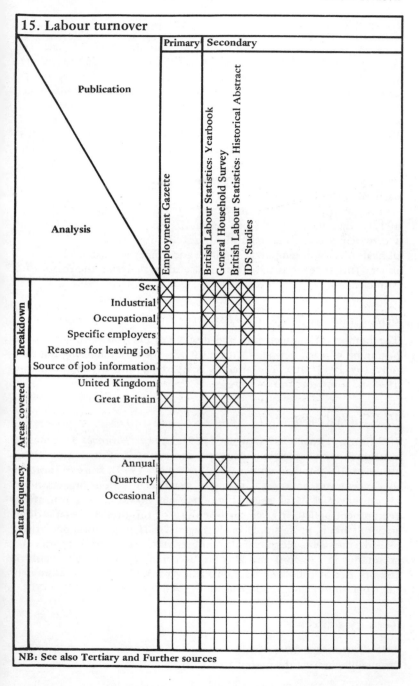

NB: See also Tertiary and Further sources

General Household Survey

This has contained some information on the percentage of males and females (separately) changing jobs in a 12 month period and the average number of job changes per person working, all by a range of age groups. Also there is analysis (for Great Britain only) of the source from which the sample of employees in the GHS first heard about their present job and any other job started in the 12 months before the interview. It lists the various ways of finding out about jobs (employment office; private employment agency; advertisement; relatives/friends; direct approach to/by employer; and other) and shows the percentage of males and females (separately) and by six age range divisions that used each method.

For Great Britain only, the percentage of males and females (separately) giving one of six reasons for leaving their last job are given. The six reasons are: made redundant/sacked; dissatisfied with last job; ill health; last job temporary; retired; and domestic reasons/pregnancy/other. This type of analysis can be useful in analysing the reasons for turnover.

British Labour Statistics: Historical Abstract 1886-1968

The number of engagements and discharges per 100 employed at the beginning of each period is shown by sex, for manufacturing industry only (by 1948 SIC). The analysis is quarterly and covers the period 1948-68, for Great Britain only.

IDS Study (Numbers 199 and 201)

IDS Study Number 199 (August 1979), *Labour Turnover 1*, is mainly concerned with the various concepts and methods of measuring labour turnover. IDS Study Number 201 (September 1979), *Labour Turnover 2*, concentrates on what happens in practice in various organisations, the turnover rates of specific groups, and how turnover can affect recruitment policy. It gives some analysis of turnover in specific occupations (that is, professional and managerial staff, production operatives, skilled craftsmen, technicians, computer staff, office staff, typists and secretaries in London) and also the 'Records' section shows details of the practice at collecting data on turnover for 22 organisations, mostly large ones but including some medium-sized ones as well.

Tertiary sources

IMS Manpower Survey
(annually, covering the period 1973-78)

This was a survey covering a broad selection of occupations carried out for six years but discontinued in 1979. Nevertheless, the six year run of data includes useful analyses of recruitment and wastage.

The *Manpower Trends: The Key Indicators Report* contains accumulated details of the percentage of employees with less than one year's service (at the end of the year), the recruitment rates during the year, and the average age of the recruits. Losses are also given comprehensive analysis including retirements. All are by broad occupational groups and the sampling details are given for each.

✕ Labour Turnover and Retention
(Pettman, B O, Gower Press, 1975, price £6.50)

This contains material on methods of turnover analysis and some of the reasons behind high turnover, in a collection of papers. Also useful is the extensive bibliography.

The Economic Causes of Labour Turnover: a Case Study
(Woodward, N, *Industrial Relations Journal*, Vol. 6, No. 4, Winter 1975/76, pp19–32)

This article looks at some of the major causes of labour turnover drawing on information collected in a chemicals firm. It specifically tries to analyse the changes in labour turnover over time and the differences in the quit rates experienced in different plants.

The Measurement of Turnover
(by Price, J L, *Industrial Relations Journal*, Vol. 6, No. 4, Winter 1975/76, pp33–46)

An article which gives some useful guidelines on the measurement of labour turnover, presented in a thoughtful way and based largely on experience in the USA.

Labour Turnover: Manufacturing Industries
(*Employment Gazette*, June 1977, pp606–09)

This contains a time series analysis of engagements and discharges in Great Britain, by sex, quarterly for the period 1966–1977 (first quarter only).

Finding a Way to Predict Wastage of Craftsmen and Apprentices
(*Employment Gazette*, July 1977, pp699–703)

A useful article describing the research carried out by the operational research department of the British Steel Corporation to predict casual wastage among craftsmen and apprentices (casual wastage taken to include dismissals, voluntary leaving and deaths). The approach is described and some of the results (the latest for 1975) are tabulated.

Factors Associated with Labour Turnover
(Williams, A, *et al, Journal of Occupational Psychology*, Vol. 52, No. 1, pp1–16)

This reports on an investigation into the incidence and causes of labour turnover among the ancillary staff at two London hospitals, each displaying different locational pressures. There is some analysis of the methods of recording turnover and discussion of some key facts surrounding the results.

Labour Turnover Costs: Measurement and Control
(Cavesey, T F and Wedley, W C, *Personal Journal*, February 1979, pp90–96)

An article describing a practical way of defining labour turnover within a company through the identification of cost centres and the eventual establishment of regular controls.

Pinpointing Avoidable Turnover with Cohort Analysis
(Lowman, J and Snediker, T, *Personnel Journal*, Vol. 59, No. 4, April 1980, pp310–15)

This outlines a method of identifying turnover and presents a range of uses for the information so obtained.

⌐ ## The Study of Turnover
(Price, J L, Iowa State University Press, 1977)

This book provides a record of literature codification, definitions and concepts across the whole subject of labour turnover.

Further sources

Department of Employment
Manpower Services Commission
Department of Manpower Services
National Economic Development Office
Institute of Manpower Studies
Industrial Training Boards

16. Earnings

Introduction

Most of the regular data available on earnings in the UK are prepared by the Department of Employment for England, Wales and Scotland and the Department of Manpower Services for Northern Ireland, from sample surveys carried out either monthly, half-yearly, or annually. Other organisations involved with the gathering of earnings information include some private companies, the OPCS (in the census and the General Household Survey) and the Board of Inland Revenue. The DE uses the following as a broad definition of earnings:

> 'Earnings are the total remuneration which employees receive from their employers in the form of money, either as wages or as salaries, including overtime and other premium payments, bonuses, commission or other payments of any kind; and before the deduction of income tax or of the employees' contributions to national insurance or superannuation funds. Earnings (as here defined) do not include employers' contributions to national insurance or superannuation funds. Income in kind is also generally excluded apart from a few exceptions which are noted.'*

There is a distinction to be made between what are known as *earnings* and *wage rates*. Information on wage rates is presented either on a weekly or hourly basis and they represent the basic amount paid to a particular person in a particular occupation/industry; many of the rates are negotiated nationally (via voluntary collective agreements) or are laid down by wages councils or boards. Earnings information is presented either in money amounts (usually per employee but some of the statistics show total costs to either the industry or economy as a whole), or in the form of indices to show movements in the earnings scales over time taken, from a fixed point at the beginning of the time period (the base year).

* From *British Labour Statistics: Yearbook*, HMSO

The DE monthly statistical series examines average earnings, and basic rates of wages; the two are compiled along slightly different lines so it requires some explanation. A large scale monthly survey is carried out on average earnings in various industries (with the exception of agriculture as these details are supplied directly by the Ministry of Agriculture, Fisheries and Food) which covers (at present) information relating to about 21 million employees (about 85 per cent of the working population). This has been the case since January 1976 when the so-called 'new series' was introduced. Prior to this date what has now come to be called the 'old series' was only based on the production industries, transport and communication and some miscellaneous service industries employing about 11 million people in all. The basic rates of wages are drawn from the results of collective national agreements or rates laid down by wages boards or councils, and preclude any locally-reached agreements, and nor do they take into account changes in such factors as bonus, overtime or short-time working. In both cases the data drawn from employers by the DE are kept completely anonymous.

The DE's annual or half-yearly surveys vary in their techniques. Perhaps the most influential and thorough survey is the DE's annual New Earnings Survey carried out each April (since 1970 on the present wide-ranging scale) and based on a one per cent random sample of all employees in employment. Many NES results appear in other periodicals and statistical sources and provide the basis for some further studies.

Many users of earnings data will be interested more in, for example, how local earnings levels compare, rather than in national or even regional data. Earnings between areas can diverge sharply even where there are nationally agreed rates, but information on the extent of this divergence is poor. In most cases it will be necessary to look to occasional studies (see Tertiary sources below) or to contacts with the local ESD office, for example. This is also the case with earnings of the self-employed.

The regular information available has been broken down as follows:

☐ sex
☐ age
☐ manual/non-manuals — where this distinction is made
☐ indices — many of the earnings data are presented in index form
☐ amounts — where the earnings are presented in money amounts
☐ industrial
☐ occupational
☐ collective agreements — usually reached on a national basis.

Points to note

1. The use of sampling to provide many of the regular statistics on earnings has the familiar problems associated with taking only a small section of the total 'population'. The major surveys only reflect the situation as seen at a particular point in time and hence cannot show sudden changes affecting earnings. The NES, for example, looks at a one per cent random sample during one pay-week or longer pay-period in April each year.

2. It should be pointed out that too much weight should not be attached to a single month's earnings figures, and the month-to-month changes are regarded as being the more important indicators.

3. Sudden or wild movements in average earnings could be due to changes in the composition of the workforce, especially when there is a sudden influx of, say, low income earners such as school-leavers. To some extent these changes should occur with a certain amount of seasonal regularity and so it becomes possible to adjust figures seasonally where appropriate to show the underlying trend. This has been the case with the old series (pre-January 1976), but since that date and the introduction of the new series, seasonal adjustments have been limited by the absence of a long, consistent run of statistics.

4. Average wage rates presented in the statistics may understate the wage rates received by many employees. This is due mainly to the differences in national and locally negotiated rates, the official statistics generally only reflecting the former. It could also be due to skill differences and general problems of definition (whether to include piecework, bonus, incentive payments and the like).

5. Most of the earnings data over time are presented in current prices, but some are shown at constant prices and as a general rule the latter series usually includes the base year used.

6. The DE analysis of methods by which increases in wage rates were achieved into five categories obviously involves some arbitrary judgement and this should be borne in mind when using such data.

Primary sources

Department of Employment Press Notice

A monthly press notice is issued (usually on the third Wednesday in the month) giving details of the latest indices of average earnings (for two months previous) and basic rates of wages (for the previous month). For the indices of average earnings, there is a short statement giving the year ending percentage change for employees in Great Britain. The latest month's figure is then incorporated into a table of monthly indices covering 14 consecutive months, which also shows the percentage increase over the 12 month period. A smaller analysis but on similar lines

16. Earnings

Analysis \ Publication	Primary					Secondary												
	DE Press Notice	Employment Gazette	New Earnings Survey	Time Rates of Wages and Hours of Work	Changes in Rates of Wages and Hours of Work	British Labour Statistics: Yearbook	British Labour Statistics: Historical Abstract	Monthly Digest of Statistics	Annual Abstract of Statistics	Economic Trends	Social Trends	Social Security Statistics	Regional Statistics	Scottish Abstract of Statistics	Scottish Economic Bulletin	Digest of Welsh Statistics	Welsh Economic Trends	Digest of Statistics – N. Ireland
Breakdown																		
Sex		X	X			X	X						X			X	X	X
Age		X	X			X	X									X	X	X
Manual/non-manuals		X	X			X	X						X			X	X	X
Indices	X	X				X	X	X	X	X						X	X	
Amounts	X	X	X			X	X						X			X	X	
Industrial	X	X	X			X	X									X	X	
Occupational		X	X			X	X											
Collective agreement		X				X	X											
Areas covered																		
United Kingdom	X	X				X	X	X	X	X						X		
Great Britain	X	X	X			X	X	X					X					
Northern Ireland								X										X
England																X	X	
Scotland														X	X			
Wales																X	X	
Standard regions	X	X				X	X						X			X	X	
Sub-regional													X			X	X	
Data frequency																		
Annual	X	X	X			X	X	X	X	X	X		X	X	X	X	X	
Half-yearly	X	X				X	X									X		
Quarterly		X						X										
Monthly	X	X				X	X	X										X
Weekly	X	X	X			X	X											
Hourly	X	X	X			X	X											

NB: See also Tertiary and Further sources

shows the indices of average earnings in production industries and some services (about 11 million people in all) based on the old series, and covers eight months.

Employment Gazette

Regular monthly series cover many of the analyses of earnings that are available and provide the input into many other published statistical series.

An index of average earnings covering the whole economy and with an industry analysis (by SIC order) for the latest two months, is shown against the percentage change over 12-monthly periods (based on six periods). There is an index of wages and salaries per unit of output in manufacturing industry (with base year 1975), monthly for ten years.

Basic rates of wages for manual workers (weekly and hourly rates of pay) are given for all industries and services for six months, with the percentage change in these over the previous 12 months. There is also a short report on the principal changes reported during the previous month.

Analyses by amount show, for UK manual workers, average weekly and hourly earnings by SIC groups, by sex, annually for four years. A further analysis shows annual figures for three years broken down into full-time women, part-time women, full-time boys and full-time girls, for all manufacturing industries and all industries separately. Based on the April NES results, there is an analysis of manual and non-manual earnings (weekly and hourly), by sex, for manufacturing and all industries and services, for about seven years' surveys. Further indices show, for Great Britain, average salaries for non-manual workers (males and females together and separately) annually for nine years, for all industries and manufacturing industry separately. Average earnings for all employees are shown by SIC industry groups monthly for about six years, and there is an occupational analysis for manual men in certain manufacturing industries (usually just three) further sub-divided to show the skilled/unskilled mix, those on payment-by-results (PBR), etc, but only for three years (at half-yearly intervals).

More generally, indices of average earnings for all employees are given monthly for 13 years, with manufacturing industries shown separately. For the UK, wage rates of manual workers (weekly and hourly) are shown in index form by 19 SIC order groups, monthly for three years and annually (averages) for four years. The monthly series is completed by a graph showing average earnings, wage rates, retail prices, and wages and salaries per unit of output plotted over seven years and based on the average monthly indices for these measures.

An annual appraisal of the results of the manual workers' earnings and hours survey (carried out each October) is given, usually in the following February issue. A somewhat shorter survey, limited to only a few industries, is carried out in April with results published in the October issue. The results contain commentary on the trends and statistics produced, as well as comprehensive tables on the industrial classification of earnings by broad SIC order and with MLH analysis. Further analysis is by UK standard region, and in most cases by sex, with divisions into youths and boys, girls, and full- and part-time women are also frequently shown.

The October issue carries an article on the key results of the New Earnings Survey carried out the previous April, with much of the summary and streamlined analyses shown as they appear in Part A of the NES itself (for full details see Primary sources below).

A regular survey of earnings in engineering, shipbuilding and chemicals is taken in June each year and published in the October or November issue.* The survey covers manual workers and includes analyses of skilled and unskilled labourers, general workers and craftsmen, with further divisions by timeworkers, PBR workers, and for overtime earnings. There are regional analyses by UK standard region for timeworkers and PBR workers, by skill. Another analysis also provides the skills breakdown by average size of firm, with three divisions based on numbers of employees.

New Earnings Survey

Since 1968 this annual survey has been a major source of comprehensive earnings data. Part A is perhaps the most useful for general information on earnings, while the subsequent five parts (B to F) concentrate more on specific analyses of the data.

Part A (general results; streamlined results; descriptions of survey methods, classifications, terminology, etc), contains for the survey year summary results for full-time men and women (separately) and manual and non-manual workers, the broad distribution of earnings, broad details of those receiving overtime, PBR, and shift payments (showing the percentage receiving them and average weekly amount), and some broad sectoral results (eg the situation in public corporations, local government, and such). Summary tables showing average gross weekly earnings and the proportion represented by overtime, PBR and shift payments, a broad distribution of earnings and some comparison with the previous year, are given for those collective agreements and wages councils in operation, with a comprehensive industrial analysis and a broad occupational analysis, all by age group and for standard regions of Great Britain (with some sub-regional analysis covering the GLC, or metropolitan county areas), and by sex with manual/non-manual distinctions.

---

* A similar survey for just shipbuilding and chemicals, carried out in January and usually published in the May issue, was discontinued in 1980

Further summary analyses show the estimated numbers of men and women with earnings below specified amounts (about 32 earnings ranges) giving the percentages under each, with separate figures including and excluding overtime earnings. The dispersion of gross weekly earnings over the years since 1970 shows those percentages in and the amounts represented by six divisions. Increases in average earnings over the previous year are given with amounts and percentages, weekly and hourly rates, and with or without overtime payments. Finally, there are summary tables showing the numbers in the sample in a wide range of earnings ranges, and with each group shown (ie full-time men, women, youths and boys, girls and part-time men and women).

Part B, earnings of particular wage-negotiation groups, covers in more detail gross weekly earnings including and excluding overtime pay; gross hourly earnings including and excluding the effects of overtime pay; and average weekly earnings of those who received overtime pay, those on PBR etc, and those on shift premium payments.

Part C, earnings for particular industries, gives detailed analyses of gross weekly earnings including and excluding overtime payments; gross hourly earnings of those who received overtime pay, and similar analyses of those who received PBR etc, and those who received shift payments. The analyses are usually by detailed MLH, although there are some broader groupings.

Part D, earnings for particular occupations, contains analyses (mainly by KOS) of gross weekly earnings including and excluding overtime pay; gross hourly earnings including and excluding overtime pay; and average weekly earnings of those who received overtime payments, with similar analyses of those who received PBR etc, and those who received shift payments.

Part E, earnings in regions, counties and age groups, contains regional analyses (in general Great Britain standard regional data but also some sub-regional analysis) covering gross weekly earnings and gross hourly earnings including and excluding the effects of overtime pay. The analysis by age group gives, for Great Britain, gross weekly earnings including and excluding the effects of overtime pay; gross hourly earnings including and excluding the effects of overtime pay; average weekly earnings of those who received overtime pay, with similar analyses for those who received PBR etc, and those who received shift payments. Most of the data is presented by nine divisions of age. Also in this part there is an analysis of the employees represented in the sample survey, and these are shown by occupation, industry, and region (broad groups used).

Part F, earnings of part-time women workers and types of collective agreement, concentrates mainly on part-time women and shows for this group analyses by collective agreement wages board or council; by industry group; by occupation; by age group; and by region. An analysis of the distribution of earnings is given for all employees, with

12 earnings ranges, for weekly and hourly payments, and with a similar table for weekly earnings exclusive of any additional payments such as overtime or shift premia. Also there are analyses covering the numbers of workers affected by types of collective agreements shown by agreement; by wages board or council; by industry; by occupation; by region; and by age group

Some NES results are published in the *Employment Gazette*, with most of the summary analyses and streamlined results appearing in the October issue. The results for Northern Ireland are first published in the *Digest of Statistics — Northern Ireland*.

Time Rates of Wages and Hours of Work

This contains details of wage rates which are the result of national collective wage agreements or laid down in wages orders made by statutory wages boards and councils. The information mainly relates to manual workers and can be said to represent the situation as at April each year. Most of the analyses are given by SIC order and MLH within that order (but there is some sub-grouping) and show the occupations to which the wages relate. Appendices list additional analyses such as younger workers' wages broken down by five single years (16–20), and overtime rates of pay showing the rates in operation for weekdays and weekends. In all cases the sources of the information and the operative dates on which the provisions took effect are also shown.

Changes in Rates of Wages and Hours of Work

This updates the annual analysis of nationally agreed wage rates etc on a monthly basis and contains much the same range of information as *Time Rates of Wages and Hours of Work*.

Secondary sources

British Labour Statistics: Yearbook

A series shows the weekly rates of wages as set out in various collective agreements, with separate tables for men and women and covering (annually) the last three years plus one other year. Changes in basic weekly rates of wages of manual workers, by 19 broad industry groups, show the net increases (£000s) annually for ten years, and monthly for two years, all for the UK. A similar industrial analysis is given for the indices of basic weekly and hourly rates of wages of manual workers, for two years annually and one year monthly, and there is also a general table covering the total UK economy by men, women, juveniles, and all workers. Annual changes in indices for all industries and services and manufacturing industries only are also given for ten years. Another table gives some idea of the methods by which increases in basic weekly rates of wages or minimum entitlements were achieved over ten years. The five methods used are: direct negotiation; joint industrial councils; wages councils and other statutory bodies; arbitration; and sliding-scale agreement (based on the official index of retail prices).

The NES summary results and streamlined analyses given are similar to those first published in the October issue of the *Employment Gazette*. See NES Part A (Primary sources above) for details of the actual range of results presented.

Average weekly and hourly earnings of manual workers are analysed by broad industry groups annually for six years, with men, women, youths and boys, and girls shown separately, and by comprehensive MLH (men and women only separately but another table gives a similar analysis for just part-time women) for the review year. There are regional analyses (by UK standard regions) for all employees in manufacturing industry only and in manufacturing and certain other industries, annually for three years, and for the review year only there is a regional breakdown by broad industry groups, but for males only.

First appearing in the *Employment Gazette*, the separate analyses for engineering, chemicals and shipbuilding are reproduced in an annotated form with analyses by occupation, skill and region for the review year only (January and June). Finally, there are monthly indices of average earnings by broad industry groups in Great Britain (with males and females together) for four years, with some analysis also given of changes in weekly and hourly rates and the dispersion (income ranges) over a number of years.

British Labour Statistics: Historical Abstract 1886-1968

This contains details of earnings over a long period with some of the older series covering basic wage rates (at current prices) and indices of average earnings. For over 100 years to 1968, the rates of wages in certain industries by a few occupations are given (fitters, turners and labourers; bricklayers and bricklayers' labourers; compositors; journeymen in the furniture industry; footwear male manuals; and agriculture ordinary labourers) by major city in Great Britain, in current prices. There are indices of weekly wage rates in manufacturing only and all industries and services by men, women, juveniles and all workers, over the period 1947–68, with two distinct periods as far as the base year is concerned of 1947–55 (base 1947), and 1956–68 (base 1956). The figures are monthly and for the UK. A similar analysis, but by 18 broad industry groups, is also given. Indices of basic hourly rates of wages for all manual workers for all industries and services are given for the period 1920–68 (monthly from 1934, annually before that). Another analysis shows the same by manufacturing and all industries and services for men, women, juveniles and all workers, for the periods

1947-55 (base year 1947) and 1956-68 (base year 1956), monthly for the UK, with a further analysis by 18 broad industry groups (based on the 1948 SIC) but covers all employees.

The average hourly earnings of manual men and women by 20 industry groups are given twice yearly over the periods 1948-59 (base 1948) and 1959-68 (base 1958), and the average weekly earnings (indices and amounts) for certain industries surveyed over 1956-68, with an additional analysis of administrative, technical and clerical staff, by sex.

Average weekly and hourly earnings of manual men for the UK standard regions are given twice yearly for the period 1960-68, and this is supplemented by analysis of certain industries (engineering, chemicals, shipbuilding and shiprepairing, iron and steel, and construction) by occupation, twice yearly over the period 1963-68 (for Great Britain only).

There are comprehensive results covering 1968 only and mostly based on the first NES (published in 1970 but relating to 1968) which include analyses of the distribution of earnings by industry, occupation, region (both weekly and hourly earnings) and age structure, with the effect of national agreements also documented. Finally there are indices of earnings and comparable wage rates and salaries plus total wage and salary costs over the period 1938-68, annually.

Monthly Digest of Statistics

Regular tables show the average weekly earnings of manual workers, with divisions by men, youths and boys, women (full- and part-time) and girls, and the amount of earnings (current prices) and percentage increase represented by this over October 1966. These are all shown for manufacturing and certain other industries and for manufacturing alone, annually for nine years. Another table shows manual weekly earnings, by sex, for 19 industry groups, annually for ten years. Indices are given for average earnings of all employees (Great Britain) based on the monthly enquiry — old series and new series, with the former covering all industries and services covered by the data range (see the introduction to this section), and all manufacturing industries, as well as by 23 industry groups, annually and monthly for four years. The latter covers the whole economy and is by full SIC order, for two years annually and three years monthly. Basic weekly rates of all manual workers are shown in index form for all industries and services and by 19 industry groups, annually for four years and monthly for about one and a half years, with an additional table giving weekly and hourly wage rates (with manufacturing shown separately), annually for three years and monthly for over one year. Also the changes in basic weekly rates of manual workers are given in a table with increases and decreases shown in £000s for all industries and services and by seven broad industry groups annually for three years and monthly for one year.

Annual Abstract of Statistics

Indices are given of the basic wage rates of manual workers (with separate tables for hourly and weekly rates) by all industries and services and manufacturing only, quarterly for two and a half years and twice yearly for five years, by all workers, men, women and juveniles. An index of average salaries of non-manual employees in Great Britain is given annually for 12 years (based on the DE October surveys) by sex, with manufacturing shown separately. Average earnings indices are given for the old series monthly enquiry (manufacturing, all industries covered and by 23 broad industry groups) and for the new series (with a similar breakdown) for a number of years annually and the latest year monthly.

The average weekly earnings of manual workers (annually for 12 years) are given with manufacturing and all industries, shown by sex. Weekly and hourly earnings (the latter including and excluding overtime pay) are also shown by a similar breakdown but with a more extensive treatment of full- and part-time and manual/non-manual workers, for six years annually. All the data are for Great Britain only. Gross weekly and hourly earnings of full-time adults are given annually for eight years by sex and by manuals/non-manuals. There are separate tables for Great Britain and Northern Ireland. Gross weekly earnings and the distribution of earnings (by 24 divisions) is given for men and women, manuals and non-manuals, for the review year and shows the distribution by millions of workers in the UK under each division. An analysis by age group for Great Britain only, gives the average earnings by sex, and manuals/non-manuals, and shows the amount of overtime pay for the review year only. There is a separate table (located in the 'Agriculture and food' section) on the weekly earnings of agricultural workers in Great Britain, for a long twice yearly series, by males, youths, women and girls.

Economic Trends

This contains a table on wage rates and earnings indices which gives basic weekly wage rates for manual workers by all industries and services and for just manufacturing industry. Average earnings indices for Great Britain, with yearly percentage increases, are also given but with a different base year. Seasonally adjusted figures cover production industries and some service and manufacturing industry separately, with indices and with percentage yearly increases shown. There is also an index of wages and salaries per unit of output for the whole economy and for manufacturing industry separately. All indices are are presented monthly for 18 months, quarterly for six years and annually for about 11 years.

A composite graph plots indices of retail prices, gross domestic

171

product, and the indices of wage rates and earnings featured in the table for a six year period (based on the monthly figures).

Economic Trends Annual Supplement contains similar information to the monthly series but for a longer period.

Social Trends

A table shows the cumulative distribution of earnings based on the annual NES in Great Britain and the numbers of men and women (separately) who fall within a range of income bands, for the latest year only and with manuals/non-manuals and full/part-time distinctions. The analysis is supported by a graph showing the distribution and bar charts showing an age group breakdown of those in the upper, median or lower quartiles of earnings. Median earnings by age and occupational groups are also given in tabular form, with six age groups and a range of broad occupations represented, again based on the NES.

Average weekly earnings for the UK are given for administrative, technical and clerical and manual workers for seven years annually, with manual earnings plotted on a graph alongside weekly wage rates and retail prices, but covering a longer period. There is also some analysis of personal incomes (before and after tax) with numbers in broad income bands over about eight fiscal years, accompanied by a graph.

Social Security Statistics

This contains some comparative analysis of earnings in relation to pensions, supplementary benefits, and such. The percentage increases in the average earnings of male manual workers are presented in a comparative table with pensions and retail price figures annually for eight years and an additional odd ten years (but no further back than 1948). A similar table compares supplementary benefit and retail price percentage increases with increases in average earnings of male manuals. The average earnings (again of just male manual workers) and income when employed is compared with benefit income when sick or unemployed, annually for 15 years, for a single man, married couple with no children and married couple with two children. A similar analysis (but just for a single person and a married couple) compares average earnings of male manual workers with the standard rates of retirement pensions. There is a general analysis showing the average gross annual earnings of employed persons, by sex and age distribution, for two years. Also there is some analysis by level of NHI contributions paid during the previous year, by age group and sex, annually for ten years.

Regional Statistics

In the 'Regional profiles' section there is some commentary on earnings (usually of the region versus Great Britain), with figures (by sub-region) on NES results showing average gross weekly earnings of full-time employees, by sex. Tables give the average weekly earnings of full-time male manuals by 12 broad industry groups for each standard UK region, annually for two years. NES results are summarised for each region and metropolitan county within the regions, by sex and manuals/non-manuals, giving the average gross weekly earnings with amounts of overtime, PBR and shift payments; hourly earnings (excluding overtime effects) with four levels and percentages earning under each; and the distribution of gross weekly earnings (by three divisions) and percentages earning under each. Bar charts of the regional distribution of weekly earnings of full-time men and the average gross weekly earnings of men and women are also included.

Scottish Abstract of Statistics

This contains the average weekly earnings of adult male manual workers by a selection of MLH industries annually for eight years plus one odd year (men and women together). There is also a range of results from the NES including average gross weekly earnings by SIC order (by sex and manuals/non-manuals) and the distribution and the amounts represented by overtime, PBR and shift payments. Percentage distributions and quartiles of gross weekly earnings are given by sex and manuals/non-manuals, with a further extension to broad occupational groups, all shown for Scotland and Great Britain. Medians and quartiles of average gross weekly earnings are also shown by full SIC order for Scotland and Great Britain.

Scottish Economic Bulletin

There is some commentary on the key trends in Scottish earnings, especially versus Great Britain, with graphs over ten years plotting the average weekly earnings of manual and non-manual males twice yearly as a percentage of the UK averages. Tables show the NES results for Scotland, with average weekly earnings by full SIC order by sex, with amount, standard error from the sampling, and the percentage increase over a three year period, for Scotland compared to Great Britain. Average weekly earnings by sex and manuals/non-manuals are given by local government region annually for four years. Basic and overtime average weekly earnings are given annually for four years, with a one year comparison with Great Britain, males and females separately.

Digest of Welsh Statistics

This shows the earnings of male manuals by 23 broad industry groups (average weekly and hourly earnings) for Wales and the UK. Similarly for all industries and services and manufacturing, gross weekly earnings are shown but for a longer run of four years and by sex and manuals/non-manuals. The distribution of gross weekly earnings of males (manual/non-manual distinction) is shown for Wales, England, Scotland and Great Britain, with 11 income levels and the percentages earning less in each. A similar table is shown for women. Average gross weekly earnings of males and females are presented in separate tables by statistical sub-division, annually for two years, for manuals/non-manuals and with some comparisons with Great Britain. Finally overtime earnings by sex are given, with effects on average weekly earnings annually for five years and with comparative data on Great Britain.

Welsh Economic Trends

This contains an industrial analysis by 23 broad groups of average weekly earnings of male manual workers for the review year only, with the amount and percentage of the UK average that this represents also shown. Average weekly earnings of male manuals is also shown as a percentage of the UK average for Wales alongside four other standard regions of the UK for 13 years annually and supplemented by a graph showing gross and disposable earnings (in both current and constant prices) for the same 13 year period.

There is a range of data based on the NES including average gross weekly earnings, by sex and manuals/non-manuals, for Wales, the assisted regions, the unassisted regions and Great Britain annually for four years, with a graph. The distribution of gross weekly earnings, by sex and by manuals/non-manuals, with the percentage with earnings less than each of eleven divisions, is shown for England, Scotland, Wales and Great Britain for the review year; a bar chart is also given. The components in the make-up of the pay of men and women, (manuals and non-manuals separately) for Wales, Scotland, England, Great Britain and two other standard regions is given with amounts in respect of overtime, PBR and shift payments shown and percentage proportions represented by these amounts, together with an illustrative pie chart.

The average gross weekly earnings of men and women (separate tables) by manuals and non-manuals for each statistical sub-division is given annually for three years, together with maps showing the percentage of the average earnings for Great Britain represented by each area for gross and disposable earnings. Overtime earnings are shown separately in a table distinguishing between manuals and non-manuals in Wales and Great Britain, annually for four years (with corresponding graph). Finally the distribution and change in gross weekly earnings of men and women is shown for Wales and Great Britain for one year, with a bar chart.

Digest of Statistics — Northern Ireland

Given here are figures on the gross earnings of full-time adults in all industries and services, by sex and manuals/non-manuals, to show the distribution of those falling within percentage ranges and the percentages falling within certain earnings ranges. The analysis is for weekly and hourly earnings and covers the latest available year.

Gross earnings figures are presented for all industries and services, manufacturing only and non-manufacturing, by sex and manual/non-manual distinctions, with weekly and hourly earnings and the numbers in sample also shown. A shorter analysis covers the results of surveys for five years for all industries and services and manufacturing only. An industrial analysis (by 20 industry groups) shows the average weekly and hourly earnings for manual workers for about ten years, for males only. By way of comparison, there is a UK index of weekly wage rates monthly for 15 years.

Tertiary sources

Family Expenditure Survey

This annual survey includes some analysis of household income with averages by family member (husband, wife, etc) and source of income (wages and salaries, social security benefits, etc), the distribution of household income (by source and income group) and the composition (single man, married with two children, etc). A broadly-based analysis by occupation and age is also included.

A separate but similar report, *Northern Ireland Family Expenditure Survey*, concentrates on Northern Ireland only.

General Household Survey

The survey of Great Britain contains some data on education and earnings, showing the level of gross annual earnings by the highest qualification attained (from first degree downwards), with some additional analysis by age, although such analysis has not appeared in every survey to date.

Survey of Personal Incomes

This is a comprehensive survey of incomes based on income tax data and covers such areas as distribution of incomes by county and region, status (eg single, pensioner, etc) and the total number of incomes falling within certain ranges. The survey is especially useful as a guide to numbers in specific income ranges.

Incomes Data Report

This contains articles of topical interest on earnings and provides details of settlements reached by individual employers. Regular (twice monthly) statistics show indices of basic weekly wage rates, average earnings (older series, seasonally adjusted), with monthly figures for six years (including current year) and some percentage increases over the previous year shown. The data are derived from the DE series.

Economic Progress Report

This lists the average earnings indices for the older series and for the whole economy monthly for the latest two months, quarterly for the latest five quarters, and annually for the previous full year in the 'Economic indicators' section.

Incomes Data Studies

One-off studies of various occupations appear regularly in this series and they concentrate on commenting upon the particular conditions in the occupation and an analysis of rates of wages and salaries of the key occupations from a sample of individual companies. Recent studies have included the following occupations:

- ☐ 171 *Canteen Workers' Pay* (June 1978)
- ☐ 174 *Computer Staff Pay* (July 1978)
- ☐ 180 *Financial Sector Pay (banking and insurance)* (October 1978)
- ☐ 190 *Toolroom Workers' Pay* (March 1979)
- ☐ 193 *Drivers' Pay and Bargaining* (May 1979)
- ☐ 194 *Warehouse Workers' Pay* (May 1979)
- ☐ 196 *Technicians' Pay* (June 1979)
- ☐ 197 *Clerical Pay in London* (July 1979)
- ☐ 198 *Apprentices' Pay* (July 1979)
- ☐ 212 *Security Staff Pay* (February 1980)
- ☐ 213 *Maintenance Craftsmen's Pay* (March 1980)
- ☐ 215 *Drivers' Pay* (April 1980)
- ☐ 216 *Maintenance Craftsmen's Pay 2* (April 1980)

Other useful studies have appeared on various aspects of earnings, including the following:

- ☐ 170 *Payment-by-Results* (May 1978)
- ☐ 172 *Relativities* (June 1978)
- ☐ 200 *Cost of Living Arrangements* (August 1979)
- ☐ 214 *Staff Benefits* (March 1980)

Especially useful is the annual *Salary Survey* (the latest for 1979, study 209, January 1980) which provides information on individual occupation surveys that range from manual and clerical grades through to the top levels of management. The list is by no means exhaustive but about 40 UK surveys are shown with a mixture of those from professional or trade bodies (for example, the Royal Institute of British Architects) and those from commercial organisations (for example, Accountancy Personnel Limited). Details on each survey are by necessity brief, but are sufficient to decide whether or not the individual survey is worth further investigation. A directory of addresses is also given.

Trends in Earnings: 1948–77
(*Employment Gazette*, May 1978, pp520–30)

This examines, through a series of tables, graphs and bar charts, the main trends in earnings in several broad groups of employees highlighting the outstanding points. It is a useful article for the period up to 1977.

The Effect of Rising Prices on Low Income Households
(*Employment Gazette*, March 1979, pp250–53)

An article which effectively shows the plight of low-income households in the face of higher inflation. The analysis does not concentrate solely on those earning money, but includes pensioner households and the like.

Further sources

Department of Employment
Manpower Services Commission — Employment Services Division (especially local offices), and Professional and Executive Register
Office of Population Censuses and Surveys
Department of Manpower Services (Northern Ireland)
Board of Inland Revenue
Incomes Data Service
Reward Regional Surveys Ltd and other organisations in the field (see Incomes Data Studies above)
Trades Union Congress (and individual trade unions)
Confederation of British Industry
Individual professional bodies

17. Labour Costs and Productivity

Introduction

Labour costs are usually presented in the regular statistical series either as total costs or broken down into their component parts. The level of detail given in the structured analyses varies, with the widest range being found in the triennial EEC Labour Costs Survey which gives the following divisions:

- ☐ direct remuneration (wages and salaries) plus bonuses
- ☐ payment to workers' savings schemes
- ☐ other bonuses and gratuities
- ☐ payments for days not worked
- ☐ social security costs (statutory and voluntary separately)
- ☐ benefits in kind
- ☐ other expenses of a social nature
- ☐ vocational training
- ☐ taxes and subsidies.

The range of information on labour costs is presented either in actual amounts (usually per hour or per month) or in index form to show the trend in costs over time. Most of the regular statistics are of the latter type, with the exception of the EEC Survey and the Census of Production which concentrate on actual amounts and costs per employee.

Labour productivity is usually expressed in the regular statistics as output per head (or per employee), and most give the components of this ratio (total output and total employment) alongside the ratio itself. The Department of Employment carries out a regular monthly inquiry into the production details of selected firms, with further inquiries quarterly and annually.* Employment and output data are also derived from the annual Census of Production. Many of the data relate to manufacturing industry only or more widely to the Index of Production industries since these are the sectors where production can

---

*For an introduction to this series, see *Employment Gazette*, October 1968, pp801–06

be easily identified. Most of the series also give figures for the whole economy and here the total output is synonymous with the gross domestic product.

The regular statistics have been broken down into the following categories:

☐ sex — only to be found in the EEC Labour Costs Survey (and the summary in the *Employment Gazette)*
☐ output per·head — sometimes called output per person employed or per employee, this being the commonly used measure of productivity
☐ total labour costs — all components together
☐ labour costs structure — by the various components, the main one being wages and salaries
☐ industrial — mostly in broad industrial groupings
☐ indices — for both labour costs and output per head
☐ actual labour costs — costs given in amount rather than in index form.

Points to note

1. Output per head is not the only measure of productivity that is used, although it is the most common one found in the regular statistics.
2. Output per person employed (per head) in the official UK statistics takes as the denominator employees in employment, self-employed persons (with or without employees), including both full-time and part-time workers as full units, and H M forces.
3. The EEC Labour Costs Survey is based on a sample of about 71,000 establishments in the UK which employed over seven million people in the 1975 survey, so the sample is considered large.
4. The EEC Labour Costs Survey uses the NACE classification for its industrial analyses which is not directly comparable with either the ISIC or the SIC, although when the results are presented in domestic publications (such as the *Employment Gazette*), adjustments to bring them into line with the SIC are generally made.

Primary sources

Employment Gazette

Regular monthly tables show, for the UK, indices of output with total output, employment, and output per person employed separately, and indices of labour costs, with wages and salaries separately for: the whole economy; the Index of Production industries; manufacturing industry; mining and quarrying; metal manufacture; mechanical, instrument and electrical engineering; vehicles; textiles; and gas, electricity

17. Labour costs and productivity

Analysis \\ Publication	Primary			Secondary								
	Employment Gazette	EEC Labour Costs Survey	Census of Production	Monthly Digest of Statistics	Economic Trends	National Institute Economic Review	British Labour Statistics: Yearbook	OECD Economic Indicators	Regional Statistics	Scottish Abstract of Statistics	Welsh Economic Trends	British Labour Statistics: Historical Abstract
Breakdown												
Sex	X	X										
Output per head	X		X	X	X	X	X			X	X	
Total labour costs	X	X	X	X	X		X	X				
Labour costs structure	X	X	X				X					
Industrial	X	X	X	X	X	X	X					
Indices	X			X	X		X					
Actual labour costs	X											
Areas covered												
United Kingdom	X	X	X	X	X	X	X					
Great Britain	X						X			X		
Northern Ireland	X	X										
England	X								X			
Scotland	X								X	X		
Wales	X								X		X	
Standard regions	X								X			
Data frequency												
Annual	X	X	X	X	X	X	X			X	X	
Quarterly	X	X			X					X	X	
Monthly	X			X		X						
Occasional	X	X										

NB: See also Tertiary and Further sources

and water. All this is quarterly for five years (the latest quarter being about two quarters prior to each issue) and annually for ten years (from the latest full year back). There are also monthly details of wages and salaries per unit of output in UK manufacturing industry, showing the monthly index of change over the latest ten years.

Results of the EEC Labour Costs Survey (carried out every three years) are published in summary form in the *Gazette*. The first survey involving Great Britain was in 1975 and results were published in 1977, with reports in the *Gazette* of September (pp927–40) carrying overall results, November (pp1221–38) with separate analyses for manual and non-manual workers, and December (pp1358–67) giving regional analyses. A more detailed idea of the content can be found under *Labour Costs in Industry* below.

EEC – Labour Costs in Industry

This is a triennial survey of labour costs in each individual EEC country, and the UK was included for the first time in 1975. Results are published in four separate and specialised volumes as follows: detailed results by industry; structure of labour costs; detailed results by size classes of establishment; and results by regions.

The first two volumes appear about three years after the survey (so for the 1975 survey they were published in 1978), while the third and fourth take about one year longer. Labour costs are analysed by monthly and hourly costs in most cases, for manuals and non-manuals separately and together, and are presented in both local currency and the equivalent (at the time of the survey) in European Units of Account (EUA).

Each volume uses this basis for analysis and Volume 1 gives detailed breakdowns by industry based on the *General Industrial Classification of Economic Activities within the European Communities* (NACE) – see Points to note 4. Volume 2 concentrates on the structure of labour costs giving the components of such costs in detail. Volume 3 analyses labour costs by size of establishment (measured by employee numbers), and Volume 4 shows the results by standard regions with some analysis by industry and by the structure of labour costs, though not in as much detail as the individual volumes dealing with these specific analyses.

Some of the results are summarised in the *Employment Gazette* before the more detailed reports appear in the Eurostat series.

Census of Production

The summary tables published in the *Business Monitor Series* (PA 1002) show the wages and salaries of operatives and others (separately), in total and per head, for each MLH industry, although the summary usually appears about four years after the actual census year (the one for 1976 being published in 1980).

The *Business Monitor PA Series* also provides individual industry reports (based on MLH) on the Census of Production which usually appear about two years after the census year. Each shows, for the UK, the net output per head, the wages and salaries of operatives and others separately, both in total and per head, all for five census years. For the latest Census of Production year operating ratios are given showing gross output per head; net output per head; gross value added per head; wages and salaries as a percentage of gross value added; wages and salaries per operative; wages and salaries per administrative, technical and clerical employee; and net capital expenditure per head.

Secondary sources

Monthly Digest of Statistics

This shows an index of output for the UK with total output, employment, and output per head separately for the whole economy; all production industries; manufacturing industries; mining and quarrying; metal manufacture; mechanical, instrument and electrical engineering; vehicles; textiles; and gas, electricity and water. All are presented quarterly for the latest eleven years (seasonally adjusted, with the latest quarter being about one quarter prior to publication), and annually for the latest eight full years. Labour costs in the UK are shown with total costs and wages and salaries separately, together with labour costs per unit of output, all in index form and for the whole economy quarterly for 11 years and annually for nine years. An index of wages and salaries per unit of output in UK manufacturing is also given monthly, quarterly and annually for 12 years.

Economic Trends

Indices show the output per person employed for the whole UK economy, the index of production industries, and manufacturing industry separately, quarterly for about seven years, and annually for 11 years. Also there is some analysis of the percentage change in output per person employed from quarter to quarter for a few years, together with a graph plotting the course of output per person over about six years.

A longer series of the above statistics appears in *Economic Trends Annual Supplement*, giving extensive quarterly and annual indices.

National Institute Economic Review

The statistical appendix includes a table on productivity in the labour market which shows indices of output per person employed in the sectors of manufacturing, mining, and construction separately, in addition to total output of all industries. Also there is an index of output per person hour worked in manufacturing. The data are usually given quarterly for the latest eight quarters and annually for the latest ten full years. An international comparison of the UK and six other OECD countries (usually USA, Canada, Japan, France, Germany and Italy) shows indices of output per person hour in manufacturing, wage costs per unit of output, and labour costs per unit of output, all quarterly for the latest eight quarters and annually for the latest seven full years.

British Labour Statistics: Yearbook

A monthly index of UK wages and salaries per unit of output in manufacturing industry is given for the latest five years (including the year of the yearbook). Labour costs are further analysed showing total costs per unit of output and wages and salaries per unit of output for: the Index of Production industries; manufacturing industries; mining and quarrying; metal manufacture; mechanical, instrument and electrical engineering; vehicles; textiles; and gas, electricity and water, annually for the latest ten years. For the whole economy, the statistics are given quarterly and annually for the same ten years. Indices of total output, employment and output per person employed are given for the same industrial sectors as above, quarterly (seasonally adjusted) for the latest ten years (which includes the year of the yearbook) and annually (but unadjusted) for the same ten years.

OECD Main Economic Indicators

For each of the 25 OECD member nations (including the UK), a graph plotted over about 13 years shows the trend in unit labour costs in manufacturing industry, together with a curve showing the average weekly earnings in manufacturing. Also a table of key economic indicators for each nation includes indices of weekly earnings and unit labour costs (for the UK this means wages and salaries per unit of output) quarterly for the latest four quarters available and annually for the latest four full years.

Regional Statistics

Based on the latest EEC Labour Costs Survey, the total labour costs are shown in pence per hour and the structure of these costs is shown by component, with the percentage of total costs taken up by wages and salaries; statutory NHI contributions; regional employment premium; provision for redundancy; employers' liability insurance; private social welfare payments; payments in kind; subsidized services; and training, all shown separately. The statistics are for all manufacturing industries; coal, petroleum, chemical products and metal manufacture; engineering and allied industries (including vehicles and metal goods not elsewhere specified); and other manufacturing, all by standard region of Great Britain.

Scottish Abstract of Statistics

Drawing on the data from the CBI Industrial Trends Survey, the percentage of firms in Scotland operating below capacity is shown by the type of constraint on output (namely labour — either skilled or other). The figures are given quarterly for about seven years and in less frequent intervals for further years back. A similar series appears in the 'Main quarterly economic series' section of the *Scottish Economic Bulletin*.

Welsh Economic Trends

Based on the Census of Production, the net output per employee is shown by industry group (SIC) in £ per employee, for Wales, the assisted regions, the unassisted regions, and the UK in total for the latest census (which is usually about four years prior to the year of the publication). This analysis is supplemented with bar charts showing a comparison of the UK total with Wales, the assisted regions and the unassisted regions, and for all manufacturing industry but by standard regions of Great Britain (which include Wales).

British Labour Statistics: Historical Abstract 1886-1968

This contains analyses of labour costs in Great Britain showing total labour costs and their components (wages and salaries; statutory NHI; private social welfare payments; payments in kind; subsidised services; recruitment and training; and other costs) by selected industry groups (based on the 1958 SIC) for the year of 1964 only. Indices of total labour costs and wages and salaries per unit of output are given for the whole economy, the Index of Production industries, and manufacturing industry separately, annually for the period 1950-1968, and for the whole economy only wages and salaries per unit of output are given quarterly for the period 1955-1968.

Also indices of output, employment and output per person employed are given separately for the whole economy, the Index of Production Industries, and manufacturing industry, annually for 1950-1968, with quarterly analysis of output per person employed given for the Index of Production and manufacturing industry only, over the period 1960-1968. Finally, selected statistics from the UK Census of of Production over the period 1907-63 (selected years) show the net output per person employed for all industries and for manufacturing industries only.

Tertiary sources

Output, Employment and Labour Productivity in Europe since 1955
(Jones, D T, in *National Institute Economic Review*, August 1976, pp72–85)

This article puts the UK Industrial performance into a European context, with many useful comparative statistics over a long period and includes some industrial analyses.

Post War Trends in Employment, Productivity, Output, Labour Costs, and Prices by Industry in the UK
(Wragg, R and Robertson, J, Dept of Employment Research Paper No. 3, 1978)

A comprehensive presentation of the main UK trends drawing on the official series of statistics on output per head and unit labour costs in a range of industries, since the last war. A shorter version appeared in the *Employment Gazette*, May 1978, pp512–19, entitled 'Britain's industrial performance since the war'.

IDS Study (Numbers 162 and 186)

Study Number 162 (January 1978), *Productivity Bargaining*, looked at the productivity agreements in operation in both the public and private sectors and examined the differing bases of each. Study Number 186 (January 1979), *Productivity Schemes*, looked at the productivity schemes in existence and the future for such schemes through case studies.

The UK and West German Manufacturing Industry 1954–72
(NEDO, London 1978)

This report analyses and compares the UK and West German manufacturing sectors with the objective of explaining the difference in standards of performance by outlining differences in industrial structure and the like.

Productivity Growth in the UK Food and Drink Manufacturing Industry
(NEDO, London 1978)

This study examines the major determinants of productivity in this particular sector and the problems surrounding the labour force and the realisation of increased productivity.

Further sources

Department of Employment
Department of Manpower Services, (Northern Ireland)
EEC Commission
Confederation of British Industry
National Institute of Economic and Social Research
British Institute of Management
National Economic Development Office
Sheffield Centre for Innovation and Productivity
Organisation for Economic Co-operation and Development

18. Trade Union Membership

Introduction

This section covers statistics on the number of individual trade unions and the aggregate membership of each. Statistics on the aggregate membership of trade unions in the UK are compiled officially by the Department of Employment and are based on data supplied to it directly by the individual trade unions and from various other sources such as the Register of Friendly Societies in Northern Ireland. The figures on membership supplied by the individual unions are reckoned to be fairly accurate and reflect the payment of union subscriptions quite closely.

The broad definition of trade unions includes all those organisations of workers which are known to include in their objectives, that of negotiating with employers on issues of wage regulation and the conditions that members work in. This latter objective must feature in a trade union's stated policy if it is to be entered in the statutory list of trade unions.

None of the sources listed below gives a regional breakdown of membership and here it would be necessary to approach either the individual trade unions directly or the Trades Union Congress (TUC). Most unions produce an annual report and some also produce a report of their annual conference. In addition, in many cases newsletters and papers are printed and most are generally available from the head office of the union concerned.

The available information has been broken down in the following ways:

- ☐ sex — although the distinctions are not always featured in some unions' statistics — see Points to note 4
- ☐ union membership — that is those paying contributions
- ☐ number of individual unions
- ☐ sizee of union — measured by the number of members and usually presented in broad bands of membership
- ☐ union finances — showing total contribution income, funds available or affiliation fees to the TUC.

Points to note

1. The official DE figures on membership cover the total including members in branches of the union overseas, but all have their head offices situated in the UK. The number of members of UK-based trade unions living or working abroad for most or all of their time is considered to be small as a proportion of the total.

2. Those members of trade unions with their head offices outside the UK are not included in the official DE figures.

3. Some workers belong to more than one union and so there is an element of double-counting in the total membership figures for the UK. However, the DE considers this duplication to be relatively insignificant.

4. It is sometimes the case that the sub-division of the total membership of a trade union into males and females is partly estimated because some trade unions are unable to state the precise sex split in their total membership.

5. It should be remembered that the TUC does not have all trade unions affiliated to it and so the membership details produced by it (see Secondary sources below) will not reflect the full extent of unionisation. However, the difference in total membership is not great although the difference in the number of individual unions is much more significant. For example, comparing the relative figures for 1977 the official (DE) membership was put at 12,707,000 and the TUC figure was slightly lower at 11,865,390. But the number of trade unions showed a much bigger gap, with the DE giving 480 and the TUC only having 112 affiliated to it.

Primary sources

Employment Gazette

Regular figures on the membership of trade unions appear annually, although there is some inconsistency as to the actual month of publication. The latest data available were published in the December 1979 issue in a provisional form and relate to the membership for 1978. The aggregate membership of trade unions in the UK is given by sex for the year, together with the relative change from a year previous. The number of trade unions is also given.

Comprehensive tables also show membership at the end of the year, with the number of unions and membership measured by 12 size bands (based on number of members) given as percentages of the total in each case. Changes in the membership over a ten-year period are given showing the number of unions, membership (males, females and total all separately) and percentage change in membership over the previous year, for the UK only. The number of trade unions in 12 size bands is given for 11 individual years with corresponding aggregate membership

18. Trade union membership

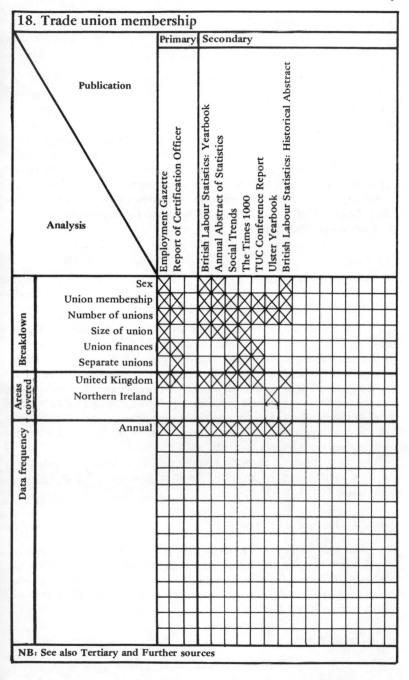

Analysis \ Publication	Primary		Secondary						
	Employment Gazette	Report of Certification Officer	British Labour Statistics: Yearbook	Annual Abstract of Statistics	Social Trends	The Times 1000	TUC Conference Report	Ulster Yearbook	British Labour Statistics: Historical Abstract
Breakdown									
Sex	X		X	X	X	X	X	X	
Union membership	X		X	X	X	X	X		
Number of unions	X		X	X	X	X	X		
Size of union				X	X	X	X		
Union finances	X		X	X	X	X	X		
Separate unions		X			X	X	X		
Areas covered									
United Kingdom	X		X	X	X	X		X	
Northern Ireland							X		
Data frequency									
Annual	X	X	X	X	X	X	X		

NB: See also Tertiary and Further sources

for the same bands and years.

Annual Report of the Certification Officer

This contains data on those trade unions recorded in the Certification Office for Trade Unions and Employers' Associations in accordance with the Trade Union and Labour Relations Act 1974. The names of all the trade unions are listed and for each one with 100,000 or more members, the membership, total income and expenditure are given as well as a fuller analysis of the balance sheet (including political funding). For unions of less than 100,000 members there are also membership details and broad totals for the financial operations of the unions.

Before 1974, similar information was given in the *Report of the Chief Registrar of Friendly Societies, Trade Unions and Employers' Associations* (HMSO, annually).

Secondary sources

British Labour Statistics Yearbook

The UK membership of trade unions (males, females, and total separately) and the number of individual unions at the end of each year is given for 16 consecutive years (from the previous year back) together with the percentage increase or decrease on membership over the previous year. There is further analysis of aggregate UK membership and the number of unions by size of membership with 12 size bands, showing the numbers in each and the relevant percentages of the total. For the latest year only. The numbers of unions in the 12 size bands are also given for 11 years annually.

Also there is a table showing membership by the 12 size bands plus the total membership by sex and the average membership per union. All annually for 11 years.

Annual Abstract of Statistics

This gives the number of UK trade unions by 12 size ranges, annually for 11 years (usually the latest year being about three years prior to publication). Also, for the same periods membership numbers are shown with males, females and total separately, and the thousands of members in each of 12 size divisions.

Social Trends

A bar chart shows the total union membership by size of union (measured by membership) and another shows the change in membership of six selected trade unions (some of the largest) giving the percentage change over a long period. Both charts cover the UK and are for 20 to 23 years, depending on the year of issue.

The Times 1000 1979–80
(Times Books Ltd, London, annually, price (1979 edition), £11.50)

This lists the top 25 UK trade unions (as measured by size of membership) and gives for each the name of the union and the general secretary, the number of members, the total contributions of members, net income, and current funds. The figures relate to one year prior to publication.

TUC Conference Report
(Trades Union Congress, London, annually)

The introduction to each annual conference report gives a brief appraisal of the membership changes over the previous year for the affiliated unions only (see Points to note 5). In the 'Statistical statement' towards the end of the report are listed the names and addresses of the secretaries of affiliated societies, the number of delegates appointed to attend the conference and the total membership they represent with their affiliation fees for the previous year (ending December).

A summary table gives total membership and the number of unions by 18 broad trade groups (mining and quarrying; railways; transport other than railways, etc). Also details are given of past congresses from the first (1868) to the present one, listing the number of delegates, the number of societies represented, the total income and, of course, the venue.

Ulster Yearbook

This gives the total membership and the number of trade unions in Northern Ireland for the latest year available.

British Labour Statistics: Historical Abstract 1886–1968

The number of trade unions and the membership of each (males, females and total separately) as at the end of each year are given for the UK only, annually for the period 1892–1968.

Tertiary sources

The French Trade Unions
(*Employment Gazette*, May 1977, pp451–54)

A useful article on the French trade union movement giving details of their structure and confederation with some membership details. The differences compared to the UK structure are highlighted.

The Enterprise Unions of Japan
(*Employment Gazette*, August 1977, pp808–11)

An examination of the Japanese trade union movement which goes into detail about the structure and membership of some of the larger bodies and looks at the general industrial relations scene. A further article on Japanese trade unions appears in the next issue, September 1979, pp922–26.

Time Off for Trade Union Duties and Activities
(*Employment Gazette*, March 1978, pp289–91)

An article by Michael Mellish of ACAS giving an appraisal of the implications of sections 57 and 58 of the Employment Protection Act which came into force on 1 April 1978, and which made provision for lay officials of trade unions to have time off in order to carry out their duties. A useful discussion of some important issues.

The Extent of Closed Shop Arrangements in British Industry
(*Employment Gazette*, January 1980, pp16–22)

A concise report on the first major study for a number of years to establish the extent of the closed shop in Great Britain, carried out by Messrs Gennard, Dunn and Wright of the London School of Economics, Industrial Relations Department. There is some industrial analysis and estimates of the extent of the closed shop now.

More historical analysis and discussion of this study appears in *The Content of British Closed Shop Agreements* (*Employment Gazette*, November 1979, pp1088–92).

The Fifth Estate: Britain's Unions in the Seventies
(Taylor, R, Routledge & Kegan Paul, 1978)

A book which assesses the role and position of the trade unions in Britain with some useful statistics. Two further books which are still useful even though now somewhat dated are: *Trades Unions* (McCarthy, W E J (ed), Penguin, 1974), and for a wider appraisal *The Labour Movement in Europe* (Kendall, W, Allen Lane, 1975).

Further sources

Department of Employment
Department of Manpower Services (Northern Ireland)
Trades Union Congress
Individual trade unions

19. Strikes

Introduction

Covered in this section are stoppages of work as a result of industrial disputes arising out of terms and conditions of employment, more commonly called strikes. Other temporary stoppages of work due to reasons other than industrial disputes are covered in subject heading 14. Statistics on strikes are collected by the Department of Employment on information received from a variety of sources such as the Department's regional manpower advisers and local employment office managers, some of the nationalised industries and other public bodies. They appear regularly measured in the following three ways:

- ☐ number of stoppages
- ☐ number of workers involved in the stoppages
- ☐ number of working days lost.

There is also a monthly table compiled of stoppages by cause — the ostensible cause that is — which gives some indication of the reasons behind the stoppage. Currently there are nine categories used, as follows:

- ☐ pay — wage rates and earnings levels
- ☐ pay — extra wage and fringe benefits
- ☐ duration and pattern of hours worked
- ☐ redundancy questions
- ☐ trade union matters
- ☐ working conditions and supervision
- ☐ manning and work allocation
- ☐ dismissal and other disciplinary measures
- ☐ miscellaneous

The official statistics do not record all stoppages (see Points to note 2) and so must be seen as only giving a partial view of the whole strike picture.

The main series of statistics has been broken down into the following analyses:

□ number of stoppages
□ workers involved
□ working days lost
□ stoppages by cause — using the nine categories listed previously
□ industrial — mostly by SIC groups
□ duration — how long the strike lasted.

The Secondary sources all use the regular statistics compiled by the DE for their analyses.

Points to note

1. DE statistics on stoppages include those resulting from official (ie with full trade union recognition) and unofficial disputes.
2. The official statistics record those stoppages which involve at least ten workers or last at least one day, or where the total of working days lost exceeds 100. Naturally this precludes a certain amount of short stoppages and disputes usually affecting firms with a small labour force.
3. Those workers who are participating directly or indirectly in a strike at the same establishment are included in the number of workers involved, but excluded are those laid off at other establishments (for example, due to a shortage of supplies from the striking establishment) who are not participating directly in the stoppage.
4. The total number of working days lost includes all stoppages in progress during the period.
5. The official statistics relate only to stoppages arising out of disputes about terms and conditions of employment.
6. Categorisation of disputes by cause obviously involves some arbitrary judgement as to the reasons behind the stoppage, given the multifarious nature of disputes, although it must be said that the categories are quite broad.

Primary sources

Employment Gazette

Official statistics on stoppages first appear in the *Employment Gazette* with a regular series covering industrial disputes in the UK. Each month the three measures are shown by full SIC industry groups for the month (that preceding publication month) and cumulatively for the year to date. Causes of stoppages for the last month and cumulatively for the year to date are also given by the usual nine categories of cause. The approximate duration of stoppages is given (1–2 days, 2–3 days, 3–6 days, 6–12 days, over 12 days) for each of the three measures.

A series is also published monthly giving annual figures of the three measures for 18 years (from the previous full year back) and for

19. Strikes

Breakdown / Analysis		Primary		Secondary									
		Employment Gazette	British Labour Statistics: Yearbook	Monthly Digest of Statistics	Annual Abstract of Statistics	Social Trends	Regional Statistics	Scottish Abstract of Statistics	Scottish Economic Bulletin	Digest of Welsh Statistics	Digest of Statistics – N. Ireland	Social and Economic Trends in N. Ireland	British Labour Statistics: Historical Abstract
Breakdown	Number of stoppages	X	X	X				X					X
	Workers involved	X	X	X		X							X
	Working days lost	X	X	X	X	X	X	X	X	X			X
	Stoppages by cause	X											
	Industrial	X			X		X	X	X	X	X		X
	Duration	X											
Areas covered	United Kingdom	X	X										X
	Great Britain			X									
	Northern Ireland						X				X	X	
	Scotland							X	X				
	Wales									X			
	Standard regions		X				X						
Data frequency	Annual	X	X		X	X	X	X	X	X	X	X	X
	Monthly	X		X									

NB: See also Tertiary and Further sources

approximately four years monthly. This series attempts to distinguish 'official' disputes and gives an industrial analysis (with 6 broad divisions of mining and quarrying; metals, engineering, shipbuilding and vehicles; textiles, clothing and footwear; construction; transport and communication; and all other industries and services) of working days lost only. Each month there is also brief commentary on the more significant disputes recorded.

Usually in the January issue each year, provisional annual figures are given for the previous year by all three measures, with commentary on the more significant trends and individual industry performances. This forms the basis of a final review of the previous year usually in the June or July issue giving a more detailed analysis by cause for 13 broad industry groups. Also there is an analysis by prominent stoppage showshowing the length of individual stoppage, numbers involved, working days lost, type of worker involved, and cause. There is also some analysis by duration of stoppage and by standard region in 13 broad industry groups. All this is supplemented by commentary on trends and the methodology used.

British Labour Statistics Yearbook

This contains summary statistics on stoppages for a ten year period by all three measures for all industries (with coal-mining shown separately) and by 12 broad industry groups. The distinction between official and other disputes is given for working days lost only by six major industry groups. For the review year the three measures are also shown by cause and by UK standard region, for 12 broad industry groups. There is also a comparison of the review year with the previous year by SIC/MLH industry listing (but not the complete classification).

Secondary sources

Monthly Digest of Statistics

This shows figures on the number of workers involved in industrial stoppages and, by six major industry groups, the total working days lost, all monthly for the latest six years.

Annual Abstract of Statistics

This contains figures on all three measures by seven broad industry groups annually for 11 years, with workers involved also shown by duration of stoppage, and working days lost by numbers involved in the stoppage.

197

Social Trends

The number of working days lost in the UK only is given for the latest seven years and by way of comparison one earlier year.

Regional Statistics

This contains the number of working days lost in each standard region (including Northern Ireland) by 13 broad industry groups for the latest two years.

Scottish Abstract of Statistics

The number of stoppages for a 12 year period and for the first six months of the current year are shown. For the same period workers involved and working days lost are given by ten broad industry groups.

Scottish Economic Bulletin

This contains working days lost only by ten broad industry groups annually for ten years, supplemented by a bar chart showing the average number of working days lost per 1000 employees by major industry groups.

Digest of Welsh Statistics

All three measures, with the addition of working days lost per 1000 employees, are shown by six broad industry groups annually for the latest ten years.

Digest of Statistics — Northern Ireland

This contains workers involved and total working days lost (the latter only by five industry groups) in stoppages in Northern Ireland, monthly for two years and annually for 17 years.

Social and Economic Trends in Northern Ireland

A simplified format shows the number of working days lost per 1000 employees by broad industry groups annually for three years. Also the percentage of the work force involved in the disputes is given annually for three years. In both cases statistics are supplemented by bar charts.

British Labour Statistics — Historical Abstract 1886-1968

This provides statistics covering the three measures annually for the period 1893–1968, with Great Britain and Northern Ireland shown separately. For the period 1960–1968 UK figures, monthly for three years and annually for six years, are given for all three measures by principal cause and by major SIC industry groups.

Tertiary sources

Industrial Relations Digest

This contains a monthly commentary on trends and overall stoppages generally in a magazine-type presentation.

Strikes in Britain
(Smith, C T B, Clifton, R, Makeham, P and Creigh, S W, DE Manpower Paper No. 15, HMSO, London 1978, price £6)

This is a major study of strike activity in Britain over the period 1966 to 1973, with most aspects covered in detail. Behavioural aspects of strikes cover such topics as the relationship between strike activity and establishment size, and the concentration of stoppages. A summary article appeared in the *Employment Gazette* of November 1978, pp1255–58, while certain aspects of the study were reported during its evolution in February 1976, pp115–16 ('Incidence rates'); November 1976, pp1219–24 ('Distribution and concentration'); and February 1977, pp111–15 ('Concentration in manufacturing industry').

International Comparison of Industrial Disputes
(*Employment Gazette*, January 1979, pp28–29)

An article looking at the problems inherent in making international comparisons of strike activity, with reference to ILO and EEC data. Another similar article covering the period 1969–1978 appeared in the *Gazette* of February 1980 (pp161–62).

Strikers' Occupations: an Analysis
(*Employment Gazette*, March 1980, pp237–39)

An article by Stephen Creigh and Peter Makeham of the DE, drawing on data over the period 1966–73 and analysing the percentage of stoppages attributable to certain occupational groups (based on broad CODOT).

Further sources

Department of Employment
Department of Manpower Services (Northern Ireland)

Trades Union Congress
Individual trade unions
Nationalised industries
Industrial Relations Services Ltd

Index of Key Publications

The regular information series referred to in Part I are listed below giving the publisher, frequency of update and the latest price. Prices are given as a guide to the relative cost of the information source in 1980 as this is useful to know when considering purchase. However, the prices of most publications listed below are reviewed regularly.

Annual Abstract of Statistics
HMSO, annually, price £10.

Many subject areas are covered in varying levels of detail. The yearly volume usually appears at the beginning of the applicable year, although many of the tables on labour market information are at least two years old.

Annual Report of the Certification Officer
HMSO, annually.

A report-type format with most of the statistics contained in the appendix. The information is quite recent.

BACIE Journal
British Association for Commercial and Industrial Education, monthly (except August), price £2 to non-members, free to members.

Magazine-type publication which incorporates a bibliography four times a year.

British Journal of Industrial Relations
London School of Economics and Political Science, three times a year (March, July, November), single copies £4, annual subscription £11.

British Labour Statistics: Historical Abstract 1886–1968
HMSO, 1971, price £7.

An extremely useful publication for any historical analysis up to 1968 (after which the yearbooks take over). Most aspects of LMI are covered in detail, although most detail is given for the post-war period.

British Labour Statistics: Yearbook
HMSO, annually, price £20.

The best composite volume covering most aspects of LMI. It includes many of the series first appearing in the monthly *Employment Gazette* but presents them together which can help the user considerably. Most of the detailed information relates to the year of the yearbook, although they tend to appear two to three years after the cover year.

Bulletin of Labour Statistics
ILO (Geneva), quarterly, single copies £3.45, annual subscription £11.25.

An international collection of some of the major labour market indicators covering many member countries of the ILO. Years used tend to vary for different subjects.

Census of Population 1971
HMSO, decennial, prices vary — see below.

The census information is published in a series of volumes which appear at varying intervals after the census year. Some take up to four or five years to appear, depending to a large extent on the level of detail and the priority attached to each set of figures. Those volumes referred to in Part I of this Guide are given below:

> *England and Wales: Advance Analysis County Leaflets*, prices vary
> *England and Wales: County Reports*, prices vary
> *England and Wales: Economic Activity — New Towns*, price £4.90
> *England and Wales: Economic Activity — Sub-regional Volume*, price £14
> *England and Wales: Migration Regional Reports*, prices vary
> *England and Wales: New County Reports as Constituted April 1973*, prices vary
> *England and Wales: Preliminary Report*, price 60p
> *England and Wales: Workplace and Transport to Work Tables*, Part I £13.50, Part II £8.70
> *Great Britain: Advance Analysis*, price £4.50
> *Great Britain: Age, Marital Condition and General Tables*, price £1.55
> *Great Britain: Economic Activity*, Part I £1.90, Part II £5.45, Part III £7.65, Part IV £9.50, Part V £5.70
> *Great Britain: Qualified Manpower Tables*, price £5.70
> *Great Britain: Summary Tables*, price £3.60
> *Scotland: County Reports*, prices vary

Scotland: New Region Reports, prices vary
Scotland: Economic Activity — New Towns, prices vary
Scotland: Economic Activity — Sub-regional Volumes, prices vary
Scotland: Migration Tables, Part I £3.20, Part II £4.50, Part III
£6.80, Part IV £11, Part V £6
Scotland: Preliminary Report, price 30p
Scotland: Scottish Population Summary, price £3.70
Scotland: Scottish Preliminary Report, price £2.55
Scotland: Workplace and Transport to Work Tables, price £3.60

Note: Some of these volumes are now out of print and may only be available through a library.

Census of Population 1971 (Northern Ireland)
HMSO Belfast, decennial, prices vary — see below.

The Northern Ireland decennial census runs parallel with the Great Britain census but produces its own set of statistical volumes. Those mentioned in Part I of this Guide are shown below:

County Reports, prices vary
Economic Activity Tables, price £7.50
Education Tables, price £2
Preliminary Report, price 30p
Summary Tables, price £1.90
Workplace and Transport to Work Tables, price 75p

Census of Production
HMSO, annually, prices shown below.

The Business Monitor PA series covers most industry groups and appears monthly and quarterly. A monthly series for *one* industry costs £3.06 per year; a quarterly series £1 per year. There are rates for complete sets.
The *Summary Tables (PA 1002)* are useful for a less detailed analysis of each industry and they appear annually, price £6.25.

The Census of Production is carried out annually but the results appear a few years after the year of the census.

Changes in Rates of Wages and Hours of Work
HMSO, monthly, single copies 40p, annual subscription £5.64.

An up-to-date account of changes in pay and hours reached through negotiation, etc. The monthly reports update the annual *Time Rates of Wages and Hours of Work*.

Compendium of Health Statistics
Compiled by Chew, R C and Wells, N E J, Office of Health Economics, biennially, price £8.50.

The latest edition of this publication (1977) is the second. The pages are loose-leaf but tables and graphs are clearly presented with further charts where appropriate.

Department of Employment Press Notices
DE, free to certain users.

These are designed for the quick release of a whole range of labour market information, but regular series cover separately, unemployment, vacancies, and training measures. They represent the most up-to-date information on many of the key labour market indicators.

Department of Industry Press Notices
DI, free to certain users.

Designed for the quick release of information emanating from the DI. There is a limited range of relevant LMI, although they are especially useful for information on changes in regional policy.

Department of Manpower Services (Northern Ireland) Gazette
DMS, six-monthly (spring and autumn), free to certain users.

A publication devoted solely to LMI, containing up-to-date statistics on the major subject headings (such as unemployment, employment, vacancies, etc) for Northern Ireland only. Good up-to-date detail in the issues published so far (the first issue appeared in spring 1978).

Department of Manpower Services (Northern Ireland) Press Notices
DMS, free to certain users.

Designed for the quick release of information especially on unemployment and vacancies, and as such represents the most up-to-date information usually available.

Digest of Statistics — Northern Ireland
HMSO Belfast, six-monthly, price £3.75.

A comprehensive collection of statistics on NI covering a wide range of subjects. Publication of the volumes is fairly swift (in March and September), with much of the labour market information relating to the previous year and beyond.

Digest of Welsh Statistics
HMSO, annually, price £5.25.

This contains a wide range of statistics on Wales including some of the more obvious LMI data. There is a clear emphasis on comparison with the rest of Great Britain. Statistics are in the main fairly recent.

Economic Progress Report
HM Treasury, monthly, free.

These pamphlets give details of recent changes or developments in economic policy. Included are some statistical series (mostly in index form) of key economic indicators. They can be obtained on application to PDSD Distribution Unit, Central Office of Information, Hercules Road, London, SE1 7DU.

Economic Trends
HMSO, monthly, price £5.40.

These contain recent information on the key economic indicators, mostly in index form. The tables are supplemented by graphs and/or charts in most cases.

Economic Trends Annual Supplement
HMSO, annually, price £2.80.

Publication began with No. 1 in 1976 and they contain a similar set of statistics to the monthly *Economic Trends* but for a longer run in most cases, and without the graphs and charts. The information is very recent.

Education and Employment 1980
by Hutt, R, Parsons, D and Pearson, R, New Opportunity Press, 1980, soft back £9.95, hardback £15.

This contains statistical tables, graphs and other charts together with commentary on the key indicators in educational supply. Good clear presentation is a key feature of this book.

Education Statistics for the United Kingdom
HMSO, annually, price £6.

This draws together some of the statistical series of the constituent countries of the UK and saves the job of collecting information from three separate volumes. The latest information contained in the volume is recent to the relevant year, although publication is usually about three or four years after the cover year.

EEC Labour Force Sample Survey
EEC Eurostat, biennial, Vol. 1 £5.75, Vol. 2 £3.30.

This survey began in 1973 for the UK and is of around 100,000 households in the country. Similar surveys run parallel in other EEC countries.

The results of the last survey (for 1977) were published in two volumes: *Methods and Definitions*, and *Statistical Tables*. Publication of the results is about two years after the survey date.

EEC Labour Costs in Industry
EEC Eurostat, triennial, Vol. 1 £8, Vol. 2 £4, Vol. 3 £4, Vol. 4 £4.

A detailed survey of employers in the UK which runs parallel to those in other EEC countires. The 1975 survey in the UK (the latest available) sampled about 71,000 establishments employing in excess of seven million people. The results are published in four volumes as follows: Vol. 1 Detailed results by industry; Vol. 2 Structure of labour costs; Vol. 3 Detailed results by size classes of establishment; and Vol. 4 Results by regions.

Volumes 1 and 2 appear about three years after the census year; Volumes 3 and 4 take about a year longer.

Employment Gazette
HMSO, monthly, single copies £1.65, annual subscription £23.52.

This is the official journal of the DE and as such contains the best series of many of the labour market statistics, together with articles and news of a wide range of employment topics. This must be seen as the primary reference publication for those interested in LMI.

Family Expenditure Survey
HMSO, annually, price £4.75.

Over 10,000 households in the UK are sampled each year for this survey with the emphasis on the financial aspects of each household. The survey was introduced in 1957. The Northern Ireland results are published separately, price £1.85.

First Destination of University Graduates
Universities' Statistical Record, annually, price £6.95.

This contains the latest information on the destinations of graduates from UK universities. Usually the information relates to the full academic year, two years' previous, so, for example, the issue published in 1980 would relate to 1977/78.

General Household Survey
HMSO, annually, price £7.

This survey is a continuous survey based on a sample of private households in Great Britain and carried out by the OPCS. The sample size is about 15,000 households each year, and the questions asked are wide ranging. Publication of the results is about three years after the survey date.

Health and Personal Social Service Statistics for England
HMSO, annually, price £8.50

Contains a wealth of information on health-related topics with recent information for a number of years in most instances. A similar volume is published for Wales, price £5.25.

Incomes Data Report
Incomes Data Services Ltd, twice monthly, price on application.

These are regular information bulletins covering many different subjects and aimed primarily at employers. They are useful for keeping up-to-date on basic statistics such as unemployment and production.

Incomes Data Study
Incomes Data Services Ltd, twice monthly, price £1.50.

These are regular studies each devoted to an analysis of a particular subject. They are very good on coverage of pay in different occupations, and a useful feature of most of the studies of employing organisations is giving good, up-to-date information.

Industrial and Labour Relations Review
Cornell University, USA, quarterly (October, January, April, July), single issues US $ 5, annual subscription US $ 16.

Industrial Relations Digest
Centurion Publications International Ltd, monthly, annual subscription £27.50.

Presented in a magazine-type format with topical articles and a few statistics on some labour market indicators, most of which relate to the previous month.

Industrial Relations Journal
Business Publications Ltd, bi-monthly, single copies £4, annual subscription £20.

Industrial Relations Review and Report
Industrial Relations Services Ltd, twice monthly, annual subscription £100.

A frequent publication which attempts to present up-to-date information including recent changes in, for example, employee law. It relies heavily on case study material, which makes it particularly useful for some areas.

IMS Manpower Survey
Institute of Manpower Studies, annually from 1973 to 1979, prices vary — see below.

This was a survey of employing organisations carried out from 1973 to 1979 (inclusive) and covered a wide range of industries employing around half a million workers. The survey produced a wide range of LMI. The following reports are available: *Key Indicators Report*, £45, and *Standard Report*, £70. Reduced rates apply to participants in the survey and IMS contributors. Special analyses are also available. For further details contact IMS.

Journal of Occupational Psychology
British Psychological Society, quarterly, annual subscription £25.

Labour Force Statistics
OECD, quarterly, annual subscription £5.40.

This contains details of the major LMI statistics for each OECD member nation (for the latest available periods). Useful for international comparisons. The quarterly data is condensed into the annual publication.

Labour Force Statistics
OECD, annually, price £9.80.

A yearbook containing the major measures of the labour force for each member nation. The quarterly series provides a regular update.

Local Authority Vital Statistics (Series VS)
HMSO, annually, price 85p.

This gives a disaggregated view of England and Wales with some of the statistics being about two years old.

Main Economic Indicators
OECD, monthly, single copies £2.20, annual subscription £21.60.

The presentation of the main economic measures for each OECD country is supplemented with graphs. The statistics generally are quite recent although there is variation from country to country.

Manchester School of Economic and Social Studies
The Manchester School, University of Manchester, four per year, single copies £4.50, annual subscription (libraries and institutions) £13, (personal) £9.

Monthly Digest of Statistics
HMSO, monthly £2.95.

This contains a wide range of statistics covering many topics, most of which are presented in a detailed periodic analysis.

Monthly Labour Review
Bureau of Labour Statistics, US Department of Labour, monthly, single copies US$ 2.50, annual subscription US$ 22.50.

National Institute Economic Review
National Institute of Economic and Social Research, quarterly, single copies £4, annual subscription £14.

A useful publication containing articles and statistics on a wide range of economic issues.

National Travel Survey
HMSO, periodic, price £6.50.

This is a periodic survey of travelling patterns in Great Britain with results available for the 1975/76 survey. Previous survey results were published in three volumes: *Cross-sectional analysis of passenger travel in Great Britain; Number of journeys per week by different types of households, individuals and vehicles; A comparison of the 1965, 1972– 73 surveys.*

New Earnings Survey
HMSO, annually, six parts, each £6.50.

This is a regular survey of a 1 per cent sample of employees covered by PAYE schemes chosen from National Insurance numbers, and has been carried out each April since 1970 in Great Britain (and a year later in Northern Ireland). Results are now published in six parts: Part A, Summary analysis of major results; Part B, Analyses by agreement; Part C, Analyses by industry; Part D, Analyses by occupation; Part E, Analyses by region and age-group; Part F, Hours, earnings by length of service, and earnings of part-time women workers. Appearance of the results is fairly quick by survey standards, with Parts A, B and C usually appearing by the end of the year and the other parts in the first quarter of the following year.

Northern Ireland Education Statistics
HMSO Belfast, annually, 2 volumes, each £4.

Volume 1 covers schools, pupils, teachers, scholarships and awards, and volume 2 covers further education.

OECD Economic Outlook
OECD, six-monthly (July and December), price £7.80 (two issues).

This gives an assessment of the future trends in the main economic measures for the OECD member nations.

OECD Economic Surveys
OECD, annually, price £1.50.

For each OECD member country an economic survey of the past year is produced.

OPCS Monitors
HMSO, occasional, free to certain users.

The *Monitors* are designed for the quick release of information emanating from OPCS which includes, for example, population, births, deaths and migration. The frequency of publication differs according to the statistics, but some indication is given below for those mentioned in this Guide: *Population Estimates* (ref PP1) — occasional; *Population Projections* (ref PP2) — occasional; *Deaths and Mortality* (ref DH1) — occasional; *Deaths by Cause* (ref DH2) — quarterly; *Deaths from Accidents* (ref DH4) — quarterly; *Births* (ref FM1) — occasional; *Births and Deaths* (ref VS) —weekly, quarterly ;*Migration* (ref MN)—occasional. *OPCS Monitors* can be obtained direct from OPCS, Information Branch, St Catherine's House, 10 Kingsway, London WC2B 6JP.

Open University Digest of Statistics
Open University Press, annually, Vol. 1: *Students and Courses.*

This relates purely to the statistics of the Open University but covers a number of years. Results are usually for the previous year.

Personnel
American Management Associations, bi-monthly, price US$ 4.

Personnel Journal
A.C. Croft Inc., monthly, annual subscription US$ 45.

Personnel Management
Institute of Personnel Management, monthly, single copies £1.75, annual subscription £20.

A regular magazine-type publication which concentrates on personnel-related matters, with succinct articles.

Polytechnic First Degree and HND Students — Statistical Supplement
Committee of Directors of Polytechnics, annually, price £4.

This contains details of the first destination of students from the polytechnics of England and Wales. It usually appears about one year after the reference year.

Population Projections (Series PP2)
HMSO, annually, price £2.75.

Projections are given for the UK and its constituent countries beyond the end of the century and are based on a recent annual population estimate.

Population Trends
HMSO, quarterly (September, December, March, June), price £3.

This refers to England and Wales but covers a number of measures in addition to population alone. Similar information for Scotland and Northern Ireland can be found in the relevant publications of the Registrar General.

Quarterly Return of the Registrar General, Scotland
HMSO, quarterly, price 90p.

This contains the latest details of population components in Scotland.

Regional Population Projections
HMSO, annually, price 34p.

A short summary of the population projections by standard regions and sub-regions of England and Wales, with recent statistics.

Regional Statistics
HMSO, annually, £7.50.

Publication of this volume is usually quick with the relevant year appearing in the first few months of that year. In addition to comprehensive tables, there are plenty of useful charts. Worthy of special mention are the regional profiles for each UK standard region.

Report of the Chief Registrar of Friendly Societies, Trade Unions and Employers' Associations
HMSO, annually (until 1974).

A report which was superseded by the Annual Report of the Certification Officer.

Scottish Abstract of Statistics
HMSO, annually, price £6.25.

This covers a wide range of subjects including many relevant to LMI. Publication is slow, however, and many of the series lack enough detail to be very useful.

Scottish Economic Bulletin
HMSO, four-monthly, price £1.75.

Useful articles on the main trends in the Scottish economy and recent statistics are given.

Scottish Educational Statistics
HMSO, annually, price £5.15.

Publication is about five years after the reference date with detailed statistical series on Scotland only.

Scottish Journal of Political Economy
Longman Group Ltd, Edinburgh, three per year (February, June, November), single copies £4.50, annual subscription £12.

Social and Economic Trends in Northern Ireland
HMSO Belfast, annually, price £3.

This covers a broad range of topics in little detail. Most are presented in diagrammatic form.

Social Security Statistics
HMSO, annually, price £7.

This covers all aspects of Social Security provision and related subjects, with recent detailed statistics.

Social Trends
HMSO, annually, price £7.90.

A well-presented collection of social statistics containing ample graphs and charts to illustrate the text. Also there is occasional commentary for each section. Although many are for the year previous to publication, the age of the statistics tends to vary from year to year as do the subjects covered.

Statistics of Education
HMSO, annually, six volumes priced as follows: *Schools* £4.75; *School Leavers, CSE and GCE* £4.25; *Further Education* £4.50; *Teachers* £7; *Finance and Awards* £2.70; *Universities, UK* £8.75.

The statistics are usually fairly old by the time they reach publication; it can be up to three years.

Statistics of Education in Wales
HMSO, annually, price £4.50.

The publication of this volume tends to be about one year after the date of the relevant statistics, but this is the most comprehensive collection of Welsh educational statistics.

Survey of Personal Incomes
Board of Inland Revenue, main results 1975-76, price 70p.

This presents the results of a special survey carried out in 1975-76 based on income tax data.

Time Rates of Wages and Hours of Work
HMSO, annually, price £6.50.

A thorough collection of data on the previous years' agreements on wages and hours of work which appears fairly quickly after the end of the year. This is updated by the monthly *Changes in Rates of Wages and Hours of Work*.

Transport Statistics, Great Britain, 1966-76
HMSO, annually, price £5.75.

A collection of transport and travel data which is updated each year, although there is still a three year gap between statistics and publication.

Ulster Yearbook
HMSO Belfast, annually, price £6.

Welsh Economic Trends
HMSO, annually, price £4.25.

A well presented collection of key economic statistics for Wales with graphs and charts put to good use. Publication is fairly quick.

Yearbook of Labour Statistics
ILO, Geneva, annually, price £23.75.

A mammoth volume containing labour statistics from around 180 countries or territories, although years between countries tend to vary. Statistics are usually about two years old by the time of publication.

PART II:
Directory of Labour Market Organisations

1. Labour Market Institutions

The main bodies concerned with labour market issues are listed below with a description of their functions and organisation, together with points of further contact.

Department of Employment (DE)

The Department of Employment is responsible for ensuring that the best possible uses are made of Britain's manpower resources. It has overall responsibility for the drafting and implementation of labour legislation. Many of its specific powers are directed through independent statutory bodies such as the Manpower Services Commission (described below).

The main areas of operational concern for the Department now range over:

- ☐ race relations
- ☐ equal opportunity
- ☐ redundancy payments
- ☐ payment of unemployment benefit
- ☐ labour market statistics
- ☐ work permits
- ☐ international labour matters
- ☐ employment research

Main offices:

Caxton House
Tothill Street
London SW1H 9NA
01 213 3000

Regional offices:

Midlands
2 Duchess Place
Hagley Road
Birmingham B16 8NT
021 455 7111

South East
Hanway House
Red Lion Square
London WC1R 4NH
01 405 8454

Northern Wellbar House Gallowgate Newcastle-upon-Tyne NE1 4TP 0632 27575	*South West* The Pithay Bristol BS1 2NQ 0272 291071
North Western Sunley Building Piccadilly Plaza Manchester M60 7JS 061 832 9111	*Wales* Dominion House Queen Street Cardiff CF1 4NS 0222 32961
Scotland 43 Jeffrey Street Edinburgh EH1 1UU 031 556 8433	*Yorkshire and Humberside* City House New Station Street Leeds LS1 4JH 0532 38232

Other useful points of contact include:

The Work Research Unit
Almack House
26 King Street
London SW1Y 6RB
01 214 6600

The Work Research Unit was set up in 1975 with the purpose of providing information, advice and consultancy to organisations wishing to improve the quality of working life. Its services are available to all relevant parties with special interests in firms and trade unions. The unit is also a focus for research into many aspects of work and the people involved.

Statistics Office
Orphanage Road
Watford
Herts WD1 1PJ
0923 28500

Department of Employment Library
12 St James's Square
London SW1
01 214 8145/8476

Advisory, Conciliation and Arbitration Service (ACAS)

This became a statutory body in 1976 under the provisions of the Employment Protection Act 1975, and can assist in formulating company policy on redundancies, advising on ways of reducing labour turnover and improving manpower planning and recruitment and selection procedures.

Head office:

Cleland House
Page Street
London SW1P 4ND
01 222 4383

218

Regional offices:

Northern
Wellbar House
Gallowgate
Newcastle-upon-Tyne NE1 4TP
0632 27575

Yorkshire and Humberside
City House
Leeds LS1 4JH
0532 38232

South Eastern
Hanway House
Red Lion Square
London WC1R 4NH
01 405 8454

South Western
The Pithay
Bristol BS1 2NQ
0272 291071

Midlands
Fiveways House
Islington Row
Middleway
Birmingham B15 1SG
021 643 9868

North Western
Sunley Buildings
Piccadilly Plaza
Manchester M60 7JS
061 832 9111

Scotland
109 Waterloo Street
Glasgow G2 7BY
041 221 6852

Wales
2-4 Park Grove
Cardiff CF1 3QY
0222 45231

Health and Safety Executive

This is the operational arm of the Health and Safety Commission set up in 1975 and it deals with working conditions generally in a wide variety of places of employment. Legislation on health and safety at work is administered through the Executive.

Head office:

Baynards House
1 Chepstow Place
London W2 4TF
01 229 3456

The Department of Manpower Services (DMS)

In Northern Ireland, similar functions to the DE and its associated bodies are carried out by this body.

Address:

Netherleigh House
Massey Avenue
Belfast BT4 2JS
0232 63244

Manpower Services Commission (MSC)

The Manpower Services Commission (MSC) was set up on 1 January 1974 under the Employment and Training Act 1973 to run the public employment and training services. The commission, which is separate from government but accountable to the Secretary of State for Employment (and for its operations in Scotland and Wales, to the Secretary of State for Scotland and Wales respectively) has ten members appointed by the Secretary of State to serve for a term of three years: a chairman, three members appointed after consultation with the TUC, three after consultation with the CBI, two after consultation with local authority associations and one with professional education interests.

The Commission has three operating divisions: Employment Service Division, Training Services Division and Special Programmes Division; and two support divisions: Corporate Services Division, and Manpower Intelligence and Planning Division.

Head office:

Selkirk House
166 High Holborn
London WC1V 6PF
01 836 1213

(MSC will be moving to new offices at Moorfoot, Sheffield S1 4PQ from January 1983.)

Employment Service Division (ESD)

The aim of the Employment Service Division is to help people to choose, train for and obtain the jobs they want and to help employers to get the recruits they need as quickly as possible. ESD operates through a network of over 1000 Jobcentres and employment offices and these are listed in the telephone directory and should be regarded as the first point of contact when seeking information about the local labour market. The local manager can deal with a wide range of enquiries himself, but is also able to draw upon the resources of specialist staff at one of the 18 area offices (listed below), or the ESD head office itself. He is also able to indicate other sources of help and advice in the other divisions of MSC. He also has a stock of leaflets dealing with most aspects of employment legislation and MSC services. The local office deals with vacancies of all kinds apart from those for the professionally qualified, executives, and senior managers. These are dealt with by Professional and Executive Recruitment (PER) which operates on commercial lines and has a separate network of offices (see below). The services of the local office are entirely free.

Vacancies handled by the local office may be skilled or unskilled, and may be in manufacturing, transport, nursing, distribution, catering, security, clerical, commercial, etc, occupations. Advice is available on labour supply, local wage rates and recruitment problems. Often interview facilities can be made available to employers at the local office free of charge. This is particularly useful during a recruitment drive and when a new company is engaging the initial labour force prior to the opening of new premises.

Advice and assistance can be given on request if the recruitment of workers from other parts of the country is considered desirable. In certain cases workers taking jobs away from their home are eligible for financial help from the ESD. Details should be discussed with the manager before making engagements.

The Disabled Persons (Employment) Act requires employers of 20 or more to have a percentage of disabled people. Advice on the problems of employing disabled people, or of rehabilitation after sickness or injury, can be given by the Disablement Resettlement Officer (DRO) at the local office.

The area offices can give information on the location of the local offices or provide contact points for other parts of the Department of Employment group.

Head office:

Pennine Centre
20-22 Hawley Street
Sheffield S1 3GA
0742 739022

Area offices:

Eastern
Anglia House
North Station Road
Colchester CO1 1SB
0206 49801

East Midlands
Lambert House
Talbot Street
Nottingham NG1 5NP
0602 411411

East Pennine
City House
Leeds LS1 5JH
0532 38232

London North East
Room 502
Bryan House
76 Whitfield Street
London W1P 6AN
01 636 8616

London North West
Room 208
Bryan House
76 Whitfield Street
London W1P 6AN
01 636 8616

North West
Red Rose House
Lancaster Road
Preston PR1 1SQ
0772 54537

Scotland East & North
10 Canning Street
Edinburgh EH3 8EX
031 229 9151

Scotland West
West Block
5 Elmbank Gardens
Charing Cross
Glasgow G2 4PN
041 221 6913

Southern
4th Floor
Telford House
Hamilton Close
Basingstoke RG21 2UL
0256 67111

South East
1-3 Langney Road
Eastbourne BN21 3QF
0323 21399

London South
3rd Floor
Bryan House
76 Whitfield Street
London W1P 6AN
01 636 8616

Manchester
Bolton House
Chorlton Street
Manchester M1 3HY
061 228 6161

Merseyside
Graeme House
Derby Square
Liverpool L2 7SU
051 227 4111

North East
Plummer House
Market Street
Newcastle-upon-Tyne NE1 6NU
0632 28543

South West
St Stephens House
9 Catherine Street
Exeter EX1 1TN
0392 32341

Wales
Companies House
Crown Way
Maindy
Cardiff CF4 3UU
0222 388588

Western
The Pithay
Bristol BS1 2NQ
0272 291071

West Midlands
2 Duchess Place
Hagley Road
Birmingham B16 8NT
021 455 7111

Professional and Executive Recruitment (PER)

This is a separately managed branch of the Employment Service, dealing with professional, administrative, managerial, executive, technical and scientific staff in a wide range of industries. This is the only part of the Employment Service which charges employers a fee for services, as is the practice of other agencies. The address of the nearest PER office can always be obtained from the local Jobcentre or employment office.

Head office:

4-5 Grosvenor Place
London SW1X 7SB
01 235 7030

Training Services Division (TSD)

The Training Services Division aims to assist in the development of the national training system to meet the manpower needs of the economy, to offer training to individuals consistent with their abilities and wishes in skills for which there is a demand, and to promote the efficiency and effectiveness of training generally.

TSD supports training in industry through the Industrial Training Boards and other industry training bodies and itself trains large numbers of individuals in a wide variety of occupations in the Training Opportunities Scheme (TOPS). TSD also offers training facilities to employers and these include training employees at skillcentres; training supervisory staff and instructors, and a special course on international trade procedures and documentation. It is also possible to hire the services of a mobile instructor to train workers on the employer's own premises. Employers are charged a fee for these services.

Head office:

162-168 Regent Street
London W1R 6DE
01 214 6000

Special Programmes Division (SPD)

The Special Programmes Division is responsible for two major programmes for the unemployed — training and work experience for young people (Youth Opportunities Programme) and temporary employment for long-term unemployed adults (Special Temporary Employment Programme). SPD also oversees a third, much smaller programme, Community Industry, for young people with special employment difficulties.

YOP schemes are sponsored by a wide variety of bodies but mainly private employers, local authorities and Local Education Authorities and voluntary and charitable organisations. The MSC pays the allowances received by the young people and other financial assistance is available to sponsors, except in the case of work experience on employers' premises. STEP employees are paid a wage which is reimbursed by the MSC.

Head office:

Selkirk House
166 High Holborn
London WC1V 6PF
01 836 1213

Manpower Intelligence and Planning Division (MIPD)

The Manpower Intelligence and Planning Division carries out, *inter alia*, special studies of the labour market and research into employment matters generally. Each of the Commission's regional directors has a small team — Regional Manpower Intelligence Unit (RMIU) — which collects, analyses and disseminates information on the labour market in the region.

Regional offices:

Scotland
2-3 Queen Street
Edinburgh EH2 1JS
031 225 1377

South West
The Pithay
Bristol BS1 2NQ
0272 291071

Wales
4th Floor
Companies House
Crown Way
Maindy
Cardiff CF4 3VH
0222 388588

Midlands
24th Floor
Alpha Tower
Suffolk Street
Queensway
Birmingham B1 1TB
021 632 4451

South East
Hanway House
27 Red Lion Square
London WC1R 4NH
01 405 8454

North West
Sunley Buildings
Piccadilly Plaza
Manchester M1 4AA
061 832 9111

London
Tavis House
1-6 Tavistock Square
London WC1H 9PS
01 430 8296

Yorkshire & Humberside
Jubilee House
33-41 Park Place
Leeds LS1 2RL
0532 446299

Northern
Wellbar House
Gallowgate
Newcastle-upon-Tyne NE1 4TP
0632 27575

Industrial Training Boards

The present Industrial Training Boards have their origins in the Industrial Training Act of 1964 amended by the Employment and Training Act of 1973. There are now 24 boards and one statutory committee in operation.

Apart from the collection and publication of regular series of information on their own industries, the boards are a focus for advice on all aspects of training within the firm and in the industry as a whole. Many are involved in research into training policy and practice, although the amount that is carried out does vary from board to board. All the boards are listed below.

Agricultural Training Board:

Bourne House
32-34 Beckenham Road
Beckenham
Kent BR3 4PB
01 650 4890

Air Transport and Travel Industry Training Board:

Staines House
158-162 High Street
Staines
Middx TW18 4AS
0784 57171

Carpet Industry Training Board:

Eagle Star House
Alderley Road
Wilmslow
Cheshire SK9 1NX
09964 27118/9

Ceramics, Glass and Mineral Products Industry Training Board:

Bovis House
Northolt Road
Harrow
Middx HA2 0EF
01 422 7101/01 864 4311

Chemical and Allied Products Industry Training Board:

Staines House
158-162 High Street
Staines
Middx TW18 4AT
0784 51366

Clothing and Allied Products Industry Training Board:

10th Floor
Tower House
Merrion Way
Leeds LS2 8NY
0532 41331

Construction Industry Training Board:

Radnor House
1272 London Road
Norbury
London SW16 4EL
01 764 5060

Cotton and Allied Textiles Industry Training Board:

10th Floor
Sunlight House
Quay Street
Manchester M3 3LH
061 832 9656/8

Distributive Industry Training Board:

MacLaren House
Talbot Road
Stretford
Manchester M32 0FP
061 872 2494

Engineering Industry Training Board:

54 Clarendon Road
Watford
Herts WD1 1LB
0923 38441

Food, Drink and Tobacco Industry Training Board:

Barton House
Barton Street
Gloucester GL1 1QQ
0452 28621

Footwear, Leather and Fur Skin Industry Training Board:

Maney Buildings
29 Birmingham Road
Sutton Coldfield
West Midlands B72 1QE
021 355 3511

Foundry Industry Training Committee:

50-54 Charlotte Street
London W1P 2EL
01 580 0341

Furniture and Timber Industry Training Board:

31 Octagon Parade
High Wycombe
Bucks HP11 2JA
0494 32751/6

Hotel and Catering Industry Training Board:

Ramsey House
Central Square
Wembley
Middx HA9 7AF
01 902 8865

Iron and Steel Industry Training Board:

190 Fleet Street
London EC4A 2AH
01 404 5972

Knitting, Lace and Net Industry Training Board:

4 Hamilton Road
Nottingham NG5 1AU
0602 621075

Man-Made Fibres Producing Industry Training Board:

Langwood House
63-81 High Street
Rickmansworth
Herts WD3 1EQ
09237 78371

Paper and Paper Products Industry Training Board:

Star House
Potters Bar
Herts EN6 2PG
0707 50211

Petroleum Industry Training Board:

Kingfisher House
Walton Street
Aylesbury
Bucks HP21 7TQ
0296 27331/7

Printing and Publishing Industry Training Board:

Merit House
Edgware Road
London NW9 5AG
01 205 0162

Road Transport Industry Training Board:

Capitol House
Empire Way
Wembley
Middx HA9 0NG
01 902 8880

Rubber and Plastics Processing Industry Training Board:

Brent House
950 Great West Road
Brentford
Middx TW8 9ES
01 568 1062

Shipbuilding Industry Training Board:

Raeburn House
Northolt Road
South Harrow
Middx HA2 0DR
01 422 9581

Wool, Jute and Flax Industry Training Board:

Butterfield House
Otley Road
Baildon
Shipley
West Yorks BD17 7HE
0274 59551

Local Government Training Board:
(This is *not* a statutory body.)

8 The Armdale Centre
Luton
Beds LU1 2TS
0582 21111

The Northern Ireland Training Executive

The Northern Ireland Training Executive incorporates nine industrial training boards covering the following industries: Catering; Clothing and Footwear; Construction; Distributive; Engineering; Food and Drink; Man-Made Fibres Producing; Road Transport; Textiles.

Address:

ITB House
33 Church Road
Newtonabbey BT36 7LH
0232 65171

Confederation of British Industry (CBI)

The CBI was founded in 1965 and is an independent, non-party-political body that is financed by industry and commerce. Its primary function is seen as a body which can act as a focal point for the views of business and to pass these views on to government. It is also deeply involved in applying its considerable experience and expertise to economic and industrial problems in order to help members both large and small.

Headquarters:

Centre Point
103 New Oxford Street
London WC1A 1DU
01 379 7400

Regional offices:

London
Centre Point
103 New Oxford Street
London WC1A 1DU
01 379 7400

Northern
15 Grey Street
Newcastle-upon-Tyne NE1 6EE
0632 21644

North Western
Emerson House
Albert Street
Eccles
Manchester M30 0LJ
061 707 2190

West Midlands
Hagley House
Hagley Road
Edgbaston
Birmingham B16 8PS
021 454 7991

East Midlands
17 St Wilfred Street
Calverton
Nottingham NG14 6FP
0602 653311

Yorkshire and Humberside
Arndale House
Crossgates
Leeds LS15 8EU
0532 644242

South Eastern
Tubs Hill House
Sevenoaks
Kent TN13 1BX
0732 55112

Southern
Bank Chambers
10a Hart Street
Henley-on-Thames
Oxon RG9 2AU
04912 6810

Eastern
Milton Hall
Milton
Cambridge CB4 4DP
0223 861383

South Western
8-10 Whiteladies Road
Bristol BS8 1NZ
0272 37065

Northern Ireland
3 Botanic Avenue
Belfast BT7 1JG
0232 26658

Scotland
Beresford House
5 Claremont Terrace
Glasgow G3 7XT
041 332 8661

Wales
Pearl Assurance House
Greyfriars Road
Cardiff CF1 3JR
0222 32536

Trades Union Congress (TUC)

The TUC was formed in the last century and is governed by a general council composed of elected representatives. The TUC makes representation to the government on behalf of affiliated unions on all major economic and social issues, as well as preparing reports and advising generally on the conditions of affiliated unions and on employment policy in general. Not all trade unions in the UK are affiliated to the TUC, the latest figure being about 112 individual trade unions, covering a total membership of around 12.1 millions.

Headquarters:

Congress House
Great Russell Street
London WC1B 3LS
01 636 4030

The Scottish Trades Union Congress:

16 Woodlands Terrace
Glasgow G3 6DE
041 332 4946

The Welsh Trades Union Council:

Transport House
1 Cathedral Road
Cardiff CF1 9HA
0222 394521

Regional councils in England:

Northern
Archbold House
Archbold Terrace
Newcastle-upon-Tyne
0632 814355

Yorkshire and Humberside
Leeds Trades Council Club
Savile Mount
Leeds LS7
0532 620629

North West
222 Stamford Street
Ashton-under-Lyne
Lancs OL6 7YZ
061 308 2821

West Midlands
191 Corporation Street
Birmingham B4 6RU
021 236 1240

East Midlands
13 Delaware Road
Leicester LE5 6LJ
0533 415437

East Anglia
119 Newmarket Road
Cambridge CB5 8HA
0223 67691

South East
Congress House
Great Russell Street
London WC1B 2LS
01 636 4030

South West
16 The Crescent
Taunton
Somerset TA1 4EB
0832 88031

Trade Unions

There are over 400 individual trade unions in the UK of varying sizes (measured in membership), and the largest are listed below.

Transport and General Workers Union:

Transport House
Smith Square
London SW1P 3JB
01 828 7788

Amalgamated Union of Engineering Workers:

110 Peckham Road
London SE15 5EL
01 703 4232

National Union of General and Municipal Workers:

Thorne House
Ruxley Ridge
Claygate
Esher
Surrey KT10 0TL
0372 62081

National and Local Government Officers Association:

1 Mabledon Place
London WC1H 9AJ
01 388 2366

Association of Scientific, Technical and Managerial Staffs:

10-26a Jamestown Road
London NW1 7DT
01 267 4422

Union of Shop Distributive and Allied Workers:

Oakley
188 Wilmslow Road
Fallowfield
Manchester M14 6LJ
061 224 2804

Electrical, Electronic, Telecommunications and Plumbing Union:

Hayes Court
West Common Road
Hayes
Bromley
Kent BR2 7AU
01 462 7755

National Union of Mineworkers:

222 Euston Road
London NW1 2BX
01 387 7631

Union of Construction, Allied Trades and Technicians:

177 Abbeville Road
Clapham
London SW4 9RL
01 622 2442

National Union of Teachers:

Hamilton House
Mabledon Place
London WC1H 9BD
01 387 2442

Civil and Public Services Association:

215 Balham High Road
London SW17 7BQ
01 675 3331

Confederation of Health Service Employees:

Glen House
High Street
Banstead
Surrey SM7 2LH
03725 53322

Society of Graphical and Allied Trades:

SOGAT House
274/288 London Road
Hadleigh
Benfleet
Essex SS7 2DE
0702 553131

Union of Communication Workers:

UPW House
Crescent Lane
Clapham Common
London SW4 9RN
01 622 9977

National Union of Railwaymen:

Unity House
Euston Road
London NW1 2BL
01 387 4771

Association of Professional, Executive, Clerical and Computer Staff:

22 Worple Road
London SW19 4DF
01 947 3131

Amalgamated Society of Boilermakers, Shipwrights, Blacksmiths and
Structural Workers:

Lifton House
Eslington Road
Newcastle-upon-Tyne NE2 4SB
0632 813205

National Association of Schoolmasters/Union of Women Teachers:

Swan Court
Waterhouse Street
Hemel Hempstead
Herts HP1 1DT
0442 42971

Banking, Insurance and Finance Union:

Sheffield House
Portsmouth Road
Esher
Surrey
0372 66625

2. Other Sources of Information and Advice

The organisations listed below are those which might be able to provide information and are usually willing to deal with requests for advice. Naturally the amount of help that can be given will vary considerably from organisation to organisation.

Association of Graduate Careers Advisory Services (AGCAS):
(Secretary: Mrs M Jacob)

Careers Centre
University of East Anglia
University Plain
Norwich NR4 7TJ
0603 56161

British Association for Commercial and Industrial Education (BACIE):

16 Park Crescent
London W1N 4AP
01 636 5351/4

Brunel University:

Uxbridge
Middx UB8 3PH
0895 37188

Business Education Council (BEC):

Berkshire House
168–73 High Holborn
London WC1V 7AG
01 379 7088

Board of Inland Revenue:

Somerset House
Strand
London WC2R 1LB
01 438 6649

British Institute of Management:

Management House
Parker Street
London WC2B 5PT
01 405 3456

Business Statistics Office:

Cardiff Road
Newport
Gwent NPT 1XG
0633 56111

CACI Inc International:

289 High Holborn
London WC1V 7HZ
01 405 2245/6

Careers Research and Advisory Centre (CRAC):

Bateman Street
Cambridge CB2 1LZ
0223 69811

Central Services Unit (CSU):

Precinct Centre
University of Manchester
333 Oxford Road
Manchester M13 9RN
061 273 6464

Centre for Inter-firm Comparison:

25 Bloomsbury Square
London WC1A 2PJ
01 637 8406

Centre for Research on User Studies:

University of Sheffield
Sheffield
South Yorkshire S10 2TN
0742 78555

Central Statistical Office:

Great George Street
London SW1P 3AQ
01 233 3000

Civil Service Department:

Whitehall
London SW1A 2AZ
01 626 1515

Conservative Party:

32 Smith Square
London SW1P 3HH
01 222 9000

Department of Education and Science:

Elizabeth House
39 York Road
London SE1 7PH
01 928 9222

Department of the Environment:

St Christopher House
Southwark Street
London SE1 0TE
01 928 7999

Department of Health and Social Security:

Alexander Fleming House
Elephant and Castle
London SE1 6BY
01 407 5522

Department of Health and Social Security:

Central Office
Newcastle-upon-Tyne NE98 1YX
0632 857111

Department of Industry:

Ashdown House
123 Victoria Street
London SW1E 6RB
01 212 7676

Department of Trade Library:

1 Victoria Street
London SW1H 0ET
01 215 7877

Engineering Employers' Federation (EEF):

Broadway House
Tothill Street
London SW1H 9NQ
01 839 1266

European Economic Community (London Office):

20 Kensington Palace Gardens
London W8 4QQ
01 727 8090
(Also at this address, EEC Library, open Mon-Fri 10.00-1.00; 2.30-5.30)

European Economic Community (Statistical Office):

Bâtiment Jean Monnet
Plateau du Kirchberg
Luxembourg
010 352 43011

European Economic Community (Information Unit):

Millbank Tower
Millbank
London SW1P 4QU
01 211 7060

European Investment Bank:

2 Place de Metz
Luxembourg
010 352 043 50 11

Federation of Personnel Services of Great Britain:

120 Baker Street
London W1M 1LD
01 486 8264/5

General Register Office (Northern Ireland):

Oxford House
49-55 Chichester Street
Belfast BT1 4HL
0232 35211

General Register Office (Scotland):

Ladywell Road
Edinburgh EH12 7TF
031 334 6854

HMSO:

49 High Holborn
London WC1V 6HB
01 928 6977 (no telephone orders)

PO Box 569
London SE1 9NH
(Mail/telephone orders 01 928 1321)

HMSO Publications (regional bookshops):

13a Castle Street
Edinburgh EH2 3AR
031 225 6333

80 Chichester Street
Belfast BT1 4JY
0232 34488

41 The Hayes
Cardiff CF1 1JW
0222 23654

258 Broad Street
Birmingham B1 2HE
021 643 3740

Southey House
Wine Street
Bristol BS1 2BQ
0272 24306

Brazennose Street
Manchester M60 8AS
061 834 7201

Incomes Data Services Ltd:

140 Great Portland Street
London W1N 5TA
01 580 0521/9

Industrial Relations Services Ltd:

67 Maygrove Road
London NW6 2EJ
01 328 4751

Industrial Relations Training Resource Centre:

Ashridge Management College
Berkhamsted
Herts HP4 1NS
04427 3491

Institute of Economic Affairs:

2 Lord North Street
Westminster
London SW1P 3LB
01 799 3745

Institute of Manpower Studies:

University of Sussex
Mantell Building
Falmer
Brighton BN1 9RF
0273 686751

Institute of Personnel Management:

Central House
Upper Woburn Place
London WC1H 0HX
01 387 2844

International Labour Office (ILO):

CH 1211 Geneva 22
Switzerland
010 41 22 31 24 00/32 62 00

International Labour Office (London Office):

87-91 New Bond Street
London W1Y 9LA
01 828 6401

Labour Party:

150 Walworth Road
London SE17
01 703 0833

Liberal Party:

1 Whitehall Place
London SW1A 2HD
01 839 4092

Manpower Society:
(Secretary: M Roberts)

Shell UK Oil
PO Box 148
Shell-Mex House
Strand
London WC4R 0DX
01 438 3211

Ministry of Agriculture, Fisheries and Food:

Whitehall Place
London SW1A 2HH
01 839 7711

National Economic Development Office (NEDO):

21 Millbank
London
SW1P 4QX
01 211 3000

NEDO Books:

1 Steel House
11 Tothill Street
London SW1H 9LJ
01 222 0565/0676

Northern Ireland Department of Education:

Rathgael House
Balloo Road
Bangor
Co. Down BT19 2PR
0232 66311

Northern Ireland Office:

Stormont Castle
Belfast BT4 3ST
0232 63011

Office of Health Economics:

Carrington House
130 Regent Street
London W1R 5FE
01 734 0757

Office of Population Censuses and Surveys:

St. Catherine's House
Kingsway
London WC2B 6JP
01 242 0262

Office of Population Censuses and Surveys:

Census Division
Customer Services Section
Tichfield
Hants
03294 42511

Open University:

Walton Hall
Milton Keynes MK7 6AA
0908 74066

Organisation for Economic Co-operation and Development (OECD):

2 Rue Andre-Pascal
75774
Paris
Cedex 16
(UK sales agent: HMSO bookshops)

Reward Regional Surveys Ltd:

1 Mill Street
Stone
Staffs ST15 8BA
0785 834554

Scottish Business Education Council:

22 Great King Street
Edinburgh EH3 6QH
031 556 4691

Scottish Education Department:

43 Jeffrey Street
Edinburgh EH1 1DN
031 556 9233

Scottish Office:

New St Andrew's House
Edinburgh EH1 3TD
031 556 8400

Scottish Technical Education Council:

38 Queen Street
Glasgow G1 3DY
041 204 2271

Sheffield Centre for Innovation and Productivity:

Holfords House
16 Fitzallen Square
Sheffield S1 2BZ
0242 20911

Science Research Council:

Polaris House
North Star Avenue
Swindon
Wilts SN2 1ET
0793 26222

Social Science Research Council (SSRC):

1 Temple Avenue
London EC4Y 0BD
01 353 5252

SSRC Survey Archive:

University of Essex
Wivenhoe Park
Colchester
Essex CO4 3SQ
0206 862286/860570

Society For Long Range Planning:

15 Belgrave Square
London SW1X 8PU
01 235 0246

Standing Conference of Employers of Graduates (SCOEG):
(Secretary: I T Pitt)

Kodak Ltd
Research Division
Headstone Drive
Harrow
Middx HA1 4TY
01 427 4380

Tavistock Institute of Human Relations:

Tavistock Centre
Belsize Lane
London NW3 5BA
01 435 7111

Technician Education Council:

76 Portland Place
London W1N 4AA
01 580 3050

The Industrial Society:

48 Bryanston Square
London W1H 1BQ
01 262 2401

The Small Business Centre:

University of Aston
200 Aston Brook Street
Birmingham B6 4SY
021 359 4647

University Grants Committee:

14 Park Crescent
London W1N 4DH
01 636 7799

Universities' Statistical Record:

Central Record Office
PO Box 40
Cheltenham GL50 1JY
0242 519091

Welsh Office:

31 Cathedral Road
Cardiff CF1 9UJ
0222 42661

Local Authorities

Greater London Council (GLC)

There are 32 boroughs within the GLC: Barking, Barnet, Bexley, Brent, Bromley, Camden, Croydon, Ealing, Enfield, Greenwich, Hackney, Hammersmith, Haringey, Harrow, Havering, Hillingdon, Hounslow, Islington, Kensington and Chelsea, Kingston-upon-Thames, Lambeth, Lewisham, Merton, Newham, Redbridge, Richmond-on-Thames, South-wark, Sutton, Tower Hamlets, Waltham Forest, Wandsworth and Westminster. In addition there is the separate City of London.

GLC Central Offices:

County Hall
London SE1 7PB
01 633 5000

Metropolitan County Councils

Greater Manchester:

County Hall
Piccadilly Gardens
Portland Street
Manchester M60 3HP
061 246 3111

Merseyside:

Metropolitan House
Old Hall Street
Liverpool L69 3EL
051 227 5234

South Yorkshire:

County Hall
Barnsley
South Yorks S70 2TN
0226 86141

Tyne and Wear:

Sandyford House
Archbold Terrace
Newcastle-upon-Tyne NE2 1ED
0632 816144

West Midlands:

County Hall
1 Lancaster Circus
Queensway
Birmingham B4 7DJ
021 300 5151

West Yorkshire:

County Hall
Wakefield WF1 2QW
0924 67111

County Councils — England

Avon:

Avon House
The Haymarket
Bristol BS99 7DE
0272 290777

Bedford:

County Hall
Bedford MK42 9AP
0234 63222

Berkshire:

Shire Hall
Reading RG1 3EY
0734 55981

Buckinghamshire:

County Hall
Aylesbury
Bucks HP20 1UZ
0296 5000

Cambridge:

Shire Hall
Castle Hill
Cambridge CB3 0AP
0223 358811

Cheshire:

County Hall
Chester CH1 1SF
0244 602424

Cleveland:

Municipal Buildings
Middlesborough TS1 2QH
0642 248155

Cornwall:

County Hall
Truro TR1 3AY
0872 74282

Cumbria:

The Courts
Carlisle CA3 8LZ
0228 23456

Derbyshire:

County Offices
Matlock
Derbyshire DE4 3AG
0629 3411

Devon:

County Hall
Topsham Road
Exeter EX2 4QD
0392 77977

Dorset:

County Hall
Dorchester DT1 1XJ
0305 3131

Durham:

County Hall
Durham DH1 5UL
0385 64411

East Sussex:

County Hall
St Anne's Crescent
Lewes
East Sussex BN7 1SG
07916 5400

Essex:

County Hall
Chelmsford
Essex CM1 1LX
0245 67222

Gloucestershire:

Shire Hall
Gloucester GL1 2TG
0452 21444

Hampshire:

The Castle
Winchester
Hants SO23 8UJ
0962 4411

Hereford and Worcester:

County Hall
Spetchley Road
Worcester WR5 2NP
0905 353366

Hertfordshire:

County Hall
Hertford SG13 8DF
0992 54242

Humberside:

Kingston House South
Bond Street
Hull HU1 3EU
0482 27291

Isle of Wight:

County Hall
Newport
Isle of Wight PO30 1UD
0983 524031

Kent:

County Hall
Maidstone
Kent ME14 1XQ
0622 671411

Lancashire:

County Hall
Preston PR1 8XJ
0772 54868

Leicestershire:

County Hall
Glenfield
Leicester LE3 8RA
0533 871313

Lincolnshire:

County Offices
Lincoln LN1 1YL
0522 29931

Norfolk:

County Hall
Norwich NR1 2DH
0603 611122

Northamptonshire:

County Hall
Northampton NN1 1DN
0604 34833

Northumberland:

County Hall
Newcastle-upon-Tyne NE1 1SA
0632 611351

North Yorkshire:

County Hall
Northallerton
North Yorks DL7 8AD
0609 3123

Nottinghamshire:

Principal County Hall
West Bridgeford
Nottingham NG2 7QP
0602 863366

Oxfordshire:

County Hall
Oxford OX1 1ND
0865 722422

Shropshire:

The Shirehall
Abbey Foregate
Shrewsbury SY2 6ND
0743 222100

Somerset:

County Hall
Taunton
Somerset TA1 4DY
0823 3451

Staffordshire:

County Buildings
Stafford ST16 2LH
0785 3121

Suffolk:

County Hall
Ipswich IP4 2JS
0473 55801

Surrey:

County Hall
Kingston-upon-Thames
Surrey KT1 2D
01 546 1050

Warwickshire:

Shire Hall
Warwick CV34 4RR
0926 43431

West Sussex:

County Hall
Chichester
West Sussex PO19 1RQ
0243 785100

Wiltshire:

County Hall
Trowbridge
Wiltshire BA14 8JG
02214 3641

County Councils — Wales

Clwyd:

Shire Hall
Mold
Clwyd CH7 6NB
0352 2121

Dyfed:

County Hall
Carmarthen
Dyfed SA31 1JP
0267 4251

Gwent:

County Hall
Cwmbran
Gwent NP4 2XH
06333 67711

Gwynedd:

County Offices
Caernarfon LL55 1SH
0286 4121

Mid Glamorgan:

Mid Glamorgan County Hall
Cardiff CF1 3NE
0222 28033

Powys:

County Hall
Llandrindod Wells
Powys LD1 5LE
0597 3711

South Glamorgan:

South Glamorgan County Headquarters
Newport Road
Cardiff CF2 1XA
0222 499022

West Glamorgan:

Guildhall
Swansea SA1 4PJ
0792 50821

Regional and Island Councils — Scotland

Borders Regional Council:

County Offices
Newton St Boswells
Roxburghshire TD6 0SA
08352 3301

Central Regional Council:

Viewforth
Stirling FK8 2ET
0786 3111

Dumfries and Galloway Regional Council:

Council Offices
Dumfries DG1 2DD
0387 3141

Fife Regional Council:

County Buildings
Cupar
Fife KY15 4TA
0334 3722

Grampian Regional Council:

Woodhill House
Ashgrove Road West
Aberdeen AB9 2LU
0224 682222

Highland Regional Council:

Regional Buildings
Glenurquhart Road
Inverness IV3 5NU
0463 34121

Lothian Regional Council:

Regional Headquarters
George IV Bridge
Edinburgh EH1 1UQ
031 229 9292

Orkney Island Council:

Council Offices
Kirkwall
Orkney KW15 1NY
0856 3535

Shetlands Island Council:

Town Hall
Lerwick AB3 0LS
0595 3535

Strathclyde Regional Council:

Melrose House
19 Cadogan Road
Glasgow G2 6HR
041 204 2900

Tayside Regional Council:

Tayside House
26-28 Crichton Street
Dundee DD1 3RA
0382 23281

Western Isles Island Council:

County Offices
Sandwick Road
Stornoway
Isle of Lewis PA87 2BW
0851 3773

Appendix: Glossary and Abbreviations

Glossary

Academic year the education year from the beginning of the first term (autumn and usually September) to the end of the final term (summer and usually July).

Activity rate can be simply described as the ratio of the working population (those who are in or seeking work) in each age and sex group to the total population in that group.

Assisted regions those areas of the UK covered by special government measures concerned with such aspects as industrial development and employment opportunities, as part of its overall regional policy.

Base year the year chosen as the static point for indices to be based on; it is usually equated with 100.

Civilian labour force this includes those employees in employment, employers and the self-employed, but excludes HM forces.

Constant prices current prices which have been adjusted to reflect the rate of change in prices over time, using a base year as the static point of comparison.

Conurbations large built-up areas usually surrounding and including a large town or city at the centre.

Current prices those prices prevalent at the time without adjustment.

Development area those areas of the UK outlined as in need of special assistance through government regional policy.

Economically active that proportion of the working population which is either in employment (employed or self-employed) or out of employment (unemployed or temporarily sick).

Economically inactive the opposite of economically active, and includes those who are retired, permanently sick, students, housewives, etc.

Economic planning region areas which are delineated for the purpose of formulating policy.

Employment status this usually means whether in employment, self-employed, unemployed, etc.

Frictional unemployment short-term unemployment largely caused by the dynamics of the labour market when people leave one job to search or take up another. It is generally considered that some level of frictional unemployment is essential for the efficient functioning of the labour market.

Gross domestic product the usual estimate of the value of the goods and services produced by UK residents in any one period.

Index a method of representing change in a factor over time relative to a chosen static point (base year, for example). Most labour market variables can be reflected in this way (and many are).

Index of Production industries these include all manufacturing industries, mining and quarrying, construction and gas, electricity and water, which correspond to SIC orders II-XXI inclusive.

Intermediate areas areas within the UK designated as in need of special assistance but with less severe problems than other areas. Part of the government's regional policy.

Joint Manpower Watch Survey this is a comprehensive survey of employees engaged in a number of separate departments or services within local authorities. It includes civilian employees of police authorities, cadets, traffic wardens, agency staff and a few other groups not normally covered in DE figures.

Manufacturing industries these refer to SIC orders III-XIX inclusive.

Metropolitan county those counties in England and Wales based on a large conurbation which came into being following the 1972 Local Government Act.

Occupational status refers to whether the person is self-employed, an employee in employment, family worker, etc, and appears frequently in EEC statistics, for example.

Operative in the statistics this refers to those workers other than clerical, technical, professional and managerial.

Participation rate see Activity rate.

Perinatal mortality infant deaths occurring at or about the time of birth.

Sandwich course a course of further education which involves a period spent with an employer, with attendance at a further education institution before and after.

Seasonally adjusted an adjustment to the actual statistics based on past experience of seasonal effects such as holidays, which attempts to bring out the underlying trend in the statistical series.

Social class in the regular statistics this is based on occupations; the latest Census of Population used five groupings:

Class I	Professional and similar occupations
Class II	Intermediate occupations
Class III(N)	Skilled occupations (non-manual)
Class IV(M)	Skilled occupations (manual)
Class V	Unskilled occupations

Socio-economic group this grouping is intended to classify people whose social, cultural, and recreational standards and behaviour are similar. In practice this is a very difficult thing to do and many such groupings in the regular statistics are largely based on employment status and occupation.

Standard regions these are the main administrative regions for the UK with the following 12 components: South East; South West; Greater London; West Midlands; East Midlands; East Anglia; North West; Yorkshire and Humberside; Northern; Wales; Scotland; Northern Ireland.

Statistical sub-division an area whose boundaries are determined by the collection and analysis of data from that region.

Sub-regions these are areas which constitute parts of the larger standard regions. In this Guide they refer to a greater level of disaggregation than the standard regions.

Wards electoral divisions of urban areas in England and Wales.

Abbreviations

ACAS	Advisory, Conciliation and Arbitration Service
AGCAS	Association of Graduate Careers Advisory Services
BACIE	British Association for Commercial and Industrial Education
BIM	British Institute of Management
BSO	Business Statistics Office
CBI	Confederation of British Industry
CNAA	Council for National Academic Awards
CODOT	Classification of Occupations and Directory of Occupational Titles
CSE	Certificate of Secondary Education
CSU	Central Services Unit (for careers and appointments services)
DE	Department of Employment
DES	Department of Education and Science
DHSS	Department of Health and Social Security
DMS	Department of Manpower Services (Northern Ireland)
EEC	European Economic Community
ESD	Employment Service Division
EUA	European Unit of Account
FE	Further Education
GCE	General Certificate of Education
GHS	General Household Survey
GLC	Greater London Council
HMSO	Her Majesty's Stationery Office
HNC	Higher National Certificate
HND	Higher National Diploma
IDS	Incomes Data Services
ILO	International Labour Office
IMS	Institute of Manpower Studies
ISIC	International Standard Industrial Classification
ITB	Industrial Training Board
KOS	List of Key Occupations for Statistical Purposes
LEA	Local Education Authority
LMI	Labour Market Information
MLH	Minimum List Heading
MSC	Manpower Services Commission
NACE	General Industrial Classification of Economic Activities within the European Communities
NEDO	National Economic Development Office
NES	New Earnings Survey

NHI	National Health Insurance
OECD	Organisation for Economic Co-operation and Development
ONC	Ordinary National Certificate
OND	Ordinary National Diploma
OPCS	Office of Population Censuses and Surveys
PAYE	Pay As You Earn
PBR	Payment By Results
PER	Professional and Executive Register
RMIU	Regional Manpower Intelligence Unit
SCE	Scottish Certificate of Education
SCOEG	Standing Conference of Employers of Graduates
SED	Scottish Education Department
SIC	Standard Industrial Classification
STEP	Special Temporary Employment Programme
TES	Temporary Employment Subsidy
TOPS	Training Opportunities Scheme
TSD	Training Services Division
TTW	Travel To Work
TTWA	Travel To Work Area
TUC	Trades Union Congress
UGC	University Grants Committee
UMS	Unit for Manpower Studies

Index

Index

Distributive Industry Training Board, 225

district councils, 26, 33

earnings, 13, 14, 15, 16, 17, 144, 147, 148, 161-77, 178, 179, 181, 182, 183, 187, 194, 203, 220; and education, 175; by industry, 162, 165, 166, 167, 168, 169, 170, 171, 173, 174, 175, 176, 177; by occupation, 162, 167, 168, 169, 170, 172, 173, 175, 176, 177; definition of, 161; in local government, 166

economic activity, 16, 27, 35-41, 47, 50, 55, 246

economic planning regions, 123, 246

Economic Progress Report, 68, 176, 205

Economic Trends, 49, 65, 77, 145, 171, 182, 205

Economic Trends Annual Supplement, 49, 66, 77, 145, 172, 182, 205

educational supply, 11, 14, 16; further education, 91-100; school leavers 82-90; universities, 101-10

Education and Employment 1980, 88, 97, 107, 205

education, manpower in, 46

education system, 11

Education Statistics for the United Kingdom, 87, 96, 106, 205

EEC Labour Costs in Industry, 178, 179, 181, 183, 206

EEC Labour Force Sample Survey, 29, 35, 39, 43, 47, 52, 58, 64, 72, 79, 139, 144, 205-6

electoral divisions, 27

Electrical, Electronic, Tele-communications and Plumbing Union, 231

electrical engineering industry, 115, 179, 182, 183

electricity industry, 46, 50, 179, 182, 183

employees in employment, 24, 36, 39, 42, 43, 46, 47, 48, 49, 50, 51, 112, 114, 144, 149, 150, 155, 161, 162, 165, 170, 178, 179, 181, 184, 247

employees, *see* employees in employment

employers, 42, 44, 47, 48, 49, 50, 51, 53, 55, 144, 149, 150, 153, 155, 158, 161, 162, 176, 206, 207, 220, 222, 223, 247

employers' federations, 17

employment, 14, 17, 35, 42-56, 70, 76, 97, 124, 178, 179, 182, 184, 185, 204, 223

employment agencies, 72, 73, 79, 81, 158

Employment and Training Act 1973, 112n, 219, 224

employment conditions, 11, 13, 15, 16, 17, 187, 194, 195

employment exchanges, *see* employment offices

Employment Gazette, 31, 40, 41, 42, 46-7, 55-6, 57, 58n, 61, 69, 70, 71, 75, 80, 81, 87, 90, 98, 99, 100, 101, 107, 109, 110, 114, 116, 117, 124, 132, 139, 142, 145, 147, 148, 150, 154, 156, 159, 165, 168, 169, 177, 178, 179, 181, 184, 188, 191, 192, 195, 199, 202, 206

employment offices, 57, 58, 59, 62, 72, 73, 75, 76, 77, 78, 79, 80, 124, 155, 158, 177, 194, 220, 221, 222

employment office areas, 52, 61, 119

Employment Prospects for the Highly Qualified, 99, 109

Employment Protection Act, 192, 218

Employment Service in the 1980s, 80-1

employment status, 27, 35, 36, 38, 39, 79, 115, 246, 247

employment structure, 12, 16

Employment Transfer Scheme, 131

engagements, 80, 155, 156, 158, 159, 221

Engineering Employers' Federation, 235

engineering industry, 49, 50, 86, 100, 114, 116, 130, 142, 145, 153, 166, 169, 170, 197

Engineering Industry Training Board, 100, 226, 228

equal opportunity, 217

establishment, size of, 43, 51, 52, 132, 166, 181, 199, 206

European Economic Community, 29, 39, 47, 56, 64, 66, 71, 144, 148, 181, 186, 199, 205, 235, 247; Information Unit, 236; Statistical office, 236

European Investment Bank, 236

European Units of Account, 181

expansion, 13, 14

experience, 13, 14

external labour market, 11, 12, 13

extractive industry, 52, 153

Family Expenditure Survey, 175, 206

family workers, 47, 52, 55, 144, 247

Federation of Personnel Services, 81, 236

fertility, *see* births

First Destination of University Graduates, 106, 206

flexible hours, 136

Food, Drink and Tobacco Industry Training Board, 226

food and drink industry, 114, 185, 228

footwear industry, 114, 169, 197, 228

Footwear, Leather and Fur Skin Industry Training Board, 226

Ford Motor Company, 130

Forestry Training Council, 114

Foundry Industry Training Committee

Index